Shangri-La

A Travel Guide to the Himalayan Dream

Michael B

edition
I

www.bradtguides.com

Bradt Travel Guides Ltd, UK
The Globe Pequot Press Inc, USA

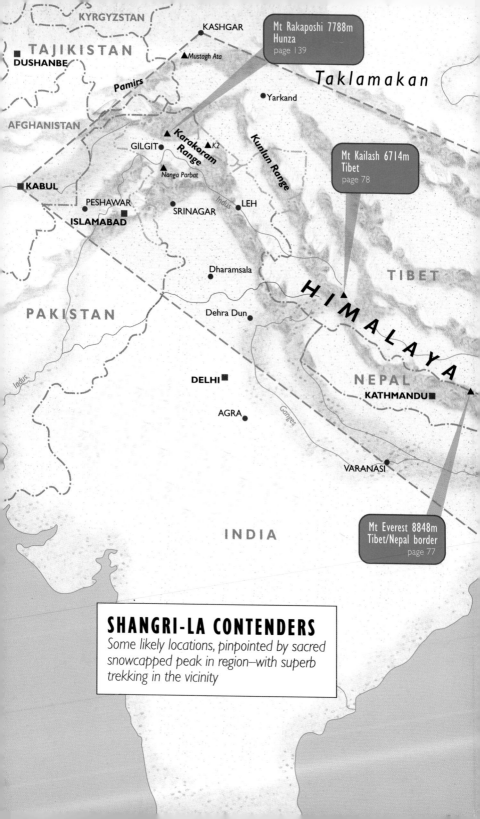

KYRGYZSTAN

KASHGAR

Mt Rakaposhi 7788m
Hunza
page 139

TAJIKISTAN

DUSHANBE

Mustagh Ata

Taklamakan

Pamirs

Yarkand

AFGHANISTAN

Karakoram Range

K2

Kunlun Range

GILGIT

Nanga Parbat

Mt Kailash 6714m
Tibet
page 78

KABUL

Indus

LEH

PESHAWAR

SRINAGAR

TIBET

ISLAMABAD

Dharamsala

H I M A L A Y A

PAKISTAN

Dehra Dun

NEPAL

DELHI

KATHMANDU

Indus

AGRA

Ganges

VARANASI

Mt Everest 8848m
Tibet/Nepal border
page 77

INDIA

SHANGRI-LA CONTENDERS
*Some likely locations, pinpointed by sacred
snowcapped peak in region—with superb
trekking in the vicinity*

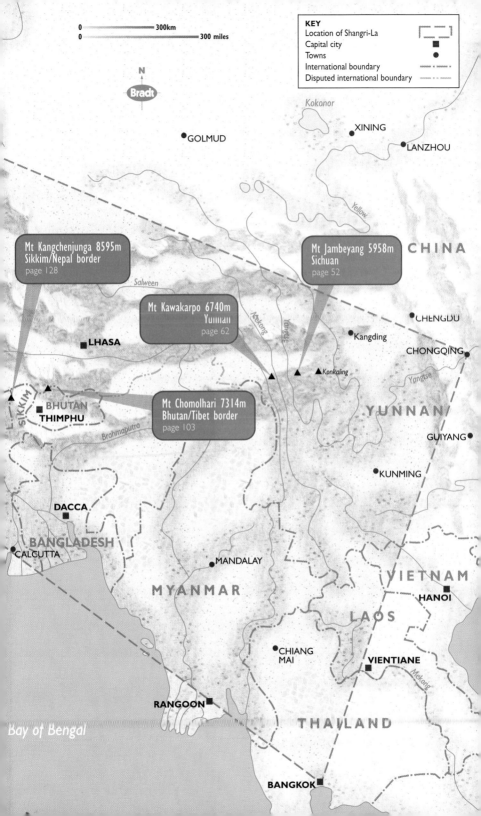

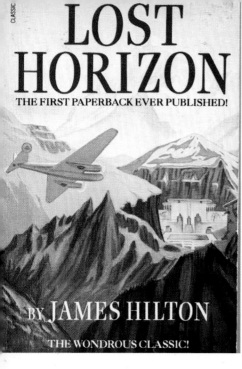

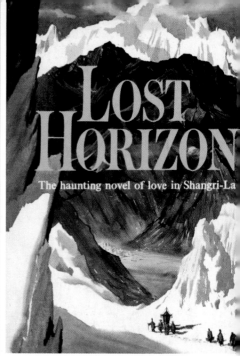

Imagining Shangri-La, in book cover designs

above Covers of Pocket Books USA editions of *Lost Horizon*

below left *Shangri-La* sequel, with an oddly Islamic touch to the buildings

below right The cover uses a photo of Chiu Gompa, with Mount Kailash as a Shangri-La setting

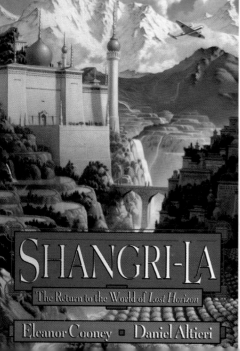

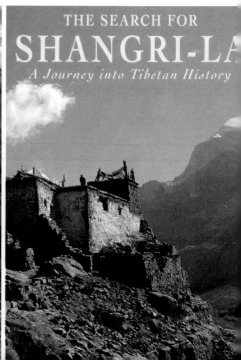

MYSTICAL SHANGRI-LA

神秘的
秘境シャングリラ　香格里拉

above Cover of a Chinese book about Shangri-La, with Mount Meili Shan dropped on top of Sungtseling Monastery, Zhongdian

below A Chinese DVD cover, with the north face of Mount Everest grafted onto the Potala Palace in Lhasa

GET INTO TIBET

At the bar in Shangri-La

left — Shangri-La wine bottle label suggests a history going back to 19th-century French missionaries at Cizhong Church

below left — Bar in Lhasa

bottom left — Shangri-La Whisky, bottled in Sikkim

bottom — To go with drinks, chew on some Shangri-La dried yak jerky, made in Zhongdian

opposite page — **Sexing up Shangri-La: sex replaces spirituality as a drawcard in SW China**

top left — Shangri-La crooner, on CD cover from Yunnan

top right — Shangri-La belle on a CD label: the yellow Tibetan script means 'Senjinida' (sun and moon of the heart).

middle — Chinese dancers posing as Tibetans show a lot of leg for performance at high-end Chinese resort hotel, Sichuan

bottom left — The CD album 'Springtime in Shangri-La' shows a singer wearing Mosuo ethnic-style dress

bottom right — Model in hodge-podge of ethnic dress, on cover of China Eastern airlines inflight magazine

བཅིངས་འགྲོལ་སྐྱལ་མ།
བརྗེ་དང་གི་ཡུལ་གྱུ།
སེམས་ཀྱི་ནེ་རྫེའི་ཕྱུར་ལ་རྫེ་ལམ་འབོར།

Xiange 香格里

卓玛拉初
亚东

香巴拉 Shangri-la
心境·意境·天境 2005年第4期 总第64期

走近川川
温馨与柔美抵达的梦境

The Shambhala myth

left   Tanka artist painting a mural of Shambhala, Dharamsala

middle left   Mural from Bhutan shows planetary orbits and Tibetan universe, according to the arcane Kalachakra cosmological system

middle right   Tanka detail showing the Kalachakra deity, at the heart of Shambhala

bottom   A rare itinerant storyteller, or *lama mani*, uses tankas as teaching scrolls for audience at a temple in Dharamsala

opposite page   Shambhala tanka, showing the sacred city of Kalapa at centre. In lower section, the king of Shambhala rides forth to battle the forces of evil.

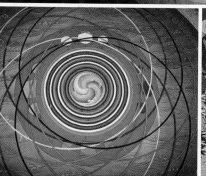

High Lamas

top   Temple mural of HH the 14th Dalai Lama, Dharamsala

above   The 13th Dalai Lama, in exile in India — the first
           Dalai Lama ever to be photographed

left   Temple mural of Tsongkhapa, regarded as the first
           Dalai Lama

opposite page

Landscapes with a definite aura of Shangri-La, but where are they?

Some clues

top   Central Tibet

middle   Hunza

bottom   Ladakh

On pilgrimage in Tibet

above Man juggling prayer-wheel and lapdog, on Lingkor Circuit, Lhasa

right Women with yak-butter offerings, making the rounds of Tashilhunpo Monastery, Shigatse

below Pilgrims prostrating outside the Jokhang Temple, Lhasa

Portraits from the plateau

top left   Woman with turquoise-studded perak headdress at festival in Leh, Ladakh

top right   Qiang woman from Songpan region with elaborate headdress, mainly of amber beads

above left   Ngakpa (shaman) with outlandish hair, from Amdo area

above right   Man with red tassels woven into hair, Everest region

BHUTAN

Creatures real and mythical, drawn from Tibet's rich mythological database

above left   Towering yeti, depicted on Bhutanese stamp

above right   Mural of naga or water deity, Tibet

left   Tibetan antelope, on Chinese stamp

below left   Wild yak, on Bhutanese stamp

below right   Mural of garuda, a bird-like deity, Tibet

BHUTAN

NU 20   YAK
BOS GUNNIENS

above left   Snow leopard from India

above right   Takin from Bhutan

below   Male and female snow lions from Tibet

Shangri-La owes a lot to the myth of Shambhala, which derives from ancient Tibetan texts

top — Novice monks study Tibetan loose-leaf texts, Sikkim

above left — The mantra Om Mani Padme Hum, carved in a mani-stone, Dharamsala

above right — Yak skulls engraved with Tibetan text, Lhasa

below — Written in stone: copying text from Tibetan book back into stone, Lhasa

Michael Buckley stumbled into this Shangri-La project a few years back – well, actually, he stumbled into a pub lunch with Hilary Bradt, who suggested publishing a guidebook. Not quite sure if she was joking, Buckley decided to take on the challenge. Buckley has trekked and travelled widely in the Himalayan and Karakoram regions. He is author of a handful of books about the Tibetan region, including *Eccentric Explorers* (2008), which profiles ten wacky adventurers bent on unlocking the secrets of Tibet; *Tibet: The Bradt Travel Guide* (2006); and *Heartlands: Travels in the Tibetan World* (Summersdale Publishers, 2002), a travel narrative about forays to the far reaches of the Tibetan plateau. In his dreams, Buckley lives in a clifftop castle with views of Himalayan snowcaps and a steady supply of yak ice-cream. In fact, this book was completed with a steady supply of Peach Blossom Tea, from a sea-level venue with views of snowcapped coastal mountains as inspiration.

www.himmies.com In support of this book and Bradt's Tibet guidebook is a special website with travellers' tales, dodgy advice, warped insights and provocative discussion related to travel in the Tibetan world. Log on to find out more.

AUTHOR STORY

Cambridge, September 2004: James Hilton won't be showing up for lunch. He's been dead for 50 years. That's why we're here – to commemorate the fact. Actually, I have gatecrashed this annual get-together of the James Hilton Society at the last minute. The long-departed writer is certainly here in spirit: I am astonished to find, seated opposite, a man who is the spitting image of James Hilton – same Roman nose, same determined jaw, same faraway look in the eyes. Turns out to be a close relative, Trevor, who is the treasurer of the Society. At this table, I'm surrounded by the Hilton clan, who are chuffed to learn a Canadian travel writer has made the pilgrimage. The Hiltons ply me with wine (a dangerous thing when jetlagged) and refuse to let me pay for anything. But despite being woozy, I am all ears – for stories about Hilton.

And why am I present at this obscure gathering of Hilton fans? Well, this author believes in applying the 'no-stone-unturned' approach when it comes to research. The concept for this guidebook evolved from a long-term fascination with Hilton's **Lost Horizon** and from a lifelong intrigue with mythology and travel to remote corners of the Himalaya. Why not put the two together in a guidebook? In the Himalaya, I have found the ultimate challenge and poetry: I have spent decades pursuing its lofty realms. And what has kept me going back is the special nature of the Tibetan people, who appear near-mythical to me because their logic seems to runs counter to everything in the West. Tibetans are extraordinary for their deep spiritualism and compassionate faith. You won't find a hardier human than a Tibetan nomad – totally dependent on yaks for survival in a harsh environment, yet cheerfully indulging in doses of ribald humour.

Shangri-La was created inside the mind of a fiction writer James Hilton. But a lot of people find his utopian vision so convincing that they want to carry it around in their heads too. I am definitely one of those converts. Shangri-La is the best place you have never been to!

PUBLISHER'S FOREWORD
Hilary Bradt

Like many great literary ideas, this book was conceived in a pub. Michael Buckley had come to Chalfont St Peter from Cambridge where he had been researching the life of James Hilton, a private passion but not surprising for someone who has immersed himself in Tibet for the last two decades. It had been 40 years or so since I'd read *Lost Horizon* but I remembered with pleasure its blend of adventure and philosophy. As Michael talked about the creator of Shangri-La, and reminded me of the story, I knew we had a potential Bradt guide. One with a difference, and one that only a writer of Michael's calibre could pull off. Re-reading *Lost Horizon* only confirmed this original gut feeling that this was a true Bradt guide.

No, Shangri-La only exists in the mind, but readers of this book will find it hard to resist the urge to set off for the Himalaya on their own quest. I don't think they will be disappointed.

First published September 2008
Bradt Travel Guides Ltd
23 High Street, Chalfont St Peter, Bucks SL9 9QE, England
www.bradtguides.com

Published in the USA by The Globe Pequot Press Inc, 246 Goose Lane,
PO Box 480, Guilford, Connecticut 06475-0480

Text copyright © 2008 Michael Buckley
Maps copyright © 2008 Bradt Travel Guides Ltd
Photographs © 2008 Michael Buckley
Illustrations © Carole Vincer
Project Management: Navigator Guides, www.navigatorguides.com

The author and publishers have made every effort to ensure the accuracy of the information in this book at the time of going to press. However, they cannot accept any responsibility for any loss, injury or inconvenience resulting from the use of information contained in this guide.

ISBN-13: 978 1 84162 204 0

British Library Cataloguing in Publication Data
A catalogue record for this book is available from the British Library

Photographs Michael Buckley
Illustrations Carole Vincer
Maps Malcolm Barnes, Steve Munns, Dave Priestley (colour map)

Typeset from the author's disc by Dorchester Typesetting Group Ltd
Printed and bound in India by Nutech Photolithographers

Acknowledgements

Some real gems for this project were provided by Tibetan expert Bradley Rowe. Pat and Baiba Morrow came up with excellent insider viewpoints on various Himalayan destinations. Simon Anholt, an advisor on national image, contributed an unusual perspective on the Shangri-La brand. Tony Williams provided details for southwest China from his extensive travels there. I would like to thank Gord and Gail Konantz for their input on Nepal, John Howarth for notes on Mustang, Sara Jackson and Karim for Hunza material, Rocky Dang and Karma Wangdi in Bhutan, and Doko in Tibet. Chung Tsering provided Tibetan script for the language section – a laborious task. For research and clues on James Hilton, special thanks go to John Hammond and Trevor Pound of the James Hilton Society (www.jameshiltonsociety.co.uk). Tony Williams provided details for southwest China from his extensive travels there. Paul Ehrlich sent me back to forage for more gems, with Matthieu and Mareile Paley providing superb photography for an expanded story on Shangri-La – the nucleus of this book. Donald Greig and Adrian Phillips at Bradt both had considerable input in shaping the material and the concept. Special thanks go to Hilary Bradt, who inspired the guidebook approach to Shangri-La, and who took a gamble on publishing this book—as she has done with many titles to exotic and off-beat destinations. For this risk-taking, she has been awarded an MBE—in recognition of her groundbreaking work in travel publishing and promoting responsible tourism. Over the decades, through the unique Bradt publishing series, Hilary has opened up wonderful new worlds for many travellers.

FEEDBACK REQUEST

The curse of the guidebook writer is that absolutely nothing stays the same. Glaciers melt, villages are flooded, forests are chopped down, hotels and phone numbers mutate. Buddhists have a word for this phenomenon: *anicca*, the impermanence of all things. So, if you notice something has radically changed, or is simply not there anymore, please drop a postcard from whichever Shangri-La it is that you are in. I welcome suggestions, comments, insights, travel tips and travellers' tales. Send snail-mail to: Michael Buckley, c/o Bradt Travel Guides Ltd, 23 High St, Chalfont St Peter, Bucks SL9 9QE, UK. Or email to: buckeroo555@yahoo.com.

Contents

Introduction

INTO THE TIBETAN WORLD

A little mythology can be a very dangerous thing. Certain books and movies leave you with a burning desire to drop everything and go. James Hilton's *Lost Horizon* – the book as well as the movie – is one of these. Before you travel, you dream – and *Lost Horizon* gets you dreaming about the Himalaya. It transports you to another world.

The novel that gave the world 'Shangri-La' starts out with the hijacking of an aircraft. A rather advanced idea for a novel set in 1931, and this is no ordinary aircraft – it has been specially modified for high-altitude flying. The plane and its passengers depart for Peshawar, but are hijacked for the voyage to Shangri-La. They crash-land in paradise – and their incredible tale gets underway.

But to some ears, this tale of Shangri-La reverberates with much deeper echoes. It would appear that Hilton hijacked the myth, borrowing heavily from the ancient Tibetan legend of Shambhala: the similarities with Shangri-La are too many and too striking to be coincidental.

No sooner did Hilton create the mythical realm of Shangri-La than he appears to have lost control of it. In short order, a Hollywood movie got under way where the director added an alluring female character, making Shangri-La a romantic escapade rather than a spiritual one. In 1942, President Franklin Roosevelt announced to reporters that bombing raids over Tokyo had originated from Shangri-La. He was referring to an idyllic hideaway he'd built in the hills outside Washington and named after Hilton's monastery. The US Navy named an aircraft carrier under construction the USS *Shangri-La*. All of which must have appalled Hilton, whose community of Shangri-La was based on peaceful and harmonious values.

Were he alive today, Hilton would be astounded by the commercial uses that Shangri-La has been put to. Thousands of hotels, resorts, restaurants and bars have been christened Shangri-La. And since Shangri-La first appeared, numerous claims have been made swearing to be the real location. Regions from Bhutan to Pakistan find Shangri-La a convenient form of branding.

The Chinese have been late off the mark, but have done so in spectacular fashion. In the late 1990s, several regions of Yunnan and Sichuan staked rival claims to being the real Shangri-La, bent on collecting tourist cash. This has led to an avalanche of Shangri-La photo books, CDs, DVDs and travel guides, all devised by Chinese spin doctors attached to local tourism authorities. And bootleg Chinese translations of Hilton's *Lost Horizon*.

In Daocheng, upper Sichuan, while gazing at shelves of books about Shangri-

La, an idea crystallised: that somebody (like myself) should write a contrary guidebook, taking on these Chinese howlers about finding the real Shangri-La – and presenting a much wider range of candidates across the Himalaya. The idea was put on ice, but something very dramatic happened to bring the idea forward again. In May 2002, in one of the most brazen rebranding exercises in history, Beijing approved the official renaming of the three counties in Yunnan to 'Shangri-La County'. Hilton had not only been pirated, his entire story had been hijacked, with an abrupt crash-landing in Yunnan.

Fortunately, the word 'Shangri-La' cannot be copyrighted or brand-named because, since Hilton's day, it has found its way into the English dictionary. In the process, the scope has widened from Hilton's novel to a general synonym for paradise in the Himalaya. Shangri-La is an elusive, mysterious realm – one where details are vague and obscure. Shangri-La is in fact more defined by what is not there. No sickness, no disease. No guns. No police. No problems with money. To which we might add the following updated shortlist: no Britney Spears, no BlackBerrys or Burberrys, no Chanels or Guccis, no Starbucks.

You will find strong elements of Shangri-La in the Himalaya, hosting the highest peaks and deepest valleys on earth. You will be enthralled by stunning settings with snowcapped peaks, verdant valleys and Tibetan monasteries. But it's highly dubious that you will find these elements all in the same location – because Shangri-La is an impossible composite created in the mind of James Hilton. If you're getting warm, getting closer to the spirit of Shangri-La, here's the litmus test: is the aura of spirituality strong? Is the place imbued with an old-Tibetan fustiness, redolent of yak-butter? Or is there a strong whiff of money in the air?

You are holding the first Western guidebook to Shangri-La. But the concept of writing guidebooks to paradise is actually nothing new. Centuries ago, Tibetan high lamas wrote tracts on how a pilgrim could reach the hidden paradise of Shambhala, though they emphasised that the way was extremely difficult. These fall into the tradition of spiritual guides. Across the Tibetan world today, pilgrimage is the prime motivation for travel. Tibetans must rank among the most devout pilgrims on the planet: they throng to sacred sites to seek spiritual fulfillment, and to gain merit.

Pilgrimage is regarded as a life-changing experience. To make a pilgrimage is to strip the self of coverings until the core shines through. And joining pilgrims on the same path will surely rub off on you, as a trekker. The pilgrim shares a lot in common with the trekker – on a quest for places of simplicity, tranquillity, serenity. Trekking is itself a form of meditation – forging a spiritual bond with nature, with few distractions and little materialism. You concentrate on the rhythm of walking, good food, good sleep under the stars. The simplicity of getting there one step at a time resets your brain, and puts you in a better space as you absorb the splendid landscapes, the vastness, the silence, the stillness.

After 75 years of searching, nobody has found convincing evidence to match Hilton's fiction with a real location for the Himalayan paradise. Which ultimately may not be the point. In this quest, what you discover along the way may turn out to be far more precious.

Hilton's flight of fancy – the plane from Baskul to Peshawar, diverted to Shangri-La via Shambhala – is beyond the pale. But there is no shortage of contenders for Shangri-La: whether pilgrim or trekker, you are bound to discover extraordinary Himalayan realms and hidden valleys by following this guidebook. The emphasis is on remote, pristine realms with high mountain ranges – located in nature reserves or national parks. Use this book as your portal to the magical Tibetan world.

Part One

THE LEGEND

Government Lamaist theocracy, founded 1734. System is hierarchical: the older the lama, the higher up the scale.

Ethnic composition Mixed Tibetan and Chinese stock for people of the valley, and mixed Latin/European/Asian stock for lamas. Brits have proved troublesome to integrate.

Religion Loose blend of Tibetan Buddhist and lapsed Capuchin (Catholic), with some Taoism thrown in.

Terrain Remote, rugged, secluded. Shangri-La cannot be seen from the air because it is well camouflaged.

Highest point Mount Karakal, estimated height over 8,500m.

Most striking features Lamasery of Shangri-La, halfway up Karakal, with fertile valley stretching below.

Time zone Time advances slowly here, with no particular rush to do anything. Lama average age: 108.

Economy Gold deposits take care of all trading needs. The lamas are not only old, they are very wealthy.

Himalayan Utopia

> A map of the world that does not include Utopia is not worth even glancing at, for it leaves out the one country at which Humanity is always landing. And when Humanity lands there, it looks out, and seeing a better country, sets sail. Progress is the realisation of Utopias.

> *Oscar Wilde*

From the dawn of time, cultures around the world have dreamed of creating the ideal society. Human beings are utopian by nature, longing for a paradise where people live in safety and peace – free from fear, disease and death – in harmony with each other and their environment. These paradises range from the mythical Garden of Eden and Plato's republic of philosopher-kings to 19th-century progressive experiments in communalism in Europe and America, and to the counter-cultural communities of the 1970s in the West. There is a dark side to these utopian visions: spurred by their faith, messianic cults have attempted to bring future visions to present life through violence. Secular utopian instigators – from the French Revolution's cult of reason to Soviet Communism and Chinese Maoism – have ended up spilling oceans of blood for their revolutionary cause. Mass murder in the 20th century has been practised by secular regimes on a scale that would make a medieval fanatic shudder.

At the forefront of creating the ideal society have been lone visionary writers. England has proved to be a rich source of ideas. In 1516, Sir Thomas More gave us the word Utopia with his work of the same name – about an island paradise with a perfect legal, social and political system. Francis Bacon's *The New Atlantis* (1626) depicts a technological paradise run by scientist-priests, developing in leaps and bounds through innovation and experimentation. Jonathan Swift took a satirical swipe at island utopias in *Gulliver's Travels*, published in 1726. In a similar vein, Samuel Butler's *Erewhon* (published in 1872) prophesied – half in jest – that machines can develop consciousness and would eventually replace humans (today no longer seen as a joke).

In the early 1930s, on the heels of the most devastating war known to history at the time, came two utopian visions from England with very different approaches – but curiously sharing the idea of genetic tinkering at their core. Aldous Huxley's *Brave New World* (1932) presents a world projected 600 years into the future, with beautiful people, no disease, designer babies, and dark overtones. And in 1933, James Hilton's *Lost Horizon* made a startling addition to the lexicon of magical dream worlds: the fabled realm of Shangri-La, set somewhere to the north of Tibet in 1931. At centre stage in Hilton's novel are adepts who have discovered how to extend their lifespan to well over a hundred.

Utopia derives from two Greek words: *u* meaning 'no', and *topos* meaning 'place'. So Utopia means 'no place', though some interpret it as 'good place'. *Erewhon* is 'nowhere' with letters scrambled. And Shangri-La, Hilton informs us,

3

will not be found on any map. The concept appears to have sprung entirely from the imagination of Hilton. This Himalayan utopia is hidden deep in snowcapped mountains, with a spiritual community at its core, and with a secret mission entrusted in its hands: to preserve thousands of years of knowledge for humankind in the aftermath of great destruction.

Hilton did not use the word 'holocaust' in *Lost Horizon* because the term was not generalised to cover mass murder and nuclear destruction until the 1950s. He wrote about 'the technique of homicide' because the word 'genocide' was not coined until the 1940s. Hilton was ahead of his time with his vision in *Lost Horizon* of mass destruction caused by aerial bombing. He lived to see destruction of terrifying proportions, when a plane commanded by General Paul Tibbetts dropped the first atomic bomb on Hiroshima on 6 August 1945. The subsequent development of nuclear strike capabilities – and development of technology that can significantly alter the course of nature – have combined to significantly alter global viewpoints. Curiously, for someone so preoccupied with mass destruction, James Hilton did not write about atomic warfare, though there was ample opportunity to do so when introducing a post-1945 reprint of *Lost Horizon*. Aldous Huxley did write about atomic warfare, in a preface for a 1946 reprint of *Brave New World:*

> The release of atomic energy marks a great revolution in human history, but not (unless we blow ourselves to bits and so put an end to history) the final and most searching revolution. This really revolutionary revolution is to be achieved, not in the external world, but in the souls and flesh of human beings.

After World War II, dystopian novels seemed to be more in vogue than utopian, in works like George Orwell's *1984* (published 1949) and Ray Bradbury's *Fahrenheit 451* (published 1953). Sinister new scenarios surfaced in the Atomic Age. In the mid-1950s, a declassified report from the Ministry of Food in the UK revealed that British contingency planners worried there would a dramatic shortage of tea in the aftermath of a nuclear attack – and that the British people would not be able to cope with such a serious situation (the lack of tea, that is).

Fritzie Manuel, co-author of *Utopian Thought in the Western World*, claims that since the A-bomb there has been a radical shift in utopian ideals: 'You don't need a vast number of people to destroy the planet anymore, and that puts utopians in a different position altogether... Utopian thinking now has to do with the preservation of the human race. Utopians of the twenty-first century are those who think we can preserve the world. And it's not one class or society: it's all of humanity... We all have to become utopian because we all have to believe we can preserve the world.'

In the early 21st century, the possibility of mass destruction looms larger than it did during World War II: worldwide, there are thought to be over 30,000 nuclear warheads in existence. Why is it that after thousands of years of chasing utopia, mankind is sinking into more and more wars? – with battles often launched in the name of religion? – wars that get deadlier and deadlier? Why is it that no way has been found to prevent genocide, or even to stop it once it has started? The UN has proved powerless in 'ethnic cleansing' situations like Rwanda or the Sudan. The UN has proved powerless to prevent genocide in Tibet, under its Chinese military occupiers.

Given this context, Hilton's *Lost Horizon* seems even more relevant today than when it was first written, because of Shangri-La's role in preserving the positive values of civilisation in the event of great destruction. Encapsulating this relevance is a statement that appeared on the Abebooks website: 'Although Hilton's sentimentality, optimism and sense of melodrama may now seem a bit old-fashioned, it still charms. Fantasy has become much darker in the post-nuclear age.'

Many utopian visions are driven by faith – often religious faith of some sort. Acting as a 'glue' for the community at Shangri-La is a strong thread of spiritualism. It is an odd mix of lapsed Catholicism and Tibetan Buddhism, with dashes of Taoism and Confucianism thrown in. Taoism and Buddhism are more philosophies than religions. Tibetan Buddhism actually does not qualify to be labelled a 'religion' – if belief in a superior deity is the prime criterion. Tibetan Buddhism is a highly evolved system of ethics and philosophy, with values like peace, compassion and harmony at its core. The ancient philosophy of Tibet has much to offer a world that seems to be constantly war-mongering. As the 14th Dalai Lama has said a number of times: 'We Buddhists believe every human life is precious. Our survival, our future is very much linked with one another. So therefore the concept of war and destroying your enemy is old-fashioned, out of date.'

And other utopian visions are driven by advances in science and medicine. The American alternative magazine *Utne Reader* published an article in June 2005 that started with a question: Is building a better human the key to utopia – or the world's most dangerous idea? With astounding recent advances in nanoscience, bio-engineering, information technology and cognitive science, researchers have been able to engineer mice that are super strong and fast, and live so long that a human equivalent would be at least 200. Futurists envisage the day when our species will be a blend of biology and machine, a race of cyborgs. They talk about satisfying the huge demand for longer lives, prettier children, better moods, instant cancer cures. Author Jeremy Rifkin, a longtime critic of life patenting and the biotech industry, warns that people are falling victim to an old misguided Western faith in human perfectability. He says the public will be seduced by new technologies whose destructive power far exceeds any benefits.

THE MYTHS

Most Tibetans haven't heard of Shangri-La, but James Hilton probably based his story on the Tibetan legend of Shambhala, which most Westerners haven't heard about. Because the two myths have many similarities, some Tibetan dictionaries define Shangri-La as being Shambhala. While Hilton must have lifted from the Shambhala legend, he modified and embellished with other ideas from the mythological database of Asia and beyond. Some possibilities are presented here.

TIBETAN LEGENDS

Shambhala As earthly paradises go, Tibet's vision is a bit different. There are several Tibetan versions of the legend of Shambhala, but they run in the same pattern. Somewhere to the north of India is a kingdom ringed by impenetrable snowcapped mountains and cloaked in mist. In this sanctuary, poverty, hunger, crime and sickness are unknown, and people live a hundred years. In the city of Kalapa there is a glittering palace where the sacred Kalachakra teachings are kept. According to the legend, about 300 years from now, when Lhasa lies under water, the world will erupt in chaotic warfare. When the last barbarian thinks he has conquered the world, the mists will lift and the king of Shambhala will ride forth to destroy the forces of evil – and establish a new Golden Age of a thousand years.

First mention of the kingdom of Shambhala appears in the Hindu epic the *Mahabharata*, dating to possibly 300BC. The legend of Shambhala took over a millennium to reach the highlands of Tibet but, when it did, Tibetans took to it with great enthusiasm, becoming the greatest guardians of the Shambhala teachings. Shambhala became part of the esoteric Kalachakra teachings, which reached Tibet from India in the 10th century AD. The teachings were handed down

DEFINITION

Shangri-la [shang gree laa] noun

1 a Tibetan utopia of eternal youth and peace, set in a hidden valley in the novel *Lost Horizon* (1933) by James Hilton
2 earthly paradise, a faraway haven or hideaway of idyllic beauty and tranquillity; ideal refuge from the pressures of modern civilisation
3 a: remote, beautiful and delightful place where life approaches perfection ('those familiar with the Shangri-las of the Atlantic coast…') b: a place whose name is not known or not given ('will fly in huge flocks from 100 unnameable Shangri-Las…')

MY SHANGRI-LA

Personalise your paradise. The dictionary does not go into details about usages like this one: 'You've come to the Shangri-La of all cheesecake lovers' dreams.' Like the Holy Grail, 'Shangri-La' can be anything you drool over or dream about. That can mean very different things to different people. The explorer's Shangri-La would surely be finding a lost kingdom. The angler's Shangri-La is lots of fish and tranquillity, but others would find that dead boring or even cruel to fish (Tibetans do not fish for this reason). And the mountaineer's Shangri-La – reaching the top of an 8,000m peak – would absolutely terrify others. Trekker's Shangri-La? Culinary Shangri-La? Book-lover's Shangri-La? Electronic Shangri-La? Here are some interpretations of what Shangri-La really means…

Scholar's Shangri-La

…The institute is a physics Shangri-La, a paradise on Earth for those lucky enough to get an appointment there…
– *as reported in US magazine* Science, *2003, referring to the Perimeter Institute for Theoretical Physics, Ontario, Canada*

Old timer's Shangri-La

We're not talking about languishing in nursing homes struggling to recognise themselves in the mirror and playing with wool here; we're talking about people in their 90s riding bikes, digging up carrots and going fishing – or doing just about exactly what it was they did back when they were 40. We're talking about Shangri-La.
– *article about centenarian islanders of Okinawa, Japan, appearing in the* South China

as spoken word, but in the 11th century, the mythical land was written up in the Tenjur and the Kanjur, the Tibetan canon. The Shambhala theme is often depicted in Tibetan temple murals in mandalic form. There are large circular Shambhala murals in the Potala and the Norbulingka in Lhasa, and also at Samye. These show a double ring of snowcapped mountains, with the palace of Kalapa at the centre of the mandala.

Many other monastic frescoes portray the Kalachakra deities. Tsongkhapa and other great Tibetan wizards and sages are thought to have visited Shambhala in the past. When the Golden Age dawns, it is said that the tomb of Tsongkhapa at Ganden will open up, and he will live again to teach true wisdom. A number of ancient, surrealistic Tibetan texts have been written on how to get to Shambhala. Some say Shambhala lies in west Tibet, near the Guge kingdom; others think it is

Shangri-La of ultimate fear

Situated in the middle of an isolated paradise, it is thought to be part of the fictional Shangri-La that James Hilton wrote about in *Lost Horizon*. In spite of the dangers, it continues to lure climbers to its slopes of dark grey rock. It is the ultimate fear and as such must be faced and overcome by climbers aiming for alpine excellence. In scaling Everest, you are a great climber to the world. Summit K2, and you are a true climber to climbers.
– *from website K2climb.net*

Spa-goer's Shangri-La

How could Frank Capra know in 1937 that Ojai, his setting for *Lost Horizon*, would today host a spa-goer's Shangri-La? Nestled in the mountains near California's coast, this idyllic 31,000 square foot spa is only a 90-minute drive from Los Angeles. The resort combines a mind/body philosophy of internal well-being (nature hikes, yoga, virtual reality biking) with sybaritic treatments (even the robes are plush).
– *review of Ojai Spa in* Hilary Online Magazine, *2007*

Photographer's Shangri-La

It seems that every photographer has his/her special place, a place where all seems in balance, we feel most alive, and the land speaks to us on a level that can only be described as spiritual. For me that place is California's Lost Coast.
– *Joseph Dickerson, story about One Photographer's Shangri-La, in* Shutterbug magazine, *April 1999*

Travel writer's Shangri-La

Shangri-La for a travel writer? Maybe staying put, not moving around at all:
… an extraordinary number of the many 'travel' books about 'abroad' in a fixed setting have been concerned with buying and doing up houses… [what you might call] 'Shangri-La' housing tales: Francis Mayes' *Under the Tuscan Sun*;…and Peter Mayle's famous – or notorious – slim volume, *A Year in Provence*. … Deep down the pursuit of happiness is the real object of the Shangri-La writer.
– *Adam Hopkins, 'A View from the Armchair', essay appearing in* The Travel

in the north, in Changtang, or much further north in the Kunlun range, or even in Mongolia. Yet others think it lies at the North Pole. Some Tibetans believe Shambhala is a mystical nirvana of the gods; others believe it is real, but that the journey is not external but internal – and that the war with ignorance is in your own heart.

Tibetan literature points the way to Shambhala. The most notable effort is the guidebook *Shambhala Lamyig*, written in 1775 by the third Panchen Lama, Lobsang Palden Yeshe. The third Panchen Lama mentions an earlier version by another lama, but points out that this lama received the contents of his guidebook from a dream, which the lama regarded as a source of delusion.

These guidebooks to Shambhala are short on practical directions, but long on talk of obstacles on the epic journey. In scenarios worthy of *Lord of the Rings*, they describe crossing burning deserts, passing through forests filled with supernatural creatures and poisonous snakes, and finding a way past mountains thronged with demigods and demons – who must be placated. For instance, to keep one demoness from destroying him, a seeker must first kill a winged lion (there are many to choose from, and all ferocious) and present the flesh to her and answer questions in a manner that shows pure motivation to reach Shambhala. Further down the road (about six months, actually) the seeker will encounter a white mountain with beautiful forests, but must not go there because 500 demonesses with copper lips will do him great harm. The odyssey goes on, with directions on how to sidestep beautiful serpent maidens, horse-faced daughters of demons, goddesses, flesh-eaters, hungry ghosts and assorted gnarly creatures.

It may well be that these dream-like guidebooks are simply offering advice on how a practitioner can overcome tremendous obstacles on the path to enlightenment. Some find them hard to take literally. The 14th Dalai Lama adds a twist on finding Shambhala. He believes Shambhala exists but it might not be on this planet – it might be found somewhere in outer space. And if it were to be found on this planet, then it would exist in another dimension, unseen by the average mortal. According to the 14th Dalai Lama, 'even if Shambhala was to be found somewhere on this planet, it can only be perceived by those who have a pure mind and pure karmic propensities.' And obviously, anybody like that is not about to divulge the location.

One reason that Shambhala might exist in another dimension is that it is not a small place. Population is estimated at 960 million by one count, and 960 million villages by another – which would be tough to tuck away in a Himalayan valley without attracting attention. The Shambhala legend did not surface in the West until the 19th century, when Hungarian scholar Csoma de Koros translated a large number of Tibetan texts (see pages 32 and 123–3).

Because of imprecise rendering from Tibetan into English, Shambhala appears in early texts as Xembala, Shamballa, Shamballah and a host of other variants.

Beyuls A parallel myth to Shambhala is the legend of the *beyuls*, or sacred hidden valleys. The myth of the *beyuls* is attributed to 8th-century sorcerer and sage Padmasambhava (Guru Rinpoche), who was instrumental in establishing Tantric Buddhism in Tibet. Although Shambhala belongs to a different tradition that has little to do with Padmasambhava, some lamas consider Shambhala to be a hidden valley – actually, the largest and most remote of all.

Padmasambhava is thought to have described the locations of scores of hidden lands to his consort, Yeshe Tsogyal, who preserved the exact co-ordinates in cryptic language written on yellow scrolls (called *terma*). These *terma* were then hidden in walls of rock, and in caves and lakes, to be discovered by later generations; also buried were magical ritual objects. A lama who discovers such a scroll is called a *terton*, or treasure-revealer, and can guide others to the hidden valley. An alternate version claims that *tertons* can discover the hidden *dharma* teachings (*terma*) through deep meditative states. These are referred to as 'mind treasures' to distinguish them from the physical treasures.

The sacred hidden valleys (*beyuls*) are scattered throughout the Himalaya because Padmasambhava travelled widely in Tibet, Bhutan, Nepal and Sikkim. A *beyul* is reputed to be a valley where plants and animals have miraculous powers, where the ageing process is halted, and where wisdom and knowledge will increase in record time. Several tracts describe miraculous water, which, when drunk, makes women not only beautiful but sexually passionate, and will cure all their illnesses. If men drink the water, they will attain youth and virility and become as strong as the warriors of King Gesar, a legendary hero.

The main purpose of the *beyul* is to provide sanctuary from the bleak conditions stemming from foreign invasion or persecution of Buddhist teachings. The *beyuls* are more than a treasure-hunt. Access involves decoding the cryptic language of the scrolls that act as guides. And each hidden valley can only be opened when the time is right – a time that is fixed and cannot be altered. In the 1960s, a Sikkimese lama attempted to lead a party to the hidden valley of Pemagang, to the side of Kangchenjunga, using a *terma* as his guidebook. But an avalanche hit the party, killing several, and he was forced to turn back. Around the same time, a Sherpa from Jumbesi related that when he tried to enter the hidden valley of Khenbalung he was forced to turn back – because the way was barred by a yeti. A yeti as a *beyul* sentinel? There's a thought: maybe yetis are safely ensconced inside *beyuls*.

Bon kingdoms Pre-dating the arrival of Buddhism in Tibet is Bon shamanism, which was heavy on magic and sorcery. The Bon heartland of Olmo Lungring shares some parallel features with Shambhala. Much of the Bon culture was obliterated, including its fabled base, known as Zhangzhung (also spelled Shangshung and other variants). The location of the Lost Kingdom of Zhangzhung has never been identified, but is associated with the region of far-west Tibet.

For more about the vanished kingdom of Zhangzhung, see 'Every Palace Has a Silver Lining', in the Tibet chapter, pages 84–5.

Mount Meru Sacred to both Bon and Tibetan Buddhism is Mount Meru, the centre of the Tibetan universe. This is closely identified with Mount Kailash in far-west Tibet, the haunt of the highly revered Tibetan sage Milarepa.

Near Kailash lies the sacred lake of Manasarovar, with holy waters. Similar in concept to sacred peaks, numerous lakes are revered in Tibet. In Nepal there is a legend of a paradisal mountain lake known as Anavatapta, from which magical healing waters flow – and where wondrous herbs and strange creatures abound.

THE AGE OF KALI

The Hindu apocalyptic legend of the Age of Kali comes from sacred scriptures. Many believe that the earth is currently in Kali Yuga (the Age of Kali), also known as the Iron Age, the Age of Despair and the Dark Age, because people are the furthest possible from god. Here are some characteristics of Kali Yuga: rulers will become unreasonable and non-spiritual, and instead of protecting their subjects, they will become a danger to the world. Taxes will be heavy and unjustified. Avarice and corruption will be rife. Animosity between men will flare to great heights. The right hand will deceive the left hand. People will not trust each other, even in their own family. There will be teenage pregnancies. People will, without reason, destroy trees and gardens. There will be no respect for animals. The list goes on...

Nobody seems sure when Kali Yuga will finish – it could go on for centuries – but in this apocalyptic vision, at the end of Kali Yuga an Avatar will arrive on earth riding a white horse. The world will suffer a fiery end where all evil will perish and demons will be vanquished. And then the new golden age of Satya Yuga will commence, characterised by virtue, wisdom and spirituality, with practically no ignorance or vice. In this age, people may live for a thousand years.

XANADU

Xanadu was Kublai Khan's deluxe summer palace, from which he ruled the Mongol Empire – at the time covering all of China, most of Asia, and all the way to eastern Europe. Marco Polo, visiting Xanadu in 1275, marvelled at the opulence and splendour of the palace, located in what is today Inner Mongolia. After the fall of the Mongol Empire, Xanadu was reduced to rubble, taking on a mythical aura – a utopian site buried in the sands of time. And a considerable time later, in a fog of opium smoking in England, Samuel Taylor Coleridge was inspired by a great vision of Xanadu. Unfortunately, by the time he awoke out of his opium haze, he was only able to remember a fragment of his dream – which was published in 1816 as the poem 'Kubla Khan'. There are some tenuous links between the legends of Xanadu and Shangri-La. In the 13th century, a great contest took place at the court of Kublai Khan to see which philosophy had the greatest power – Islam, Nestorian Christianity, Confucianism, Taoism or Tibetan Buddhism. Tibetan Buddhism prevailed, later becoming the official religion of Mongolia. In Chinese pinyin transliteration, Xanadu is rendered as Shangdu, or Shang-tu, thus sounding like the first syllable of Shangri-La.

PEACH BLOSSOM SPRING

Chinese mythology is full of stories about longevity. There are stories about discovering a 1,000-year-old mushroom and becoming immortal. In Chinese mythology there is a lost valley of the immortals in the Kunlun range: it is rumoured to be the location of a Taoist paradise where immortals live in perfect harmony.

Among the best-known longevity myths is Peach Blossom Spring. When Chinese hear the legend of Shangri-La, it reminds them of this story. In fact, when the movie *Lost Horizon* was adapted for a Chinese audience in 1938, the title was changed to 'Romance in the Peach Blossom Village'. Peach Blossom Spring is a short simple poem written by 4th-century poet Tao Qiang (aka Tao Yuan Ming) that tells of a mysterious utopia deep in the remote mountains of China. In this place, generations of Chinese had isolated themselves from China's wars and rebellions and knew nothing of the outside world. A fisherman exploring a river chanced across a forest of peach trees in full bloom. Entranced, he drifted in his boat, following the forest till it ended at the base of a mountain. He sighted a narrow opening illuminated by a shaft of light. The fisherman abandoned his boat and squeezed through the opening.

On the other side, he was amazed to find vast farmland and majestic farmhouses, fertile fields, beautiful lakes, mulberry trees, bamboo groves, and people who appeared very content with their lot. And hermits who had attained extreme longevity. The fisherman was warmly greeted by all the families in Peach Blossom Spring. They told him how their ancestors had fled to this hidden world some 500 years previously, and since then they had no contact with the outside world. The fisherman gave them details of the outside world and the people sighed, full of sorrow over the misfortunes of humanity.

After a few days, the fisherman decided he would have to go back to his own family. The villagers told him not to tell anyone what he had seen. The fisherman did his best to mark his way, and on reaching home, reported his discovery to the district magistrate. The magistrate sent men back with the fisherman to find this mysterious community, but he could find no traces of the markings he left, became disorientated, and the search was abandoned.

THEOSOPHIST LEGENDS

An enduring source of mythical mumbo-jumbo from the Himalaya is the Theosophical Society, a quasi-religious group founded in the late 19th century by Madame Helena Blavatsky, a Russian émigré who moved to the USA.

Agharti Agharti (also known as Agharta, Agarta, Agartta, Agarttha, Asgartha, Agarthi, Agarti and Agardhi) is a subterranean kingdom which possesses highly advanced technology. This myth was cooked up by Louis Jacolliot, a French consular official who served in India during the 1860s and became intrigued by oriental occultism, about which he wrote more than 20 volumes. In Calcutta,

Jacolliot heard a legend of a subterranean world beyond the Himalaya which he called 'Asgartha'.

In 1886, another French occultist, Alexandre Saint-Yves d'Alveydre, published a book entitled *Mission de l'Inde en Europe*, in which he described the underground Himalayan kingdom of Agharti in detail. Though intended as fiction, the author blurred the lines by claiming that his knowledge of Agharti was based on 'revealed' information – meaning it was received by Saint-Yves d'Alveydre himself through 'attunement'. He claimed that Agharti's crown jewel was a university that was a repository of secret knowledge, and that when the evil forces of the world were destroyed, these secrets would be revealed by mahatmas for the benefit of mankind. Apparently Saint-Yves d'Alveydre had second thoughts about publishing this work (by another account, he was sternly warned off disclosing secrets by an Indian Brotherhood), and set about destroying the copies printed.

The legend might have stopped there, but it was picked up and dusted off by Madame Blavatsky, founder of the Theosophical Society. In her work of monumental spiritual gibberish, *The Secret Doctrine* (1888), Madame Blavatsky

THE CURIOUS CASE OF THE LONG-LIVED HERBALIST

In 1933, the year that *Lost Horizon* came into the world with its incredible story about a 250-year-old High Lama, a parallel story about a feat of longevity appeared in the *New York Times*. The news story asserted that Chinese herbalist Li Chung 'Yun had died at the very ripe old age of 256. If true, that would be roughly double any previous record-breaking human lifespan ever traced. According to Chinese sources, the herbalist was born in 1677 in Sichuan, making him a tad older than the High Lama of Shangri-La.

It is said that Li Chung Yun received special recognition from the government in 1827 on his 150th birthday, and again in 1877 when he turned 200. On that anniversary, he gave a lecture about the power of wild foods and herbs at the University of China. The herbalist claims to have met a 500-year-old sage who instructed him on how to brew a special kind of herbal tea; he also consumed large amounts of wild ginseng. Unfortunately, Li Chung Yun had no documents to prove his age – but then again, photo ID did not exist in the 17th century, and nobody was issuing birth certificates to common folk either. The case of the herbalist was dismissed as ludicrous by doctors and scientists in the West. But consider this: life expectancy has dramatically risen over the last few centuries. According to anthropologists, primitive man was lucky to live past 20; in the Dark Ages, healthier people might have made it to 25 or 30. The average lifespan in the United States in the 1800s was around 25. By the year 2000, it had shot up to 80, or three times longer.

The Guinness Book of Records cites Frenchwoman Jeanne Calment as being the world's longest-lived person with verified papers, expiring in 1997 at the grand age of 122. She once met Van Gogh, and she rode her bicycle till the age of 100. In May 2008, a 76-year-old Nepalese man, Mr Serchan, reached the top of Everest – the oldest person to summit the peak. He was a few days shy of his 77th birthday.

The oldest living animal is thought to be Ming the clam – a mollusc dredged up off the coast of Iceland in 2007, and reckoned to be between 405 and 410 years of age, based on counting the rings on its shell. It was nicknamed Ming after the Chinese dynasty in power when it was born. There's no birth certificate for the mollusc, but the rings record everything.

TIBET

1903 A British invasion force of 3,000 troops and 10,000 pack animals marches into Tibet on the pretext of opening the place to trade with the British. The 13th Dalai Lama flees to Mongolia.

1904 British force pushes through to Lhasa, concludes a useless treaty and withdraws. As a result of this military action, British trade agencies are set up in Gyantse, Yatung and Gartok. Bhutan is carved off as separate entity.

1910 Chinese Army invades Tibet, 13th Dalai Lama flees to India.

1912 Tibetan uprising against Chinese.

1913 The 13th Dalai Lama returns to Lhasa to declare Tibetan independence.

1933 The 13th Dalai Lama dies in December, leaving a prophecy about a great holocaust in Tibet.

1935 The 14th Dalai Lama is born in Amdo.

1939 Tibet remains neutral during World War II, a real Shangri-La at the time, but peace is not to last.

1940 The 14th Dalai Lama is enthroned in Lhasa.

1947 India gains independence from Britain. The partitioning of India with creation of Muslim nations of Pakistan and Bangladesh costs millions of lives. Ladakh is absorbed into the Indian states of Jammu and Kashmir. Though officially independent since 1923, it is only after the British withdraw troops in 1947 that Nepal becomes truly independent.

1950 Chinese troops invade Tibet, crossing into Tibet proper in October.

1951 Under duress, Tibetan officials sign a 17-Point Agreement, which promises cultural autonomy but forfeits independence.

1959 National uprising against the Chinese on 10 March. The Dalai Lama escapes from Tibet into exile in India through Sikkim. Khampa guerrillas attack Chinese troops across southern Tibet from their base in Mustang.

1965 The Tibet Autonomous Region (TAR) is created, effectively reducing the area of ethnic Tibet by half.

1965–76 The madness of the Cultural Revolution hits Tibet hard, with wholesale destruction of temples.

1971 CIA withdraws support for Khampa guerrillas due to US rapprochement with China.

1974 Due to pressure from China, the Khampa guerrilla threat in Mustang is eliminated by Nepalese troops.

1975 Sikkim annexed by India; monarchy is abolished.

1974 Jigme Singye Wangchuck enthroned as fourth king of Bhutan.

1989 In March, severe rioting breaks out in Lhasa. In December, the Dalai Lama is awarded the Nobel Peace Prize.

1996 Anti-Dalai Lama campaign is launched in Tibet following fiasco over the choice of the 11th Panchen Lama.

Continued overleaf

SHANGRI-LA

1900 James Hilton born at Leigh, Lancashire, 9 September.

1920s Hilton at Cambridge University.

1932 In winter 1932, Hilton is at the British Library in London, reading up on missionaries to Tibet. He hits on the name for a lost Himalayan realm, settling on 'Shangri-La'.

1933 The manuscript for *Lost Horizon* is completed in April and published in September simultaneously on both sides of the Atlantic, to great critical acclaim.

1934 In December, film director Frank Capra picks up a copy of the novel at Union Station in Los Angeles to read on a train journey. He sets about persuading Columbia Pictures to buy the film rights.

1935 Columbia Pictures does more than buy the rights – they buy Hilton himself. Hilton is imported to Hollywood as consultant on script revisions for the movie adaptation of *Lost Horizon*.

1937 The movie *Lost Horizon* is released. Directed by Frank Capra, it is the biggest-budget movie made by Colombia Pictures of this era. The movie version spreads the fame of Shangri-La far and wide.

1938 A Chinese-dubbed version of the movie is released, with added Chinese songs like 'Peach Blossom Spring'.

1939 Pocket Books USA releases 10 titles in a new line of mass market paperbacks with eye-catching designs on the cover. The first is James Hilton's *Lost Horizon*. Other authors include Shakespeare, Agatha Christie, Samuel Butler and Pearl S. Buck.

1939 World War II breaks out. Hilton stays in Hollywood for the duration of the war, and goes on to adapt *Lost Horizon* as a radio script, a stage play and television drama.

1940s The movie Lost Horizon is shown to troops, but its pacifist message is largely removed.

1953 October issue of *National Geographic* runs a story on Hunza as a strange Shangri-La. Later *National Geographic* stories apply the Shangri-La image to Baltistan, Ladakh, Bhutan and other parts of the Himalaya – as well as parts of the USA.

1954 James Hilton dies on 20 December, at Long Beach, California. Alice Brown, his reconciled wife, is the executor of his estate. Although Hilton the author swiftly drops off the radar, the legend of Shangri-La lives on, mutating with a life of its own.

1961 Pocket Books USA paperback edition of *Lost Horizon* achieves its 47th reprint, with more than two million copies sold.

1966 October issue of *National Geographic* personalises Shangri-La in story by Desmond Doig, entitled: 'Sherpaland: My Shangri-La'.

1971 The first Shangri-La Hotel is opened in Singapore by Malaysian entrepreneur Robert Kuok. Pan Books prints a special edition of *Lost Horizon* for Shangri-La Hotel in 1972.

1973 In an era of blockbuster musicals, Colombia Pictures dusts off its *Lost Horizon* property and decides to remake it as a musical. The result is a total flop.

Continued overleaf

2002 A concrete monolith is erected in Potala Square to mark the 50th anniversary of the 'liberation of Tibet'.

2006 Railway reaches Lhasa, enabling exploitation of Tibet's vast mineral and other resources on a major scale.

2007 The Dalai Lama is awarded the Congressional Gold Medal, the highest honour bestowed by US Congress.

2008 In March, protests break out in Lhasa and spread to a huge swathe of the plateau. A vicious crackdown on Tibetans follows, as large numbers of Chinese military and paramilitary troops are mobilised and dispatched to the Tibetan region. Hundreds of Tibetans are killed, and thousands more arrested, imprisoned, or sent away for 're-education'. Scores more simply disappear: entire monasteries are emptied of monks, considered the instigators of these protests.

confirmed that not only was the network of tunnels of Agharti well-known to the Brahmins of India, but that these tunnels eventually led to a 'sacred island', the fabled Shambhala, under the sands of the Gobi Desert in Mongolia. Two legends are better than one, obviously. And for good measure, she later threw in Atlantis as being linked to Agharti – a sort of Atlantis of the Sands. She claimed to be in telepathic communication with wise men in all of them – Shambhala, Agharti and Atlantis. And those were the days before email.

The dwellers of the Aghartean realm are possessed of great powers and have knowledge of all the world's affairs. They can travel anywhere they want through ancient passageways by using flying cars of strange design.

Other Theosophists took up the search for Agharti, notably Nicholas Roerich, another Russian émigré, who launched expeditions into Central Asia. Roerich's book, *Shambhala* (1930), might well have been a source for Hilton. Theories were expounded that among the purported entrances to Agharti was one located deep in the Kunlun Mountains in northern Tibet, another between the paws of the Sphinx at Giza, and a third somewhere in the Potala Palace in Lhasa. Other hidden entrances are rumoured to exist at both the north pole and the south pole.

The Theosophists had some effect on the Nazis in Germany, who appropriated their logo (an ancient Buddhist symbol of longevity) and turned it into the swastika. In 1938, a Nazi expedition came to Tibet. It was led by Ernst Schafer and was under the auspices of the Ahnenerbe – a 'scientific' research organisation founded by Henrich Himmler to delve into the origins of the Aryan race. Himmler had modelled the SS on a Hindu warrior caste, and was fascinated by

1987 *Return to Shangri-La* published by Grafton Books, UK. The story continues some 50 years on, in this sequel by Leslie Halliwell.

1996 *Shangri-La: The Return to the World of Lost Horizon* published by William Morrow, NY. This sequel to *Lost Horizon*, written by Eleanor Clooney and Daniel Altieri, is set in Tibet and China in the 1960s.

1996 Zhongdian County in the Chinese province of Yunnan starts a campaign to change its name officially to Shangri-La County. Copies of *Lost Horizon* are published in Chinese to bolster this claim.

1999 Diqing-Shangri-La Airport opens in Zhongdian, capable of handling Boeing jets.

1999 Restored and digitally remastered version of movie *Lost Horizon* is re-issued as part of Columbia Classics series. However, there is still lost footage from the original version.

2002 Zhongdian County is renamed Shangri-La County with official approval from Beijing.

2003 *Lost Horizon* 70th anniversary edition is published by Summersdale, UK.

2005 Pocket Books USA publishes 106th reprint of *Lost Horizon*.

2006 Chinese subtitled version of digitally remastered *Lost Horizon* movie is released in Hong Kong, with jacket copy claiming that Shangri-La is located in Zhongdian.

2008 *Shangri-La: A Travel Guide to the Himalayan Dream* is published by Bradt Guides, UK, on the 75th anniversary of the first publication of *Lost Horizon*.

eastern religions. Hitler, a great believer in occultism, wanted to tap into the power of the underground race rumoured to be in Tibet.

The Lemurians Mountain-tops are believed to be the abode of deities and demons by Tibetans – with Mount Meru being the centre of the universe. A similar perspective is shared by many cultures, from Mount Olympus in ancient Greece, right up to...Mount Shasta in California.

In 1932, reporter Edward Lanser announced the sensational news that Mount Shasta, California, was home to a colony of Lemurians. The snows of Mount Shasta, 4,317m high, had been observed through a telescope by a professor who claimed to have sighted a temple of onyx and marble. The Lemurians were reported to venture into the local town of Weed to buy provisions, using huge gold nuggets, apparently derived from the mountain itself.

Apart from the gold nuggets, you probably couldn't mistake a knuckle-dragging Lemurian. Madame Blavatsky described them as a Root Race: giant apelike creatures, some with four arms, and some with a third eye in the back of their heads. A later Theosophist described Lemurians as being able to walk backwards as easily as forwards, and able to communicate through telepathy. A temple of precious stone atop a snowcapped mountain, odd inhabitants who communicate through telepathy, nuggets of gold used to pay for stores. It all has a terribly familiar ring.

Probably due to the ascendancy of television and a decline in reading skills in recent times, fiction and non-fiction have the potential to become fused – or confused. In a survey of 3,000 British adults conducted by British cable channel UKTV Gold in 2007, it was revealed that fully 23% thought Winston Churchill was a fictional character, while 58% thought that Sherlock Holmes had been a real person. Intrepid pilot Biggles of the adventure books for boys was thought by 33% of respondents to be a real person, while 23% thought Florence Nightingale was a figment of some writer's imagination. Which leads us back to Shangri-La: there are an awful lot of people who are convinced it is a real place.

'We have a collection of several hundreds, [of maps],' said Chang. 'They are open to your inspection, but perhaps I can save you trouble in one respect. You will not find Shangri-La marked on any.'
– *James Hilton,* Lost Horizon, *1933*

'It is not easy to judge, but probably some part of Tibet.'
– *according to Conway in* Lost Horizon, *1933*

Shangri-la can be found in a cup of café latte or yak butter tea if you look carefully enough... Searching for Shangri-la... Can you find it? Maybe you are not looking carefully enough...
– *Laurence J. Brahm, from the dust jacket of his book* Searching for Shangri-la, *2004*

The tragedy is Shangri-La may be lost very soon due to overdevelopment, careless tourism, and short-sightedness. In 'Searching for Shangri-la' we sought to document the 'lost horizon' before it is lost.
– *Laurence J. Brahm, ibid (prologue)*

We have located 22 elements of proof that Hilton's Shangri-La and the place we located are one and the same.
– *Ted Vaill, American mountaineer and lawyer who claims to have found Shangri-La in a valley in Kham, southern Sichuan, after 20 years of searching (quoted in* Newsweek, *26 March 2001)*

I am 100 percent sure this is Shangri-La. There is no doubt. I have all the documents.
– *Xuan Ke, Naxi musicologist, referring to the location of Lijiang, in Yunnan Province, southwest China (interview in* Utne Reader, *16 December 2002)*

If people think Shangri-La is one place, this is a mistake. They will not find it this way. Shangri-La is not just a specific place. It is also an idea, a dream.
– *Xuan Ke, quoted in the same interview*

Since Shangri-La is a mythical place based on the writings of an American anthropologist, we think the 'supposed' discovery of Shangri-La in Kham is baseless. Tibetans do not believe in the existence of Shangri-La in Tibet.
– *Thubten Samphel, spokesman for the Tibetan government-in-exile (*Newsweek, *26 March 2001)*

For thousands of years, Tibetans living on the Diqing Plateau call this beautiful land Shangrila, meaning the 'sun and moon in the heart'.
– Shangrila, *a booklet by Foreign Languages Press, Beijing, 1999*

Tsaparang and the great mother monastery of Toling are surely what Hilton had in mind when creating his fictional Shangri-La... here, if anywhere, I tend to think, is the source of the Shangri-La story.
– *Michael Wood,* In Search of Myths and Heroes *(2005), referring to the former Guge kingdom in far-west Tibet*

The abyss of contradictions between novelist James Hilton's vision of paradise in *Lost Horizon* and the actual conditions of Pemako is as deep as the Tsangpo Gorge itself.
– *Michael McRae,* In Search of Shangri-La: the Extraordinary True Story of the Quest for the Lost Horizon *(2002), referring to his 1998 exploration of the remote Tsangpo region of southeast Tibet, a place of precipitous jungles*

If there is a Shangri-La, this is it.
– *Rebecca Martin,* National Geographic *Expeditions Board, speaking of the same National Geographic-sponsored expedition to same deep Tsangpo area, although she has never been there (quoted in the story 'Tibet Discovery A Real-Life Shangri-La', in the* Chicago Tribune, *8 January 1999)*

Concealing his sources... Hilton relocated Shangri-La to Tibet's northwest frontier. But its literary origins lay firmly in the depths of the Tsangpo River Gorge.
– *Ian Baker, leader of the same 1998 expedition, who wrote an article 'Secret Heart of Shangri-La' (from a piece appearing in* Himalaya, *2006)*

2

The Book

LOST HORIZON, THE NOVEL

Lost Horizon is a short book – better described as a novella. Though short, it offers a number of innovations: it can lay claim to being the first novel in English that is set entirely in Tibet. The novel was written in just six weeks while Hilton was living at his parents' home in Woodford Green, on the outskirts of London. The serious seeker should set out armed with a copy of *Lost Horizon*. Meanwhile, to bring the book into sharper focus, here are some details about the story, characters, setting and philosophy of Shangri-La.

Berlin, spring 1932: the unnamed narrator, a neurologist, meets an old acquaintance, Rutherford, in a club. Rutherford, a writer, relates a strange tale told by Hugh Conway, former British Consul at Baskul. Rutherford recognised Conway in a mission hospital in Chung-Kiang, southwest China, and arranged for him to return to the West. Conway had no recollection of what had happened to him – he was suffering from amnesia.

The story goes into flashback mode, revealing Conway's incredible tale through notes recorded by Rutherford on a ship, as Conway regains his memory. Going back a year, the story starts with a revolution and riots in Baskul in May 1931, and the evacuation of Westerners by air. Four passengers on the last flight out of Baskul are hijacked.

THE SETTING

The characters of Shangri-La are not the driving force of the book. They are too sketchy for that. If you ask someone what they recall most after reading the book, the answer is likely to be the incredible setting of the lamasery of Shangri-La and its harmonious spiritual community. This spiritual packaging is what lingers in the mind. This is Conway's first glimpse of the lamasery:

> It was, indeed, a strange and almost incredible sight. A group of coloured pavilions clung to the mountainside with none of the grim deliberation of a Rhineland castle, but rather with the chance delicacy of flower petals impaled upon a crag. It was superb and exquisite. An austere emotion carried the eye upward from milk-blue roofs to the grey rock bastion above… Beyond that, in a dazzling pyramid, soared the snow slopes of Karakal.

Stretching far below is the verdant Valley of the Blue Moon, where a wealth of unusual flowers and medicinal plants grow. The handsome people of the valley are of mixed Tibetan and Chinese stock.

The lamasery of Shangri-La is a decidedly modern monastery, with central heating, modern plumbing, Chinese cuisine – and a brilliant collection of books, music and art. Shangri-La is a place for deep contemplation and study. Conway says it reminds him of Oxford University, where he used to lecture. There is a

HUGH CONWAY – British Consul at Baskul, steely-eyed and steel-nerved, tall and bronzed, calm and collected. A charismatic figure because of strong leadership traits and personal brand of mysticism. Feels instantly at home in Shangri-La. Conway is 37 years old.

CHARLES MALLINSON – Vice-Consul at Baskul, a hyper character who is hot-headed and prone to panic easily. At 24, Mallinson is probably the youngest of anyone at Shangri-La.

ROBERTA BRINKLOW – working with the Eastern Mission in Baskul. Her main objective in life is to convert as many heathens as possible to Christianity. She regards her 'posting' to Shangri-La as providence: she has already decided to set about converting the locals.

HENRY D BARNARD – this American is rumoured to be Chalmers Bryant, an international swindler wanted by the police in a number of countries. On the run in Baskul, and actually quite pleased to disappear into Shangri-La. He is a former mining engineer: his chief interest in Blue Moon valley is the gold mine – he has plans to increase its output.

TALU – the Tibetan pilot who hijacks the special plane from Baskul carrying the four characters mentioned. Talu dies at the controls when the plane crash-lands near Shangri-La, apparently from a heart-attack.

CHANG – liaison person and guide at Shangri-La: a philosopher who wears silk-embroidered gowns, and who conveniently speaks perfect English, though his first language is Chinese. From the plane crash, he escorts the four to the lamasery of Shangri-La and shows them around, but he is a master of vagueness – choosing not to answer certain questions or reveal certain aspects of Shangri-La. Chang

trade route linked to the outside world – and gold deposits in the valley take care of any monetary needs. There is no radio at Shangri-La, ostensibly because the surrounding high mountain barrier does not permit any reception, but a more obvious reason is that reports of war and famine would disturb the tranquillity within. The mountain barrier provides a natural deterrent to escape. 'We have no jailors, save that Nature herself has provided,' says Chang.

THE LAMAS

Time is one of the great luxuries of Shangri-La. As Conway soon finds out, Shangri-La acolytes age very slowly, looking half their age, or even younger. The minimum age for initiation into the lamahood is 100. Shangri-La hosts about 50 of these initiates, with both men and women in the ranks. The majority are Tibetan and Chinese, but there are others from European nations. So there are century-old sages reading year-old newspapers (copies of *The Times* from London – presumably the papers take that long to reach Shangri-La through irregular trade caravans). Conway and his companions are screened from the lamas, but he does hear about some of them – Meister, a German explorer; Alphonse Briac, a student of Chopin's; and an English vicar who met the Brontë sisters. Shangri-La is presided over by the bicentennial man – the High Lama – who is 250 years old. Conway explains they will have to wait at least two months for the next trade caravan to pass through before they can think of leaving. Chang arrived in the valley in 1855, at age 22, so he would be 98 years old in 1931, the year in which the novel is set.

LO-TSEN – pretty Manchu princess whose caravan got lost en route to Kashgar. She speaks no English, but charms Mallinson and Conway nonetheless. Both of them fall for her. She arrived in the valley in 1884 at the age of 18. That would make her 65 years old in 1931, though she looks far younger. Clooney and Altieri, the authors of a sequel to *Lost Horizon*, made her 80 years old, figuring that she had lied about her age!

FATHER PERRAULT – the wizened High Lama, who conveniently speaks English (or, rather, whispers it), though his native language is French. Perrault is a dedicated Capuchin monk from Luxembourg, who stumbled into the Valley of the Blue Moon around 1720, close to death. He was nursed back to health by locals: at that time he was around 40. Perrault conceived the idea of reconstructing a rundown Tibetan lamasery in the valley as a Christian monastery – the initial work was completed in 1734. Perrault embarked on a mission to refute Buddhist writings left at Shangri-La by its previous occupants. Over a century later, he is still working on that idea. He is more like a born-again Buddhist at this stage, having synthesised Tibetan Buddhism with elements of his original faith to come up with a new blend.

THE HIGH LAMA a small, frail man who is presented in darkness and shadow, but Conway glimpses a very wrinkled face. Put that down to Perrault's advanced age: he has survived to 250 through a regimen of meditation, yogic breathing practices, and eating medicinal tangatse berries, which grow in the valley. Though he has dodged his expiry date far longer than most, Perrault realises he is close to death and needs to find a successor to replace him at Shangri-La. Just after he appoints new arrival Conway as leader of Shangri-La, the High Lama passes away.

realises that, at 37, he is one of the youngest at Shangri-La – and that is the reason he has been brought here. The High Lama evidently wants some young blood in the ranks.

THE PHILOSOPHY

Shangri-La is a kind of spiritual Club Med, hosting an improbable synthesis of Eastern and Western philosophies. The main faith of the valley is Tibetan Buddhist, but Taoist and Confucian temples are indicated down the valley. There are strong hints of Zen, Taoist and Buddhist principles practised by this secret community. Perrault is a lapsed Capuchin friar, and the Western lamas in residence are described as having a 'Catholic taste' in reading. Music slants heavily to Europe, with Chopin and Mozart the most favoured. When questioned about the beliefs and practices of Shangri-La, Chang gives only vague answers and says more will be revealed later, but ventures that the practice of moderation is important to this benevolent theocracy: 'We rule with moderate strictness, and in return are satisfied with moderate obedience. And I think we can claim that our people are moderately sober, moderately chaste, and moderately honest.' Later, Father Perrault elaborates: 'We have no rigidities, no inexorable rules. We do as we think fit, guided a little by the example of the past, but still more by our present wisdom, and by our clairvoyance of the future.' Harmony is a key facet of Shangri-La – in a place where everybody gets along well, there is no need for police or army.

The High Lama's revolutionary vision is to gather the best of Eastern and Western knowledge – literature, art and music – and preserve it for times of great holocaust:

> …a time when men, exultant in the technique of homicide, would rage so hotly over the world that every precious thing would be in danger, every book and picture and harmony, every treasure gathered over two millenniums, the small, the delicate, the defenceless – all would be lost…

Perrault claims that after this destruction, the treasures preserved in Shangri-La will fuel 'a new Renaissance'.

ESCAPE FROM SHANGRI-LA

The dying High Lama appoints Conway to take over the leadership of Shangri-La. But in a surprise ending, Conway is persuaded to escape from Shangri-La by Mallinson, taking the pretty Lo-Tsen with them. They escape by a perilous high-altitude route with constant danger of avalanche. Mallinson presumably perishes, and Conway comes down with a severe case of amnesia. He is delivered to a mission hospital in Chung-Kiang, southwest China, in October 1931 by a very old Chinese woman. Later in the story, the reader discovers the woman is most likely Lo-Tsen, who, in a plot twist, has been transformed into a wizened old crone – looking her real age. She dies from fever shortly after reaching Chung-Kiang.

At the mission hospital, Conway is recognised by Rutherford and is escorted on a ship bound for Hawaii. As he regains his memory, he tells Rutherford what he knows. Then he gives his escort the slip, and jumps onto a freighter for Bangkok. He vanishes, leaving a note to say he is heading to northern Siam and the mountains of upper Burma – looking for Shangri-La again.

THE TIMES

Conway is a kind of anti-hero. He started out with a brilliant career – an Oxford don, a rowing blue. But his early promise has burned out. He was blown up while fighting in the trenches in World War I. He is one of the 'Lost Generation' – a generation of young men who survived the horrors of World War I, drifting through the heady 1920s in a daze of disillusionment and emptiness. For ten years he has been moved from one minor post to another in the British consular service. Due to his lack of ambition and drive, he is considered a failure by others.

At Shangri-La, Conway recognises what is missing from his life – spiritual fulfillment. And the High Lama recognises in Hilton a singular lack of passion. This quality, normally a drawback, is highly valued in Shangri-La. Phase one of the High Lama's training is to overcome human passions, which are considered to wreak havoc in the mind.

The character of Conway echoes the malaise of the late 1920s and early 1930s – highly volatile times. In the USA, the crash of Wall Street in 1929 bankrupted many; by 1931, it led to massive depression. Germany saw the rise of Hitler and the Nazi party, with the clouds of war hanging over Europe. In Asia, the military power of Japan was running amok, making imperialist incursions into both China and Russia.

Uncannily, James Hilton predicted the use of weapons of frightening power in *Lost Horizon*, of a holocaust of unimaginable scale. And he lived to see such weapons unleashed in 1945, with the A-Bomb dropped on Nagasaki and Hiroshima. US Secretary of War Henry Stimson described the A-Bomb as 'the most terrifying weapon ever known in human history'. War as a theme shows up again in another Hilton novel, *Random Harvest*, published in 1941, which is about a British soldier in World War I who suffers from amnesia. The title comes from a line in a German report: 'bombs fell at random'.

HILTON AND HOLLYWOOD

One thing is sure about Shangri-La – it sprang from the mind of James Hilton. Trouble is, he's been dead for over 50 years. A stumbling block on the way to finding the real Shangri-La, you might say. But is it? An ace literary detective can look for clues in Hilton's life and his writing – and the turbulent times he lived in.

James Hilton was born at Leigh, Lancashire, England, on 9 September 1900. He grew up in London, where his father had accepted a teaching post. Both parents were teachers. Hilton moved on to Leys School in Cambridge, and then attended Christ's College at Cambridge, graduating with honours in English and a history degree in 1921. His first novel, *Catherine Herself*, was published in 1920 while he was still an undergraduate. He continued to write novels, but this brought little financial reward; for the next decade, Hilton supported himself by lecturing at Cambridge, and working as a freelance writer for papers like the London *Daily Telegraph* and the *Manchester Guardian*.

Typing away in the back garden of his parents' home in Woodford Green, London, Hilton hit on the Himalayan theme that was to catapult him to fame. His big breakthrough came with the September 1933 publication of *Lost Horizon*, which was awarded the Hawthornden Prize in 1934 for most promising young novelist. Success was not instant – sales of *Lost Horizon* were slow in the UK at first, but the book took off in the US, soon winning plaudits on both sides of the Atlantic. Within a few years, the novel was reprinted 18 times, with sales of hundreds of thousands. Hilton followed this up with *Goodbye Mr Chips* (1934), a simple tale of an old schoolmaster, which was another resounding success.

In 1935 Hilton was invited to California as a consultant on the movie version of *Lost Horizon*. In 1937, he wrote in an article, 'When I first contemplated a visit to Hollywood, I was warned by many excellent people. I might fail, they told me. Worse still, I might succeed.' Although several of his books were made into movies by studios in England, Hilton decided to settle in Hollywood, becoming involved in script dramatisations as well as radio broadcasts.

Hilton knew nothing about scripts when he arrived in Hollywood, but by the 1940s he was one of Hollywood's highest-paid screenwriters. In the mid-1930s, Hollywood was home to over 1,000 writers, working for studios dominated by eight corporations. Among Hilton's screenwriting efforts were *Foreign Correspondent*, directed in 1940 by Alfred Hitchcock, and *The Story of Dr Wassell*, directed in 1944 by Cecil B DeMille. Hilton won an Oscar for his contribution to the screenplay for the 1942 film, *Mrs Miniver*. He continued writing novels, several of which were adapted as movies. In the early 1940s, at the height of his fame, Hilton was a frequent speaker on radio: he achieved great popularity for his current affairs broadcasts for CBS. While Hilton mixed with the Hollywood crowd at parties, meeting just about everybody, he identified most with a small English ex-pat contingent, becoming good friends with British actors Ronald Colman and Greer Garson (who also starred in his movies).

In Hollywood Hilton found safe haven, insulated from the worries of World War II. Here in America's own Shangri-La, where dreams are forged on the silver screen, Hilton revelled in the chance to experiment with marvellous new formats like talking movies and radio plays. In 1937 he wrote, '...I liked Hollywood and found there an exciting amount of genuine artistic enthusiasm as well as an astonishingly high level of technical competence.' Later that year he wrote, '...as for music, I would hazard the guess that there is as much musical talent on the Hollywood pay-roll as lives permanently in London, New York, Paris, or Berlin.' A keen classical musician himself, Hilton delighted in listening to some of that talent in live performances. Life in Hollywood was not always rosy: in the 1940s, Hollywood was under attack in a McCarthy-led crusade against perceived domination of the film industry by 'Communists and radicals'. Being a member on the governing boards of several academies and guilds, Hilton fiercely resisted the notion that Hollywood was overrun by radicals or Communist crackpots.

In 1951, Hilton provided a snapshot of his routine in Hollywood in a short piece about himself that appeared in the *New York Herald Tribune Book Review*:

> Among the things I once tried to be was a concert pianist; among the things I nearly became were an architect and a university don; among the things I could be and wouldn't mind being if I weren't a writer are a carpenter and an Alpine guide to the not-too-difficult mountains. I dislike organized games, swimming pools, fashionable resorts, night clubs, music in restaurants and political manifestos; I enjoy driving from coast to coast, good food and drink, a few friends, dogs, the theatre, long walks, music (except grand opera) and free conversation. I read a dozen or so books a week (if I can find that many I want to read). I spend three or four hours a week in radio listening and an hour or so with television. I came to America in 1935, liked it, decided to stay here.
>
> The way I write is this: I get up at 8, drink coffee, listen to the news bulletin, take my dogs for a walk, force myself to climb the steps to the room where I work, sit down at the typewriter and start. I never make preliminary notes or a synopsis; at the end of the day I go over with pen and ink, correcting and cutting perhaps half of the typescript. I can do three thousand words a day when the mood is on me...

Hilton didn't talk much about his private life, but he was twice married. He married Alice Brown, a secretary at the BBC, in England just before they both left for Hollywood in 1935. Probably due to the pressures of Tinseltown, the marriage was short-lived. Hilton divorced Alice in 1937 in Mexico, and a week later married an aspiring young Hollywood starlet, Galina Kopineck, whom he later divorced in 1945. In 1948, Hilton became an American citizen.

Hilton was a heavy smoker, and was ailing from various health problems when he went back to England in 1954 for a last visit to bid farewell to relatives and close friends. Accompanying him from America was his secretary, a young blonde woman with whom he appears to have been involved. Back in Hollywood, Hilton's illness got the better of him: with reconciled wife Alice at his side, he died suddenly of liver cancer at his home in Long Beach, California, on 20 December 1954. He was 54.

THE MOVIE

Hilton was keenly aware of the opportunity of telling his stories in other mediums – radio, movies, and later television – made possible by new inventions and new technology. When he was invited to Hollywood to assist with the movie script for *Lost Horizon*, Hilton immediately accepted. This turned out to be fortuitous: by moving to Hollywood, he avoided the outbreak of war in Europe. So did his parents, who dropped into California for a visit in 1939, and stayed on during the war. Staying in California probably suited his father just fine – he was a pacifist.

The late 1930s was still the era of the black-and-white movie. And Hollywood was emerging as the greatest mythmaker of all time, due to its global reach. These were the days long before *Star Wars* or *Harry Potter*. James Hilton was riding the early waves of Hollywood mythmaking. The film version of *Lost Horizon* spread the story of Shangri-La far and wide.

However, a few things got lost in translation in the shift from London to Hollywood. The movie is not the same as the book. For one thing, Hilton did not write the script. He was hired as a consultant on the project. The scriptwriter was Robert Riskin. The movie was directed by Frank Capra, who decided to cut some important facets of the story – and then spice it up with the addition of a sex siren, Sondra Bizet – who starts out by skinny-dipping in a lotus pool. The script suggests that it is not the High Lama who has ordered Conway to be kidnapped and brought to Shangri-La, but Sondra. That throws the story's focus right off – spirituality as motivation and goal is replaced by sexual intrigue and romance. It turns into 'Lust Horizon', with movie posters focusing on a classic love match. There are two love stories going on in the movie version of *Lost Horizon*, but one love-triangle in the book.

Other character changes: five people are hijacked on the plane to Shangri-La, not four. The timing is 1935, not 1931 (as in the book). An extra character, fussy fossil expert Lovett, is added to the plane – apparently for comic relief. Hugh Conway becomes Robert Conway, and the character of Charles Mallinson is altered to George, the brother of Conway, not his vice-consul. And British missionary Miss Brinklow is turned into consumptive American prostitute Gloria Stone! At Shangri-La, the pivotal character of Lo-Tsen metamorphoses into spiteful resident Maria, who claims the High Lama is insane. When Maria shrivels from old age and dies on the escape from Shangri-La, George kills himself. Weeks later, Conway stumbles into a mission hospital alone. While the book left the ending a mystery, in the movie version Frank Capra showed paradise regained, with Conway battling his way back to Shangri-La. Hilton didn't write much about the making of the movie, but we do know he was pleased by the Shangri-La lamasery set, constructed on a back-lot at Burbank, LA. In an April 1937 article for *Pall Mall* magazine, Hilton wrote about being introduced to the set by Frank Capra:

> I was speechless; I could do nothing but shake his hand.... Capra's conception of the lamasery of Shangri-La, that tranquil Tibetan refuge from the troubles of the world, was more visual than mine had ever been; but henceforth, it is part of my own mental conception also. The lotus pool fringed by flowers and lawns, and the exquisitely stylised architecture of lamasery background, caught the exact paradox of something permanent enough to exist for ever and too ethereal to exist at all. I could not help a feeling of sadness that it must, presumably, be broken up when the picture was finished; I should have liked to have added a few rooms to its unsubstantial fabric and lived there myself.

And here Hilton has put his finger on one of the big differences between the book and the movie. The book is vague about what the monastery looks like, about the details – it is left to the reader's imagination to fill everything in and conjure it up. The movie visualises it for the viewer.

Capra had considerable trouble casting the actor for the High Lama: several actors were hired for the role, and finally Sam Jaffe prevailed. Capra had more success with the lead role of Conway: he had cast British actor Ronald Colman to play the part from the time he obtained the film rights. The role of love-interest Sondra is played by Jane Wyatt. Another casting problem in 1936 (when the movie was being shot) was the Tibetans. At this time, the only Tibetans found outside Tibet would be on trading runs to neighbouring nations like India. The Tibetan parts in the movie were played by San Diego Indians, speaking gibberish (or else English). While Chinese props were easy to find, Tibetan props were not: there are no Buddha statues or Tibetan long trumpets. There is no Tibetan ritual music. There is little attempt at Tibetan-style architecture, either.

THE SHANGRI-LA BRAND

by *Simon Anholt*

Every inhabited place on earth has a brand image: and plenty of uninhabited ones do, too. What does this mean? Simply that for a number of people, the place has a particular image, a reputation. The brand image of a place may be rich and complex, or relatively simple; it may be true or false, deserved or undeserved. It may be mainly negative or mainly positive, and for most places it's a constantly shifting mixture of the two.

The brand images of countries are important because they powerfully affect the way people inside and outside the country think about it, and the way they behave towards it. Whether the brand is strong or weak, positive or negative, simple or complex, makes a tremendous difference to the way in which the world behaves towards the place, its people, its government, its sporting and cultural offerings, its tourism and heritage attractions, its products and services, its investment, business and educational potential. People trust what they hear from places with good brand images, and mistrust what they hear from others; and in the absence of reliable information, they make favourable assumptions about the places with good brands and unfavourable ones about the rest.

My quarterly global survey of national images, the *Nation Brands Index*, suggests that it is mainly the old, rich, famous and successful countries that always have the best images. But there are some exceptions: Bhutan and Tibet, for example, rank higher in some areas of the survey than you would expect from two tiny, economically and politically insignificant nations hidden away in remote corners of the world.

Why should this be? There is a parallel here with the world of commercial brands. It's certainly true that most of the world's most powerful brands, like Kellogg's, Ford, Sony and Coca-Cola, have earned their reputations through decades of successful relationships with consumers; and yet there are plenty of entirely new brands that achieve even greater profile in a matter of years. It's worth looking at the behaviour of these upstart megabrands – the Microsofts, the Amazons, the Nikes and the Googles – and see how they have managed to achieve so much profile in so little time.

It's certainly not because they advertise so much. A megabrand is one that finds itself, by accident or by design, in the path of major social change. Of course, the product itself has to be world-class, but the rest is timing and positioning. When the world discovered fitness, Nike was there as the ultimate fitness brand; when the world discovered personal computing, Microsoft was the biggest name; when the world discovered the internet, Google was there to help them find their way, and Amazon was there to help them shop.

Countries like Tibet and Bhutan could become megabrands in exactly the same way: because they are believed to have what the world wants and needs, at the moment when the world discovers what it wants and needs. Such places are beginning to register on global public opinion because that old, old urge to find Shangri-La has never been so strong – at least amongst the populations of industrialised countries, where it is starting at last to dawn on people that material wealth is not a recipe for happiness.

It's rather predictable, however, that the strongest candidates for Shangri-La should be tucked away somewhere in the fastnesses of the mysterious East. Why not in the equally glamorous North, South or West? Exoticism is really only an expression of geographical distance, and the myth of Shangri-La only happens to be located in the East because that was where the most distant, most exotic lands were in the imaginations of the Europeans who created and perpetuated the myth. But if the significant economic, political, cultural and social power of the next decades and centuries lies not in Europe but in India or China, then the truly exotic, truly idyllic Shangri-La for our modern age might just as well be the Faroe Islands, Tasmania, Suriname, Montenegro, the Laccadives or Botswana.

These are countries whose brand images really might be susceptible to significant enhancement, if only their governments can find the imagination, the ambition, the wisdom and the patience to carry out the innovations, policies and investments that would truly make them into megabrands.

But 'brand' is such a dangerous word. Most people associate branding with marketing, advertising and PR, but in fact it has as much to do with the product itself as the way in which it is sold: nothing is more false or pernicious than the view of some governments that their country can have a Nike-sized brand in a couple of months, if only they can raise a Nike-sized marketing budget. In fact, most countries have weak reputations because they aren't of any great interest to people in other countries, and the best marketing in the world will only serve to corroborate that fact.

It is theoretically possible that there are countries which are truly perfect in every respect but simply overlooked by world opinion. However, it does seem rather unlikely. With hordes of intrepid travel journalists and tour operators crawling over every inch of the planet in search of new destinations for increasingly wealthy, jaded and world-weary consumers, it seems probable that most countries, ultimately, have the brand image they deserve.

And perhaps Shangri-La needs to remain imaginary for this very reason: because an imaginary place – a brand image without a product behind it – is the only place that can't disappoint, and the only place we can't spoil simply by going there.

Simon Anholt has a very unusual job: he advises governments on how to look after their national image, with implications for tourism, foreign investment, political relation, and a slew of other things. He is the inventor of 'nation branding', author of several books on the subject (including Brand America *and* Competitive Identity*), and a policy advisor to numerous national and regional governments including those of Bhutan, Iceland, Tanzania, Jamaica, the Netherlands, Latvia and Sweden. He is also publisher of the* Anholt Nation Brands Index *and* City Brands Index*. Find out more about him on his website: www.simonanholt.com.*

Frank Capra's movie was a grand venture. Production began in March 1936 and shooting wrapped up four months later. Columbia Pictures, then a minor production company, committed US$2.5 million to the making of *Lost Horizon* – a huge amount in its day (the amount represented half the studio's annual budget). The sets were lavish: Shangri-La lamasery was built over a course of two months by 150 workmen. It was an Art Deco-style masterpiece designed by Art Director Stephen Goosson, and based on the concepts of Frank Lloyd Wright. A giant soundstage for avalanches and snow scenes was created inside a vast cold storage warehouse. Outdoor scenes were shot at various sites around California.

The rough cut for *Lost Horizon* was around six hours. When it was shown to preview audiences, it ran nearly three hours. A test screening of the movie at Santa Barbara was a disaster: the opening scenes elicited howls of laughter as the audience watched scenes of Conway, the main character, struggling to regain his memory. The director's response was to delete this embarrassing sequence, along with copious other cuts in the body of the picture. The release length of *Lost Horizon* was 132 minutes, later pared down to 119 minutes for general distribution in September 1937. The movie did well at the box-office, but not as well as Columbia expected. *Lost Horizon* picked up two Academy Awards in 1937 – for Best Art Direction, and for Best Film Editing. Heading into the World War II years, Hollywood offered a steady roster of escapist movies. *Lost Horizon* fitted right in, promising the ultimate hideaway of peace and tranquillity. But ironically, for the World War II re-issue of *Lost Horizon*, 24 minutes of the movie were cut to tone down the film's pacifist message, giving it a running time of about 95 minutes. The opening scenes were altered to show white people rushing to escape being butchered by 'the invaders from Japan'. Over time, the rest of the footage was lost, and original reels of film degraded beyond use. The case of the seven minutes of lost footage has never been solved. When the movie classic was restored in the 1970s and 1980s, still pictures were used to illustrate scenes where only the soundtrack existed.

THE SEQUELS

Hilton adapted *Lost Horizon* as a radio drama, a stage play, and a TV drama (the TV version did not show up until 1960, but this time in colour). All that remained was the musical. And that happened in 1973, long after Hilton's demise, when Columbia Pictures – which owned the movie rights to *Lost Horizon* – decided to dust off its property and cash in on the popularity of musicals. A Camelot set was adapted for Shangri-La. Despite music by Burt Bacharach and lyrics by Hal David, and an all-star cast that included Peter Finch, Liv Ullmann, Olivia Hussey and Charles Boyer, the musical was a resounding flop.

Although he left the way open for one, Hilton never wrote a sequel to his wildly popular novel. But other authors did. *Return to Shangri-La*, by Leslie Halliwell, published in 1987, picks up the trail half a century later – with Hugh Conway, Roberta Brinklow and Henry Barnard still at Shangri-La, though 50 years older. Another sequel is *Shangri-La: The Return to the World of Lost Horizon*, by Eleanor Clooney and Daniel Altieri. The book was published in 1996, but the action is actually set back in the 1960s, during the upheaval of the Cultural Revolution. Also set in the 1960s is *Messenger: A Sequel to Lost Horizon*, a work self-published by author Frank DeMarco in 1994. An American pilot in a U-2 spy plane is forced down by engine failure in remote Tibet; the pilot finds himself the guest – and prisoner – of Shangri-La, in the company of Conway, Brinklow and Barnard.

The legend goes on: Shangri-La has surfaced in a number of other books, comics and movies. Back in the real world, searching for the real Shangri-La seems to be an enduring hobby for documentary makers at the BBC and the Discovery

Channel. But the biggest impact of Shangri-La has been in the 'paradise industry'. You've read the book, seen the movie, now go there! Shangri-La is a wonderful concept for branding – paradise encapsulated.

Were Hilton alive today, he would be astonished at the uses that Shangri-La has been put to in tourism and business – countless resorts, restaurants and clubs. Enter 'Shangri-La' under a Google web search and several million web pages pop up. The largest luxury hotel chain in Asia, Shangri-La Hotel Group, started up in 1971. In Nepal, there's a company called Shangri-La Air, with a fleet of planes carrying that logo. *Shangri-La* is the name of the inflight magazine for China Eastern Airlines. In Bhutan, a company called Digital Shangri-La provides information technology solutions. In Moscow, one of the largest gambling venues is Shangri-La Casino. Shangri-La Entertainment is the name of a Hollywood film production group. In England, Shangri-La is one of the most popular house names.

Shangri-La has universal appeal and great staying power. It is reported that director Frank Capra induced Columbia Pictures to buy the film rights for *Lost Horizon* because he said the novel held up a mirror to the thoughts of every human being on earth. Advancing into the 21st century, the myth remains stronger than ever. That might be because, although a short book, *Lost Horizon* touches on major issues that preoccupy us today: saving precious culture in times of impending holocaust – due to weapons of unimaginable power; the riddle of human longevity – tinkering with time, stretching time, altering genetic codes; how to find inner peace, harmony and happiness. In the 21st century these themes may bear different names – weapons of mass destruction, genetic engineering – but the basic concepts are the same.

HIMALAYAN MIRAGE

In *Lost Horizon*, Hilton has patterned his novel after a classic adventure story, with parallels to many myths – for instance, the narrative of Greek hero Odysseus. In his book *Hero of a Thousand Faces*, Joseph Campbell maintains that many myths follow a similar pattern: the hero undergoes an arduous journey to reach a new domain or dreamworld; undergoes obstacles and ordeals to come to terms with this new domain; then leaves abruptly – but feels regret and a strong urge to return. The hero is forever transformed by this profound experience.

Hilton's narrative sleight of hand – passing us from an anonymous narrator to the writer Rutherford, who records what Conway told him – masks a very important question. Did Conway hallucinate the whole thing? After all, he suffered head injuries from an explosion in WWI, and early in the novel, we learn that Conway wakes up in a Chinese hospital with amnesia – initially, he has no memory of what has transpired during his time in Shangri-La. Another factor to consider: a sudden visit to a high-altitude zone can result in extreme disorientation, which may include hallucinations and carrying on conversations with imaginary people or even objects. Is Shangri-La real? Or is it a shimmering mirage? Hilton leaves us with a dream vision, suggesting the tantalising possibility that Shangri-La does exist – in a hidden valley somewhere over the horizon.

The Book HILTON AND HOLLYWOOD

2

3

The Quest

THE SEEKERS

A character in a novel by André Malraux puts it this way: 'Every adventurer starts out as a mythomaniac.' And looking for lost worlds is a prime obsession for mythomaniacs. Profiled briefly here are missionaries, spiritual seekers, adventurers and others who set out in search of lost Christians, Shambhala, *beyuls*, Agharti, or Shang-Shung, and, finally, Shangri-La. These are all lost kingdoms of sorts – and some get the myths mixed up, whether by accident or by design, resulting in a kind of mythological stew.

MISSIONARIES

Two missionaries appear in *Lost Horizon*. One is Father Perrault, the High Lama. The other is Miss Brinklow, freshly arrived from the Afghan Mission, and already setting her sights on converting the Tibetans of Shangri-La. The first Europeans to enter Tibet in 1624 were Portuguese Jesuits Andrade and Marques, who were searching for a group of lost Christians, possibly the lost kingdom of Prester John. It is more than coincidence that Father Perrault, the High Lama in *Lost Horizon*, was on his way from Peking to search for remnants of the Nestorian faith in the Tibetan hinterlands. He didn't find any lost Christian kingdom, but instead stumbled into an idyllic valley where he set about trying to shape his own spiritual utopia. Perrault stumbled into the valley of Shangri-La around 1720, which is historically accurate in terms of Capuchin missionary activity in Tibet. And the shelves of Shangri-La's library hold the writings of missionaries Andrade, Grueber, d'Orville, and Beligatti (the last one a Capuchin monk).

Missionaries were spectacularly unsuccessful in Tibet. This was not only 'Lost Horizon', it was The Lost Cause. In centuries of effort, only a handful of Tibetans were converted. In Hilton's novel, Father Perrault embarked upon a project of refuting Tibetan Buddhism but instead ended up accepting its basic tenets.

In 1661, the first Europeans to reach Lhasa were two Jesuits – Johann Grueber (Austrian) and Albert d'Orville (Belgian). They found their way overland from China to Tibet, heading for India. They stayed a month in Lhasa, but were not permitted to see the Dalai Lama because they had announced their unwillingness to make prostrations in his presence. Grueber's account of the journey, published in Latin in 1677, excited a great deal of interest as it made the first references to the Dalai Lamas and presented Grueber's sketches of the strange customs of the Tibetans. Grueber's drawing of the Potala is the first known image of this amazing building – then still a work-in-progress.

In the early 18th century, Tuscan Jesuit priest Ippolito Desideri reached Lhasa, at the same time that Italian Capuchin missionaries were staking out the region. The licentious 6th Dalai Lama ruled at the time; Desideri observed that he was a 'dissolute youth, addicted to every vice, thoroughly depraved, and quite incorrigible, because of the blind veneration and stupid faith of the Thibettans'. Both the Jesuits and the Capuchins were bent on establishing a permanent mission – setting the stage for a showdown over who had the right to claim the souls of the Tibetans for Rome. Jesuit Father Ippolito Desideri faced off with Capuchin friar Orazio della Penna. The rival Italians eventually waived their differences to tackle the pressing problem of Tibetan grammar. della Penna became proficient enough in the Tibetan language that he was able to present a work refuting Buddhism to the Dalai Lama. The Dalai Lama accepted it and politely advised della Penna not to condemn the religion of other people.

Despite strong opposition from the Jesuits, the Capuchins finally prevailed in the quest for souls in Tibet – the Vatican, persuaded by della Penna, backed another Capuchin mission to Tibet. della Penna had remained in Tibet for some 16 years – after he left in 1733, the Lhasa mission lapsed. In 1740, attempting to revive the Capuchin mission, friar Cassiano Beligatti approached Lhasa bearing gifts from the Vatican for the 7th Dalai Lama, including a fine drawing-room clock. But the welcome mat was no longer out, and the mission's status went from bad to worse. After some converted Tibetans disowned their allegiance to the Dalai Lama, the Capuchins were forcibly ejected from Tibet in 1745.

Jesuit priest Desideri wrote a report of his travels to Tibet – which was suppressed by the church because it did not want to create tensions between Capuchins and Jesuits. It was not published till 1904. In 1902, another long-lost narrative saw the light of day – the diaries of the Capuchin friar Cassiano Beligatti, unearthed at the library of Macerata in Italy. A manuscript of 200 pages was written in Italian, with pen and watercolour sketches of Tibetan rituals and plans of edifices in Lhasa. The narrative probably lay unpublished because proselytising had been a dismal failure in Tibet. The total number of converts for the entire Capuchin campaign could be counted on the fingers of two hands – not good numbers to broadcast for all the money spent on these missions.

Although missionaries were barred from central Tibet after the mid-18th century, there were still openings for spreading the gospel at the fringes of the plateau – in the Kham and Amdo regions, where missionary activity was tolerated because they brought much-needed skills in setting up schools and hospitals. French, Belgian, British and American missionaries of all stripes and creeds – Capuchins, Jesuits, Lazarists, Presbyterians, evangelists – all had a stab, but gained precious few converts. Tibetan Buddhism stood firm.

SPIRITUAL SEEKERS
Taking a totally opposite tack to the missionaries came a different breed of spiritual seeker from the West. They came to learn from the wisdom of Tibetan Buddhism.

The Hungarian scholar Alexander Csoma de Koros came to Ladakh in the 1820s looking for traces of his ancestors from Transylvania. Instead, he stumbled into a treasure trove of Tibetan Buddhist texts, completely unknown in the West. He set about translating these in an epic feat of scholarship, while developing a Tibetan dictionary and grammar. Csoma de Koros is credited with bringing the story of Shambhala to Western attention in his writing. In the same era, the British Resident of Kathmandu, Brian Houghton Hodgson, collected a large number of Tibetan manuscripts and introduced Tibetan Buddhist concepts to the West.

The Shambhala myth was completely warped by the imagination of Madame Blavatsky, the founder of the Theosophy spiritual group (see pages 11–14). She hyped up the notion of a hidden kingdom in the Himalaya ruled by enlightened masters, with whom she directly communicated. She appears to have travelled to India, but not to Tibet (as she claimed), nor to Shambhala (nor Atlantis).

But her disciple, eccentric Russian explorer and painter Nicholas Roerich, did make it to Tibet. He went with a severe case of Shambilitis – looking not only for Shambhala but for the subterranean kingdom of Agharti. Roerich mounted two extensive expeditions – one in 1925, and another in 1934. The second expedition was in theory a hunt for drought-resistant grasses, and was funded by a secret backer at the US Department for Agriculture, a fiasco later dubbed 'the Guru Scandal'. When Roerich showed pictures of the New York skyline to Mongolian nomads, they were unanimous in declaring this had to be the fabled Shambhala. Roerich soldiered on in his quest, spotting UFOs along the way, and eventually determined a mountain in Kazakhstan to be the source of Shambhala. Roerich was a prolific writer – and painter of many dreamy Himalayan landscapes of the Shangri-La inspirational kind. In 1929 he was nominated for the Nobel Peace Prize for this efforts to promote global harmony. His Roerich Peace Pact was an ambitious treaty that sought – shades of Shangri-La – to preserve cultural monuments from the ravages of war. It was supported by influential figures like Albert Einstein and H G Wells.

The most renowned traveller and spiritual seeker among the Theosophists was Alexandra David-Neel, who set off at the age of 54 on her grandest quest – to become the first Western woman to reach Lhasa. This she accomplished in 1924. She was well-versed in Tibetan and contributed significantly to Western knowledge about arcane Tibetan texts. At the age of 100, David-Neel renewed her passport. But she never used it – at 101, she passed on from this world.

ODDBALL ADVENTURERS OF THE 1930s

In Hilton's day, in the 1930s, Tibet was a blank on the map in many ways. It held many secrets, and adventurers were determined to unlock them. Contemporary with James Hilton was eccentric American botanist Joseph Rock, who came to collect unusual plant species but also made a career out of finding obscure Tibetan kingdoms and fiefdoms in southwest China and writing them up in *National Geographic* during the 1920s and '30s. In far-west Tibet, Italian scholar Giuseppe Tucci discovered the long-lost Guge kingdom – his remarkable findings were published in Italian in 1934 and in English in 1935, which are both after the publication of *Lost Horizon*. Tucci was one of the first people to recognise that Tibetan art was worthy of collecting. He himself made off with loads of Tibetan books and painted scrolls from monasteries around Tibet.

The 1920s and '30s saw a new breed of seeker arrive in Tibet: mountain climbers. Taking his own peculiar brand of spiritual faith to great heights was Maurice Wilson, dubbed the Mad Yorkshireman by the British press. Going to 'great heights' means Everest. Wilson believed that a combination of fasting and faith would get him to the peak of Everest. His plan was to crash-land a Gipsy Moth biplane halfway up Everest – a very Shangri-La method of getting there – and then climb from there to the top to plant the British flag on the virgin peak. Wilson reached Everest's north face in spring 1934. He hit it off with the High Lama of Rongbuk, and was privileged to have several audiences before his untimely death on the slopes of Everest. The High Lama, a jovial man of around 70, lived in an eerie at the top of the monastery, reached by a rickety ladder. The small wooden room had windows of real glass – a rarity in these parts. This was about as close as you could get to a Shangri-La moment: a lofty Tibetan monastery, backed by the biggest snowcap in the world, and an audience with the High Lama.

SHANGRI-LA SEEKERS

The end of *Lost Horizon* leaves us with the disappearance of Hugh Conway, last heard of heading back for Shangri-La. Hot on his trail is Rutherford, the writer, who spends a fruitless summer searching high and wide through central Asia for

You don't hear much about female missionaries and explorers in Tibet. A number of female adventurers gained access to 'Little Tibet' – the Ladakh area in northwest India – but very few made it across the border into Tibet proper. If it was tough for male explorers to reach Lhasa, it was doubly difficult for female explorers, as the Tibetans had a strict policy of barring Western women. This was probably a remnant of China's trade with Europeans during the 17th and 18th centuries, when no foreign women were allowed on the Chinese mainland. In Nepal a similar policy held sway. When Alexandra David-Neel reached Lhasa in 1924, she went disguised as a Tibetan beggar on pilgrimage. She was the first Western woman to reach the Holy City. But some 30 years earlier, British missionary Annie Taylor came tantalisingly close to reaching Lhasa.

The full story of Annie Royle Taylor's adventures might never have surfaced if not for a writer named William Carey, who passed through the trading town of Yatung (Sikkim–Tibet border) in 1899. Planning to write a book about Tibetan customs, he sought Annie out and noticed she referred to a slim diary to answer his questions. Carey asked if he might transcribe it. The diary duly arrived: Carey said it was 'very odiferous', redolent of the yak-butter, foxskins, goatskins, dried mutton and yak tails that it had been packed with. Carey painstakingly transcribed 160 pages of hieroglyphics by poring over the diary with a magnifying glass. Annie's diary was published in 1901 in a book compiled by Carey, entitled *Adventures in Tibet*.

Annie Taylor was the first Western woman known to enter Tibet. She embarked on the ambitious project of bringing the Presbyterian gospel to Lhasa's residents. She possessed two great assets to mount the journey – she dressed like a native, and she learned colloquial Tibetan in Darjeeling, where she taught in a mission school. In 1884 Annie transferred to the China Inland Mission, to the Amdo area. In September 1892, she set off to answer a Divine Call to reach Lhasa, with her faithful Tibetan servant Pontso, two Chinese servants, a ruffian called Noga, his Tibetan wife, and 16 horses. Annie's game-plan was roughly this: disguised as a Tibetan, she would make it through to Lhasa – where she would throw herself at the mercy of the Dalai Lama and, having won his confidence, would proceed to convert him.

both Conway and for clues about Shangri-La. Hilton has let loose the first two Shangri-La seekers even before the book finishes.

Many have followed in their wake. The chase continues with modern writers and myth hunters – specifically looking for Shangri-La, or muddying the waters by mixing up Shangri-La with other Tibetan myths, like Shambhala.

British author Charles Allen somehow equates his search for the lost Bon kingdom of Zhangzhung into a quest for Shangri-La in his book *In Search of Shangri-La* (1999). He misses both by a wide margin. Ian Baker and Michael McRae are authors of articles and books about Baker's *National Geographic*-sponsored expeditions to the Tsangpo regions of southeast Tibet, which resulted in the discovery of a major waterfall in 1998. Both authors try to make the case that Hilton used the *beyul* of Pemako (in Tsangpo) as his model for Shangri-La. However, there is not a single mention of a river or a waterfall in *Lost Horizon*, though Baker and McRae seem to harp on this (desperate to seize onto something, Baker cites a pool seen in the movie version of *Lost Horizon*).

In an article titled 'The Heart of Shangri-La', appearing in *Spa Asia* magazine

Then 36 years of age, Annie endured a harrowing four-month journey from western China, braving ice and snow, windstorms and freezing passes. She developed stomach problems and suffered from snow blindness. Harassed by bandits, she lost most of her horses and her supplies; one of her servants turned back; another died. On 4 January 1893, at Nagchu – only three days' march away from Lhasa – Annie and Pontso were arrested by Tibetan officials, who had been alerted by the treacherous Noga.

When questioned, the fearless Annie said her reason for going to Lhasa was to cross Tibet to reach Darjeeling. A magistrate from Lhasa patiently listened to her story and her accusations of horse theft against Noga. He is said to have remarked: 'Dear Me! The English people are odd creatures.' Instead of executing Annie and beheading Pontso, the magistrate compassionately supplied them with fresh horses, clothing, a tent and blankets – and an escort – and told them to go back the same way they came. The disconsolate Annie and Pontso made their way back to Sichuan, reaching Tachienlu in April 1893. In seven months, they had covered some 2,000km, surviving the rigours of a howling Tibetan winter.

Not one to give up her divine quest so easily, Annie returned to England to found the Tibetan Pioneer Mission. The advance group consisted of nine men, dressed in Tibetan robes and hats, dedicated 'to live and die for Tibet'. Within a few months of arriving in Sikkim, however, Annie had a falling-out with her pioneers, and told them to go and join the China Inland Mission.

In 1895, Annie and Pontso showed up at the town of Yatung, where they wrangled a permit to open a general store and medical supplies shop. When Colonel Younghusband entered Tibet at the head of a British army in 1903, Annie was waiting for him outside Yatung. She questioned him closely about his religious beliefs before giving her seal of approval to proceed with the invasion. Indeed, her nursing skills proved useful to Younghusband's mission. However, she was greatly disturbed that the Younghusband campaign did not open up Tibet to missionary activity. Around 1905, Annie suddenly disappeared from the scene, apparently dispatched to a lunatic asylum, and there the trail grows cold.

(January 2005), Baker starts out describing the linking of earthly paradise and *beyuls* to Shangri-La, talks about the geographical grail for British explorers being a colossal hidden waterfall, and then trails off to…the southern oceans:

Padmasambhava, the Lotus-Born author of the Buddhist texts which described the hidden lands, ultimately left Tibet and carried his vision of enlightenment to the 'southern oceans'. In these distant tropical islands, he taught that by transforming the way we see the world, the world itself transforms. My own journeys through Pemako and the Tsangpo gorges ultimately led me to Koh Samui, the island in the Gulf of Thailand renowned for its pristine beaches and healing spas. Amidst a growing tourist industry, twenty-two Buddhist monasteries still thrive amidst swaying coconut palms and lush-covered hills…. It had all the makings of a tropical Shangri-La – a place worthy of the ancient prophecies.

So there you have it – Baker's sudden transition from the remote hidden gorges of Tibet to tropical Shangri-La in Thailand, and all in the footsteps of Padmasambhava. Well, at least there is a strong water connection. The article goes on to tell us that Baker is co-founder of a multi-faceted resort on Koh Samui – a sanctuary for body, mind and spirit, which, although it is located in Thailand, was 'birthed in the Himalayas'. Baker may be spending a lot more time in Thailand. When last heard of, there was a warrant out for his arrest by Nepal Police.

Michael McRae's original story about expeditions to the Tsangpo region was entitled 'Trouble in Shangri-La: the Siege of the Tsangpo' (appearing in *National Geographic Adventure* magazine). The first US publication of his book is under the title *The Siege of Shangri-La*. But later editions somehow morphed into this title: *In Search of Shangri-La*. That's a rather large shift in meaning, from 'siege' to 'search'.

British writer and documentary filmmaker Michael Wood takes an interesting tack: he sets out in the footsteps of a lost kingdom seeker, seeking to retrace his route. He follows the route of 17th-century Portuguese Jesuit Andrade, 'hoping that it would open up new perspectives on the tales of Shambhala and Shangri-La'. The chapter 'The Search for Shangri-La' appears in Wood's book, *In Search of Myths and Heroes* (2005), which chases the real origins of four epic legends – Shangri-La, the Golden Fleece, the Queen of Sheba, and Arthur of Camelot.

Doyen of the Shangri-La spin doctors hard at work within China is New York lawyer Laurence Brahm, who has advised multinational corporations on their investments in China while liaising with Chinese officials. In 2004, Brahm went on the road and produced a hefty photo book, *Searching for Shangri-La: an Alternative Philosophy Travelogue*. In case you don't know what that last turn of phrase means, it appears to be about getting directional pointers from trendy Chinese rock stars, musicians, fashion designers and choreographers, who rip off aspects of Tibetan culture to claim as their own. There are also handy tips from Tibetan monks and yak-cheese makers on where Shangri-La might be found. Brahm then goes chasing (in no particular order) Tibetan ponies, café lattes and peach gardens beyond the realm. Brahm's book is full of corkers: he claims you might be able to find Shangri-La in a cup of yak-butter tea, if you stare hard enough. On the cover, he is photographed sitting on a high pass, composing next to a yak skull (he writes up a poem called 'Conversation with a Yak Skull' in the book).

Brahm ventures the opinion that interest in *Lost Horizon* has sparked 'an alternative scene for China's art and culture circles searching for creative space'. A movement of which Brahm himself would appear to be at the forefront: he took an entire film crew along on his travels through Tibet, Amdo and Kham. The resulting hokum spiel has been packaged into a hardback photo book, a softcover book, several music CDs, a set of six DVDs, and a postcard set. That's a formidable Shangri-La marketing machine at work. Made and published in Beijing, these products all come in Chinese-language versions too. But not in Tibetan-language versions.

To cover all bases, Brahm later sets off into the wilds of Tibet in search of the lost kingdom of Shambhala, resulting in another epic tome of turgid prose. The twist here is that Brahm has somehow come into possession of a secret Buddhist scripture called the Shambhala Sutra, stolen from a monastery. The ancient text acts as a road-map leading through west Tibet, but after beating about the bush for a hundred pages or so, Brahm tells us that the search for Shambhala has paradoxically led him back to a place deep within his own heart. Back to the drawing board: time for another intense cup of yak-butter tea and a fresh consultation with a yak skull.

Meanwhile, back at the House of Shambhala, a boutique hotel that Brahm manages in Lhasa: in through the door walks a fellow Shambhaholic – an American writer Patrick Symmes, who is on a quest to find the hidden kingdom. Or maybe he is on a quest to fill out a lot of pages in *Outside* magazine (where the story appeared in the October 2007 issue). Heading for his dawn meditations, Symmes almost steps on Brahm: 'An ascetic hedonist, Brahm slept on the roof but surrounded himself with beautiful women and the comforts of his hotel.' The comforts of the hotel include hot-stone massage therapy, dubiously linked to Tibetan tradition. According to Brahm, the timing for finding Shambhala is good because it has remained hidden during the rule of 25 kings, each lasting a century, and since the Buddha was born 2,500 years ago, then revelations could be close. Symmes sets off on his quest heading all over the map, with an *Outside* photographer called Seamus Murphy in tow.

They end up somewhere past the Kunlun mountains, over the rainbow near Urumqi, where Symmes adamantly declares he has found Shambhala. He refuses to reveal where it is, but says it is an archaeological site, some ancient Buddhist kingdom on the Silk Road, with lots of ruined temples and palaces, totally abandoned. Unfortunately, Seamus the photographer, who has thus far captured an assortment of goat herders and Tibetan pilgrims on film, does not appear inclined to photograph any part of this amazing discovery, thus leaving us in the dark. This is especially odd when you consider this is exactly what the photographer has been hired for. No mention is made of why Seamus has failed to film anything, but Symmes does inform us that the photographer is very busy throwing stones at an obnoxious urchin who is pestering him for money. Symmes then realises with a shock that he visited the same site 18 years earlier while backpacking with a Danish woman. But back then, he was exploring the Silk Road, and had never heard of Shambhala. He might have got it right the first time: this is a Silk Road site – one that has very little to do with Tibetan culture.

THE SOURCES

Wilson Mizner wrote: 'If you steal from one author, it's plagiarism; if you steal from many, it's research.' Hilton got his inspiration from many sources. He was a voracious reader, finishing as many as a dozen books in a single week. It is probable that he cobbled his account of Shangri-La together from a large number of sources.

Hilton never set foot in Asia, let alone Tibet. He got his inspiration from books. The closest he got to a Tibetan temple was the cavernous domed structure of the British Library (today the Reading Room of the British Museum). He went to the British Library in London to read many accounts of early explorers and missionaries in Tibet. In an introduction to the Universal Studios radio version of *Lost Horizon*, recorded in 1950, Hilton says that he began writing the book during the winter of 1932 while taking walks close to home, and 'climbing English hills with wild thoughts of Everest and Kangchenjunga'. He adds: 'I remember hours in libraries reading tales and legends of the great missionary travellers who explored all central Asia centuries ago.'

Hilton portrays an intimate knowledge of these missionary accounts, and not just in English. In *Lost Horizon* the lead character, Conway, is astonished by Shangri-La's delightful library, which is lofty and spacious. At a rough guess, Conway estimates there are 20,000 to 30,000 books on the shelves. He takes a closer look:

> Volumes in English, French, German and Russian abounded, and there were vast quantities of Chinese and other Eastern scripts. A section which interested him particularly was devoted to Tibetiana, if it might be so called; he noticed several rarities, among them the *Novo Descubrimento de grao cataya ou dos Regos de Tibet*, by Antonio de Andrada (Lisbon, 1626), Athanasius Kircher's *China* (Antwerp, 1667), Thevenot's Voyage à la Chine des Pères Grueber et d'Orville; and Beligatti's *Relazione Inedita di un Viaggio al Tibet*.

The library at Shangri-La may be imaginary, but the books described on the shelves are real. They deal with accounts by early missionaries and explorers to Tibet. Early accounts of Tibet were mostly by Jesuits and Capuchins, who fought over who had the rights to convert the Tibetans, although both groups were dismal failures in that respect. Hilton's Father Perrault is a Capuchin monk. Perrault grappled with Tibetan Buddhism, trying to refute it, but unable to bring himself to do so. In reality, this was the case with the Capuchin missionaries. Some of them were of the opinion that Tibetan Buddhism was the work of Satan: that only he could create a religion so outwardly similar to Catholicism, yet inwardly amounting to atheism.

Apart from the journals of frustrated missionaries, there is a wealth of material by explorers, climbers and fiction writers that Hilton could have tapped into. Hilton's spelling of the Kuen-Lun mountain range is peculiar to only a few sources (it is usually spelt Kun Lun or Kunlun). Prominent among them is *Visits to High Tartary, Yarkand and Kashgar*, by Robert Barkley Shaw, published 1871. Intriguingly, in this old travel narrative, Shaw starts his journey northward out of India to Ladakh, crossing Chang La (pass) and then traversing the Karakoram Pass toward the Kuen Lun range. With Yarkand and Kashgar thrown into *Lost Horizon*, this is a strong possibility for a source of names used by Hilton.

For plot and characters, Hilton could have taken cues from Rudyard Kipling's short story, *The Man Who Would Be King* (1888), in which two British adventurers enter the realm of Kafiristan, ruled by monks in a kind of theocracy. The story was inspired by the real experiences of American adventurer Josiah Harlan, who became a prince in Afghanistan in 1840. Theosophist and novelist Talbot Mundy's novel, *Om: The Secret of Abor Valley* (1924), introduced an all-knowing Tibetan Lama, Tsiang Samdup, cloaked in occultism and wisdom. The novel is set in India and Tibet, but the landscape and the ethnic group portrayed have little to do with Hilton's setting.

Very few explorers had managed to get into Tibet by 1933. Hilton's mention of the meditation practice where Tibetan monks raise their body temperature in freezing conditions and dry off wet sheets almost certainly derives from the work of Alexandra David-Neel (*My Journey to Lhasa*, 1927), who was the first Westerner to record this mystical practice in her writing.

As a keen mountaineer, Hilton would surely have turned to the accounts of the British expeditions to Everest in the 1920s, such as John Noel's film, *The Ascent of Everest*, and his follow-up book, *Through Tibet to Everest* (1927). In his book, Noel talked about air-dropping climbers on the top of Everest (with parachutes?) and hiking down. This was dismissed in climbing circles as unsporting, but it might have given Hilton ideas on how to get his main characters to Tibet, by cutting months of arduous overlanding to a day by plane. Some theorise that Hilton's hero Hugh Conway is modelled on George Leigh-Mallory, who disappeared on Everest in 1924. The name of Hilton's main character, Conway, could derive from Sir Martin William Conway, a British explorer and climber who in 1892 held the mountain-climbing altitude record (around 7,700m) in the course of exploring and mapping the Karakoram and Himalayan ranges.

Other explorer accounts from the highlands of Tibet: Joseph Rock wrote stories for *National Geographic* about unknown Tibetan enclaves in southwest China in the 1920s and '30s. And Giuseppe Tucci, an Italian Tibetologist, wrote about exploring the lost kingdom of Guge in western Tibet in the early 1930s. (See also page 33.)

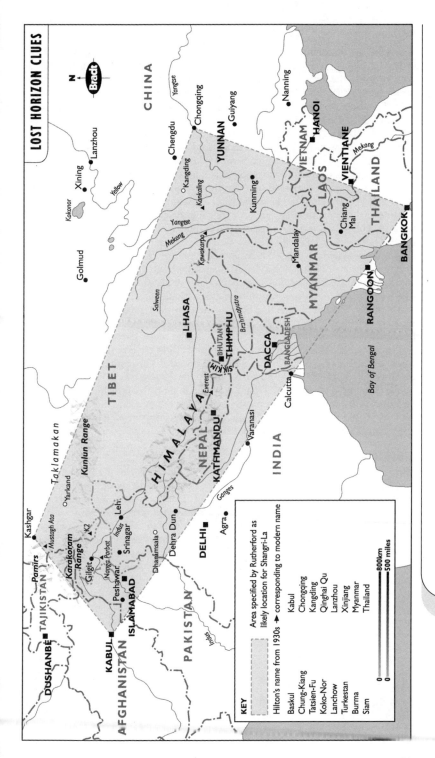

LOST HORIZON CLUES

CHINA

Lanzhou
Xining
Kokonor
Yellow
Golmud

Taklamakan
Yarkand
Kunlun Range
Kashgar
Mustagh Ata
Pamirs
TAJIKISTAN
DUSHANBE

Kangding
Kangding
Kawakarbo
Yangtse
Mekong
Chengdu
Chongqing
YUNNAN
Guiyang
Kunming
Nanning

TIBET
Salween

LHASA

Chiang
Mai
VIETNAM
HANOI
VIENTIANE
LAOS
THAILAND
BANGKOK
MYANMAR
Mandalay

HIMALAYA

BHUTAN
THIMPHU
SIKKIM
Everest
Brahmaputra
NEPAL
KATHMANDU
DACCA
BANGLADESH
RANGOON
Bay of Bengal
Calcutta

Kunlun Range
K2
Karakoram Range
Gilgit
Nanga Parbat
Leh
Peshawar
Indus
Srinagar
PAKISTAN
Dharamsala
Dehra Dun
Varanasi
Ganges
Agra
DELHI
INDIA

AFGHANISTAN
KABUL
ISLAMABAD
Indus

N

KEY

Area specified by Rutherford as
likely location for Shangri-La

Hilton's name from 1930s ➜ corresponding to modern name

Baskul   Kabul
Chung-Kiang   Chongqing
Tatsien-Fu   Kangding
Koko-Nor   Qinghai Qu
Lanchow   Lanzhou
Turkestan   Xinjiang
Burma   Myanmar
Siam   Thailand

0   800km
0   500 miles

THE CLUES

Your chances of finding Shangri-La are far greater than finding Atlantis. Both evolved as high-powered civilisations offering great promise for humanity. Atlantis sank beneath the waves, but Shangri-La is still out there on a mountainside somewhere, ageing lamas and all. The question is: where?

In *Lost Horizon*, a handful of locations are indicated by Hilton. Some, like Bangkok, Shanghai and Macao, bear the same name today. Because of political shifts, others, like 'Pekin', have changed name from the 1930s – today corresponding to 'Beijing'. The map in 1931 is not the same as it looks today. Peshawar – in the 1930s part of British India – later become part of Pakistan, while Sikkim lost its independent status and was absorbed into India. Tibet in the 1930s embraced a much larger area than is presently portrayed on maps by its Chinese overseers. The area that is today part of southwest China formerly all fell within the Tibetan realm.

Hilton fabricates some locations by juggling the spelling. The novel starts out from Baskul, which is a thin disguise for Kabul, with letters rearranged. Mount Karakal is very close in spelling to Karakul Lake, a real place along the Karakoram Highway. Tatsien-Fu is undoubtedly Tatsienlu on the 1930 map.

In *Lost Horizon*, Hilton notes 'La' is Tibetan for 'high pass'. However, 'Shangri' has no meaning in Tibetan. The closest Tibetan sounds would be 'kang ri' meaning 'snow mountain', or 'sang ri' meaning 'hidden mountain'. There are a number of passes on the Tibetan plateau that bear a similar-sounding name. There is Shingri La, to the north of Leh in Ladakh, and another pass called Chang La on the route from India up to Leh. There is place called Changri in the Everest region in Tibet, and there's a pass called Shirang-La in far-west Tibet (re-arrange the letters and you'd get Shangri-La). Who knows if Hilton looked at a map of the region and put his finger on a pass and then played around with the letters? An even larger blob on the map to put a finger on: if you follow the flight path of the hijacked plane in *Lost Horizon* from Kabul past Peshawar, heading in the direction of K2, you would pass over a district in Pakistan's North West Frontier Province known as Shangla. The Shangla district is today entirely Muslim.

GEOGRAPHY OF SHANGRI-LA

Hilton set the lamasery of Shangri-La somewhere to the north of Tibet, which is a vast area – Tibet is as big as western Europe. Tibet hosts the world's highest peaks and lakes – and its deepest gorges. Most of Tibet is over 4,000m high, with dramatic drop-offs from the edge of the plateau to forested areas. Most of Asia's major rivers are sourced on the Tibetan plateau – including the Mekong, Yangtse, Salween, Yarlung Tsangpo and Indus. The northern sector of Tibet is the forbidding Changtang, an immensely rocky and arid desert where nomads roam. To the northeast, in Amdo, the landscape turns to lush green, with rich grassland irrigated by the Yellow River. In Kham, semi-monsoonal conditions and lower elevations result in copious forest cover. Tibet's extreme altitude makes it a special place for hardy high-alpine flora, with secrets yet to be revealed. There are over 400 species of rhododendron in Tibet, and over 2,000 species of medicinal plants have been documented by Tibetans themselves because herbal remedies lie at the core of Tibetan medical practices.

Tibet is isolated by mighty mountain ranges, which James Hilton makes reference to. To the north of Tibet are the Kunlun Mountains, while to the west are the Pamirs and the Karakoram Range (which Hilton calls 'the Karakorams'). To the south are the Himalaya, with the world's highest snowline, and some 17,000 glaciers. Here, bordering Nepal, lie the 8,000-metre-plus giants of Everest, Lhotse, Makalu and Cho Oyu.

The hijacked plane in *Lost Horizon* would appear to crash somewhere in the Kunlun Range, which is often overlooked in the quest for finding Shangri-La – probably because it is bleak and deserted, with few settlements. However, the snowcapped peak where Shangri-La is located, Mount Karakal, is described as being 'over twenty-eight thousand feet' (over 8,500m) by Chang, the liaison person from the monastery. There is no peak of this height in the Kunlun Range – the highest mountain is Kunlun Goddess at 7,167 metres. In Hilton's day in the 1930s, it was unknown if peaks over 8,500 metres existed outside the Himalaya. In 1930, Joseph Rock cabled *National Geographic* with the sighting of a peak of 30,250 feet (9,220m), to the south of Tatsienlu (Kangding). The peak, Minya Konka, was climbed in 1932 by two Americans who pegged its height much lower – at 24,900 feet. Today the height of Minya Konka is officially given as 24,790 feet (7,556m). There are, in fact, only four peaks on the planet exceeding 28,000 feet: Everest, K2, Kangchenjunga and Lhotse.

JOURNEYS

In 1931, there were no roads to access the remote high-altitude region of Tibet, only caravan trails: Hilton solved the arrival problem by flying his visitors in. But the departure was overland, and much older residents arrived overland – hence dropping some hints about possible location. Here are some of the clues, in the order they appear in the novel.

At the start of *Lost Horizon*, the hijacked plane takes off from Baskul, which would be Kabul – the Afghanistan connection is confirmed when Miss Brinklow is mentioned to be teaching Afghans hymns. The plane is headed for Peshawar, which in 1931 was part of then-British India (today in Pakistan). The plane crosses the Karakoram Range, where Conway hazards a guess at the Indus Valley below, and the peaks of Nanga Parbat and K2. The plane then continues east into Tibet for some time, possibly reaching the Kuen-Luns (Kunlun Shan range). The crash-landing site is specified as Tibet.

The High Lama, Father Perrault, later tells Conway that he stumbled into Shangri-La while on his way from 'Pekin' to find Nestorian faith remnants in Tibetan hinterlands. He says he 'travelled southwest for many months, by Lanchow and the Koko-Nor' and that his three companions died. Those are real locations, with Pekin being Beijing, Lanchow being Lanzhou, and the Koko-Nor being the area around Lake Kokonor (Qinghai Qu). Perrault was close to death when by accident he found a rocky defile that led to the Valley of the Blue Moon.

Later in the novel, Conway finds out more about Lo-Tsen, who is of royal Manchu stock. According to Chang, she was 'betrothed to a prince of Turkestan, and was travelling to Kashgar to meet him when her carriers lost their way in the mountains'. Manchu royalty would come from northeast China, while Turkestan (today known as Xinjiang) is in the far northwest. Apart from Kashgar, two towns in Turkestan later mentioned by Rutherford are Yarkand (Soche) and Khotan (Hotien).

After escaping from Shangri-La, Conway tells Rutherford he went on a journey of '1,100 miles eastward to Tatsien-Fu on the China border'. Tatsien-Fu is undoubtedly Tatsienlu, an old tea-trading post, today known as Kangding. This is later confirmed by Rutherford, the narrator, who specifies Tatsien-Fu as 'a weird place, a sort of world's-end market town, deuced difficult to get at, where the Chinese coolies from Yunnan transfer their loads of tea to the Tibetans'. And then Conway ends up in Chung-Kiang mission hospital, which would correspond to Chungking or Chongqing on the map today. When Conway sets out for Shangri-La again, the route is given as departing Bangkok and heading north into northern Siam (Thailand) and Upper Burma (Myanmar).

The writer Rutherford went looking all over the region because he was writing a travel book on his search for Conway. But one big hitch: Rutherford says he never made it into Tibet because he couldn't wrangle permission to go there. Conway said he travelled 1,100 miles from Shangri-La heading east to reach Tatsienfu. If you were to draw a line due west of Kangding (today's Tatsienfu), you would arrive somewhere in Tibet, possibly in the Lhasa region. Except that travel by road would not be in a straight line.

At the end of *Lost Horizon*, Rutherford says:

> Altogether I must have done some thousands of miles – Baskul, Bangkok, Chung-Kiang, Kashgar – I visited them all, and somewhere inside the area between them the mystery lies. But it's a pretty big area, you know, and all my investigations didn't touch on more than the fringe of it – or of the mystery either.

ALTERED LANDSCAPE

One thing you must bear in mind when looking for Shangri-La is that clues from the 1930s might well have changed – or have become unrecognisable. For starters, due to greatly increased air traffic since 1930, it is highly likely that the inhabitants of Shangri-La have resorted to using some sort of camouflage for its temple rooftops to avoid detection from the air. They have also undoubtedly developed some kind of technology to avoid satellite detection, and to deflect probing devices like radar signals, magnetic sensors and electrical pulses – used to detect foundations and metal objects.

Then there is the climate change factor to consider. In an age of fast-receding glaciers, who knows if Shangri-La's Mount Karakal is completely covered in snow and ice these days? Research studies indicate that major glaciers in the Himalaya are retreating by as much as 20 to 50 metres a year, due to human interference and global warming. At this rate, a large number of Himalayan glaciers will completely melt and vanish between 2030 and 2050. According to a UN report, if current trends continue, 80% of Himalayan glaciers will be gone by 2040, leading to disaster for agricultural communities that depend on the seven river systems sourced from the glaciers for their drinking water and irrigation needs – let alone the protein derived from fishing. Melting glaciers and dried-up rivers could trigger droughts, desertification and sandstorms. In Ladakh, a project has been initiated to generate artificial glaciers which can function as a substitute for dams.

The mountains are rapidly changing, and so is the earth. Tibet has an underground layer of permafrost, which is not as permanent as the term suggests. The permafrost is shrinking due to climate change, and that means water locked in the soil during winter now melts and drains away earlier, before sprouting spring plants can send down roots to reach the water. This can dramatically reduce plant growth, causing changes to vegetation patterns over large areas.

Not helping matters here are Chinese engineers, who are good at damming and diverting major rivers, defiling sacred lakes (changing the colour scheme in the process), tunnelling through mountains to create highway access, laying down railway lines on the permafrost (in northern Tibet), and throwing up entire towns of corrugated roofing in the middle of nowhere in Tibet. This can be confusing if you are looking for wilderness. At UN climate change talks in Vienna in 2007, the official heading China's delegation to the 158-nation talks was asked what China was doing to combat global warming. His reply was that China has reduced the birth rate through the one-child policy, thereby lowering future demand for energy. He has a point, because China is heavily dependent on burning fossil fuels like coal for its energy, and coal burning is notorious for emitting the most greenhouse gases.

Another curious argument from Chinese officials: China has no plans to reduce coal-burning, arguing that coal is cheap, and the nation is entitled to experience the same coal-fired Industrial Revolution phase that Western nations passed through. China is fast becoming a toxic time bomb: it has some of the world's most polluted cities and rivers due to tonnes of sulphur dioxide being spewed out from the country's coal-burning factories, and coming back as acid rain. In fact, China is home to 20 of the world's 30 most polluted cities. This will go a long way to explaining why tourist promotions within China harp on about Shangri-La-like enclaves with pure mountain air and clean water in the sparsely inhabited western regions.

Sometime in 2006, experts believe, China surpassed the USA as the world's top emitter of carbon dioxide and other heat-trapping gases. China thus attained the dubious distinction of having the leading role in driving climate change. By 2030, if current trends continue, China and India will achieve a total of three billion in population, requiring exponentially more energy consumption.

Another factor possibly contributing to swift climate change is global wobble. This theory claims that the huge movement of goods and resources from the southern hemisphere to the northern hemisphere causes the earth to wobble. The top-heavy population weight of the northern hemisphere (over 2.5 billion for China and India alone) exacerbates the situation.

Part Two

THE CONTENDERS

4

Southwest China

CAUGHT BETWEEN MR ROCK AND A MYTHICAL PLACE IN SICHUAN AND YUNNAN

> I'm sure there's a wish for Shangri-La in everyone's heart... I just know that secretly they are hoping to find a garden spot where there is peace and beauty...oh, I just wish the whole world might come to this valley.
> – Jane Wyatt's ecstatic lines in a cherry blossom garden, in the movie *Lost Horizon*

This is what tourism authorities in southwest China are hoping too. They're peddling paradise with a big marketing campaign about being the location of the real Shangri-La. Jane Wyatt has something to do with all this. In later life, when American climber Ted Vaill caught up with the ageing actress, then 90, she revealed that on the set James Hilton had told her *Lost Horizon* was in part inspired by the writing of explorer Joseph Rock in *National Geographic*. The link has never been proven, and Jane Wyatt is no longer with us. The key words here are 'in part': Hilton used many sources – and Joseph Rock wrote about a number of Tibetan enclaves in southwest China for *National Geographic*. It is more likely that Hilton's Shangri-La had a greater impact on *National Geographic* than the reverse. Since the 1940s, *National Geographic* has run many stories referring to 'the Last Shangri-La' or variations on that theme.

In the mid-1990s, Shangri-La fever gripped southwest China with the announcement that the Himalayan utopia had finally been found. It all started with a man called Xuan Ke, a musicologist from an obscure ethnic group called the Naxi. Xuan Ke was thrown in jail for 21 years during the cultural revolution, when all things Naxi were banned. Xuan Ke's father had been hired by American explorer Joseph Rock to help him study the local culture in Lijiang. Much later, in the 1980s, Xuan Ke was given a copy of *Lost Horizon* by a friend who thought he might be interested in a Westerner's view of Tibetan areas. Xuan Ke claimed that upon reading *Lost Horizon*, it immediately reminded him of the area of Zhongdian, where his grandmother was from a Khampa family. But wait, no, *Lost Horizon* also reminded him of the town that other relatives were from, Deqin. And there were definite traces of Lijiang, the town he currently lived in. He arranged for a translation of *Lost Horizon* into Chinese, with an introduction featuring photos of Joseph Rock and his Lijiang mansion, used as a base for expeditions.

Xuan Ke decided to inform officials in the town of Zhongdian in upper Yunnan about his exciting conclusions, and they immediately saw the possibilities. A conference was held in 1996, setting in train a dizzy array of marketing gimmicks. Zhongdian commissioned a hit single, 'Stepping into Shangri-La', funded the production of lavish picture books, and began lobbying aviation officials to rename its new airport 'Zhongdian Shangri-La Airport.' At this point, Xuan Ke raised objections and tried to distance himself from the phenomenon, claiming to be disgusted by greedy officials who cared only about making money and building five-star hotels. But Xuan Ke was simply left behind in the dust as the 'Shangri-La Tourism Project' gathered momentum in Zhongdian. And in other parts of Yunnan – and neighbouring Sichuan – as well.

Amusing but true: all the Shangri-La claims in southwest China depend on Xuan Ke's theory that James Hilton was inspired by reading *National Geographic* articles written by Dr Joseph Rock – a theory partially backed up by anecdotes from actress Jane Wyatt as told to climber Ted Vaill. Doc Rock explored Yunnan and Sichuan in the 1920s and '30s. The region of Sichuan and Yunnan provided a treasure trove of unusual species for Western collectors, especially for plant hunters such as Rock. Trouble is, Rock never wrote a *National Geographic* story about Zhongdian or Deqin. He wrote about the two places in an obscure academic work, *The Ancient Na-Khi Kingdom of Southwest China,* which was published in two volumes by Harvard University Press in 1947, long after *Lost Horizon* appeared in print. Xuan Ke was (much later) a key consultant in the translation into Chinese of Rock's scholarly work on the Naxi, so it's possible Xuan Ke was confused, and he got Rock's obscure academic work mixed up with popular *National Geographic* magazines as a source for Hilton. The *National Geographic* articles that Rock did write prior to the 1933 publication of *Lost Horizon* were about Muli (1925) and Yading (1931), which are both in Sichuan Province, not Yunnan.

Ignoring this anomaly, Yunnan tourism authorities mounted a vigorous campaign to have a region officially renamed 'Shangri-La'. Branding of an area as Shangri-La would surely attract lots of income from tourism. A steady stream of glossy photo books, brochures, DVDs and music CDs followed. Joseph Rock, who had been booted out of Yunnan by the advancing Red Army in 1949, was rehabilitated and retroactively upgraded to a Communist Party poster boy. In brochures, he morphed into 'Doctor Lock' or 'Joseph Lark' or 'The Rocker'. This is all the more odd when you consider that Joseph Rock despised the Chinese, particularly the communists. Prose about James Hilton in Chinese brochures is also replete with typographical errors: some make reference to 'The Lost Horizontal' and the paradise of 'Shag-rila.'

The sillier the hype, the more impact it seemed to have. Singaporean and Hong Kong tourist agencies lapped up special Shangri-La promotions. Tourist arrivals in Zhongdian County, numbering 66,000 in 1995, shot up ten-fold to 670,000 visitors by 1998, and topped the million-mark the following year when Shangri-La Airport opened.

The meteoric rise of the Yunnan campaign sparked dogfights with Sichuan spin-doctors, who suddenly coveted the Shangri-La mantle. Eventually, it was decided in Beijing to officially bestow the name Shangri-La County on Zhongdian County in upper Yunnan in 2002. At the same time, authorities announced the creation of a huge area in western Yunnan and Sichuan, embracing all the greedy contenders, to be called the 'China Shangri-La Ecological Tourist Zone', with development projects to run to billions of dollars. This was a chunk of land about the size of Switzerland. This idea seems to have since vanished into thin air.

Although this chapter is entitled 'Southwest China', in the 1930s the regions under discussion were very much part of the Tibetan realm. In 1965, the Chinese occupiers of Tibet renamed the central section the 'Tibet Autonomous Region' and carved off large slabs – donating them to neighbouring provinces in Yunnan, Sichuan, Qinghai and Gansu. This effectively reduced the area of Tibet by half. The highland zones of Yunnan and Sichuan carry names like Ganzi Tibetan Autonomous Prefecture, Diqing Tibetan Autonomous Prefecture, and Muli Tibetan Autonomous County, but there is nothing autonomous about governance here.

I catch up with Xuan Ke at his family mansion in Lijiang: we settle in for a long interview. His Alsatian guard dog wanders in and flops on the floor, eyeing me suspiciously. Xuan Ke lights up a cigarette and cracks jokes about Chinese officialdom. Most Chinese would never dare voice such opinions, but the outspoken Xuan Ke doesn't care. In 1957 he was sent to prison for the crime of being a 'counter-revolutionary'. He languished in jail for 21 years. Xuan Ke's father was an interpreter for Joseph Rock and General Stillwell, among others, and Xuan Ke was being groomed for the same job. Both father and son were jailed for being 'spies of foreign organisations'.

Now in his seventh decade, Xuan Ke very much doubts that the authorities would attempt to put him away again. He is a celebrity with a huge following among the Chinese themselves; having toured with his Naxi orchestra in the West, he has a host of foreign supporters too. Xuan Ke is spritely, considering his advanced age – and the fact that he smokes a lot.

On the bookshelves behind him are older editions of *Lost Horizon* and old *National Geographics* that hold Joseph Rock's articles. But when I ask him to pinpoint the *National Geo* article about Zhongdian, he reaches instead for a huge volume by Joseph Rock, *The Ancient Na-Khi Kingdom of Southwest China*, which was published in 1947 – long after *Lost Horizon* appeared. He flips through the pages to find pictures of his mother's birthplace – the white limestone terraces of Baishuitai, sacred to Naxi shamans.

Here are some quotes from Xuan Ke from the interview:

> *The first time I heard about Shangri-La was, I think, in 1946. I was a student at a mission school in Kunming. The teachers were American and they showed some movies at the time. One of these was the Hollywood movie* Lost Horizon. *And then later in 1987, I was given a copy of the book by James Hilton.*

> *It reminded me of the rolling hills around Zhongdian, not the town of Zhongdian – no culture there – and not the monastery, Sungtseling. That used to be a prayer place, but today it's just a business place – not a real religious place, not for the Buddha. Just tickets for tourists, and selling souvenirs. And* Lost Horizon *reminded me of my mother's birthplace, Annan, or the Heavenly Fields, which were all controlled from Lijiang.*

> *Zhongdian at that time was still Tibetan, with many religions mixed together – Tibetan, Confucian, Taoist, Christian, shaman.*

> *I think around 1996, I was interviewed by the BBC and one American program. And they became very interested in Zhongdian and made a big story about it and the connections to Shangri-La. I told the journalists about Joseph Rock's articles in the* National Geographic.

> *Shangri-La is not a real idea on the map, but from the novel. A young Chinese guide from Kunming came to me and asked to be taken on as my student. He knew nothing about the region and he couldn't read English. I shared my knowledge about Joseph Rock and Peter Goullart and other texts about Zhongdian. But that Chinese guide had big lips – he made the story much bigger. Many journalists rushed to him. Later, the stupid writers from Hong Kong believed everything he said. Many journalists from Hong Kong and Singapore wrote about Shangri-La as the real place. They wrote stories about 'Shangri-La finally discovered'. That young guide with the big lips, he became the vice-governor of Zhongdian County.*

Southwest China MR ROCK AND A MYTHICAL PLACE

4

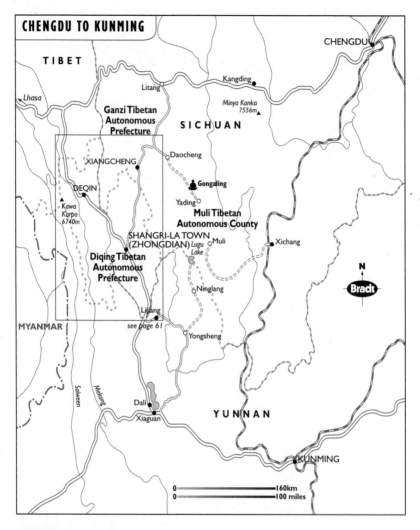

TIBET

Lhasa

Kangding

Litang

Minya Konka
7556m

**Ganzi Tibetan
Autonomous
Prefecture**

SICHUAN

Daocheng

XIANGCHENG

Gongaling

DEQIN

Yading

*Kawa
Karbo
6740m*

**Muli Tibetan
Autonomous County**

SHANGRI-LA TOWN
(ZHONGDIAN) *Lugu* Muli
Lake

Xichang

**Diqing Tibetan
Autonomous
Prefecture**

N

Bradt

Ninglang

MYANMAR

Lijiang

see page 61

Yongsheng

Salween

Mekong

Dali
Xiaguan

YUNNAN

0 ———— 160km
0 ———— 100 miles

KUNMING

SICHUAN

The borderlands of Sichuan are happy hunting grounds for Shangri-La, with a sprinkling of little-explored Tibetan areas, such as Aba. Ganzi Tibetan Autonomous Prefecture is vast – it covers about a third of the area of Sichuan. This is Khampa territory. The tall brawny Khampas have a reputation as fierce warriors. Though considerably subdued under Chinese rule, they are nonetheless not intimidated by the Chinese, and are aggressive traders who can be encountered as far off as India or Nepal. The Tibetan ethnic groups here seem to have much more freedom than in Tibet itself: people appear more prosperous, with Tibetan entrepreneurs often living in castellated structures for farmhouses.

A short aside here on the Chinese paradise market in Sichuan: it is aimed at well-heeled Chinese from the east coast, craving some fresh mountain air and drawn by 'Tibet chic'. Right up north in Sichuan, near Jiuzhaiguo national park, is the five-star-rated Jiuzhai Paradise Resort Hotel, where room rates start at US$200 a night. No need to worry about bad weather here: this place has several huge wings entirely enclosed with Plexiglas domes – including artificial hotsprings and a whole Tibetan village (that's artificial too). There's a huge theatre inside where quasi-Tibetan costumed performers cavort in modern moves, with female dancers showing lots of leg (which Tibetans never do).

YADING NATURE RESERVE

The first contender for Shangri-La presented in this book has a very strong case. It hosts a stunning Matterhorn-like pyramidal peak. It has beautiful pristine valleys. This area has long been sacred to Tibetans, as it is reputed to be one of the *beyuls* – a hidden valley consecrated by a great Tibetan lama. There is a *kora* (pilgrim circuit) around three major snowcaps, which have never been climbed. These vistas were shown in the July 1931 issue of *National Geographic*, which James Hilton may well have read.

All that is lacking to complete the Shangri-La picture is a huge active monastery. In Chinese photo books and brochures of the area, such a monastery appears, but it has been dropped into Photoshop, or whatever the Chinese version of that is. The monastery in question is actually 30km distant from the snowcaps at Yading. Known as Gongaling ('Snow Mountain Monastery'), the place does not exactly match the profile of the peaceful lamasery at Shangri-La. Back in the early 20th century, pilgrimage to this area was quite dangerous due to bandits who were in the habit of robbing pilgrims coming to pay homage to the sacred peaks. The 400 monks at Gongaling found pilgrims a handy source of revenue too. The monks used to rob pilgrims blind, and then return to their quiet meditations at the monastery – apparently not a contradiction in these parts.

The first Westerner to explore this remote terrain was eccentric American plant-collector, Doctor Joseph Rock. A number of explorers had tried to penetrate the region but failed, partly due to brutal weather conditions, but mainly due to the threat of Tibetan bandits. In mid-1928, the resourceful Dr Rock enlisted the help of the king of Muli (aka the Head Lama of Muli Monastery) who dispatched stern missives to the bandit chiefs and monk-bandits telling them to back off at least long enough for Dr Rock to photograph and write a *National Geographic* article and to collect flora and fauna samples (the title 'Doctor' was self-given: Rock never formally studied botany).

Rock rode into the region with a posse of Naxi and Tibetan bodyguards, armed to the hilt. He carried two Colt-45 pistols and a rifle – a bit of a cowboy. They visited twice during the monsoon season, experiencing torrential rain, which meant the peaks were obscured by cloud. Rock bided his time, lingering to get the photos he needed. When the clouds finally parted, the panorama knocked him out: 'In a cloudless sky before me rose the peerless pyramid of Jambeyang, the finest mountain my eyes ever beheld,' he crooned in the *National Geographic* article. Of course, Rock was pumping it up for his audience: there are plenty of snowcaps that rival Jambeyang in Bhutan, Tibet or Nepal.

Rock planned a third visit to the region in the dry season, but never made it: the area's robber chief bluntly said next time round he would murder Rock and his escorts. Rock explains: 'His reason was the obvious displeasure of the gods. Shortly after our last trip around the peaks the wrath of the deities was aroused and hailstones descended in such size and quantity as to destroy the entire barley crop of the Tonyi Besi outlaws.' Rock took the hint and stayed away.

But even so, Rock had gathered a 'mountain' of material – enough to fill a whopping 60 pages of the July 1931 issue of *National Geographic*. A lot of the *National Geographic* page count was taken up with superb colour photos. Rock was a pioneer in the use of natural colour photography, dragging along heavy plates and developing the pictures on the spot. He would have marvelled at present-day Chinese tourists with their featherweight digital cameras, video-cams, and collapsible tripods.

Horsing Around in Shangri-La

There are plenty of those (Chinese tourists with cameras) on the way into Yading. Yading Nature Reserve is a kind of paradise for well-heeled Chinese tourists coming from as far afield as industrial Shenzhen or Shanghai. It embraces a realm of crystal-clear gurgling streams, and luxuriant forests of larch, pine, cypress, fir and oak, and majestic snowcaps with cascading glaciers and odd-coloured glacial lakes. Human habitation is minimal: there are no permanent residents inside the reserve apart from roving Tibetan shepherds. The nature reserve, first designated in the late 1990s, is pristine and pollution-free; the superb mountain vistas are a tonic for the senses. Shielded by the mountain range, the region has created its own micro-climate, with an ever-changing show of clouds dispersing over the snowpeaks, and a great interplay of lighting conditions revealing new colours.

If that doesn't take your breath away, the altitude will. It's over 4,000m here. Chinese tourists come armed with oxygen pillows, oxygen canisters and traditional herbal remedies to counter the debilitating effects of high-alpine air.

Several options for Yading: you could hike in, or go by horseback to a viewpoint at Luorong, which is 14km from the trailhead, and then return by the same route. A more strenuous option is to keep going from Luorong and complete a *kora* of the peaks of Yading. This would require having your own tent and food to complete the journey.

Chinese tourists usually opt for a horseback ride of 14km to the viewpoint known as Luorong pasture. Tourists are led by Khampa wranglers, and seated on woven Tibetan carpeted saddles. The first photo-op stop is near tiny Tsengu Gompa, the only temple in the area. Within a few hours by horse, you reach Luorong pasture, where overnight camping in rudimentary tents is provided. There are eye-popping views of Jambeyang from this point – especially dramatic toward sunset. From Luorong, you can hike up toward a 4,700m pass to see pristine tarns, including one magical lake where, it is said, the future can be divined.

Those are the Chinese tourists. Tibetan pilgrims aspire to doing a *kora* (complete walking circuit) of the sacred peaks, taking several days. If you have the time and the supplies, the *kora* is the way to go. Fifteen *koras* is said to be equal to the accumulated virtues of 100 million murmurings of the sacred mantra *Om Mani Padme Hum*, so some very strenuous hiking could save considerable wear and tear on the voicebox for Tibetans.

Tibetans named the three major peaks of the region after deities thought to reside atop them. Depicted in Tibetan *tankas* (religious paintings), the trinity of deities are: Chenrezig (the Bodhisattva of Compassion), Chanadorje (a wrathful deity, the Holder of the Thunderbolt), and Jambeyang (Manjusri, deity of learning, shown wielding the Sword of Knowledge). The three peaks lie close to each other, arrayed in a rough triangle.

To mountaineers, the three lofty main peaks provide a tantalising challenge. Chenrezig (6,032m), Chanadorje and Jambeyang (both just under 6,000m) are all virgin peaks: they have never been scaled, though a number of expedition attempts have been mounted. There's something to be said, however, for keeping the mountains pristine, with the summit snows untrampled by the boots of mountaineers.

MULI

American lawyer and climber Ted Vaill, who claims to have researched the location of the real Shangri-La for over 20 years, swears that Muli is the right spot. In fact, he once offered to guide tour-groups into the area for a cool US$15,000 a head, on one condition: that they do not reveal his secret location. Ted Vaill promised to publish a book and produce a documentary proving many points of convergence between Muli and *Lost Horizon*, but he has since disappeared off the radar. Maybe his research will take another 20 years to complete, who knows?

Muli was once a Tibetan fiefdom, ruled over by a king. Seeking to write a story for *National Geographic*, Joseph Rock managed to reach the unknown kingdom of Muli in 1924, running the gauntlet through bandit territory. He found the kingdom of Muli comprised about 340 houses and 700 monks, and the king's authority extended over a region of some 15,000 km^2.

In these remote parts, status and rank had to be established: it was important to keep up appearances and earn the respect of local leaders. So Rock arrived as a true leader would: by limousine. The limo of these remote areas was the sedan chair – a compartment borne on two long poles and carried either by four porters or four ponies. It was accompanied by an armed escort. On arrival, Rock would dramatically alight in a white shirt, tie and jacket. He acted like royalty – and carried a business card in Chinese.

Probably his grandest entrance like this was his meeting in January 1924 with Chote Chaba, the king of Muli – who doubled as High Lama of Muli Monastery. The king of Muli – six-foot-two and corpulent – towered over Rock, who stood five-foot-eight. Chote Chaba ruled over his tiny kingdom with absolute authority – which included frequent public executions. He employed spells and magical incantations to reinforce his power. Rock played down the nasty aspects of Chote Chaba and harped instead on the theme of a long-lost kingdom. This was perfect prose for *National Geographic* – it appeared in the April 1925 issue under the title 'Land of the Yellow Lama'. Rock relates how the inquisitive monarch of Muli peppered him with inane questions like: Did Rock have binoculars that could see through mountains? Could a man ride a horse from Muli to Washington? Rock tried to keep a straight face when the king demanded to know where the kingdom of Puss in Boots was located. When Rock showed Chote Chaba a picture of an aeroplane in flight, the monarch inquired if the Americans could fly to the moon. Back in the 1920s, that made the monarch sound like a dum-dum, but today his comment would be viewed in an entirely different light.

Joseph Rock rarely talked about food or what the local people ate in his writings, but there are some prize snippets in the *National Geographic* story:

After the lecture, the king urged me to partake of Muli delicacies. There was a gray-colored buttered tea in a porcelain cup set in exquisite silver filigree with a coral-studded silver cover. On a golden plate was what I thought to be, forgetting where I was, Turkish delight, but it proved to be ancient mottled yak cheese, interspersed with hair. There were cakes like pretzels, heavy as rocks. It was an embarrassing situation, but, in order not to offend His Majesty, I took a sip of tea, which was like liquid salted mud.

Later, Rock was given gifts by the king:

There were eggs in plenty; a large bag of the whitest rice, two bags of beans for the horses and one of flour; one wormy ham; dried mutton; lumps of gritty salt, more of that doubtful yak cheese, and butter wrapped in birch bark. All the gift-bearers stood as I distributed silver coins. Three cakes of scented soap were presented to the prime minister. As the king's porters left, a hungry mob of beggars gathered outside our gate. The dried legs of mutton and yak cheese were literally walking all over the terrace of our house, being propelled by squirming maggots the size of a man's thumb. I was informed these were the choicest delicacies from the king's larder. As none of my party wanted the lively food, we gave it to the beggars, who fought for it like tigers.

On a second visit in 1928, Rock curried favour with Chote Chaba by bringing him copies of *National Geographic*, with photos of the king prominently displayed. Appealing to the king's great vanity, Rock used the *National Geographic* issues as a ploy to get leverage to enter Yading.

Chote Chaba was executed by the Chinese in 1934. The tiny kingdom of Muli was carved up by competing warlords in the lawlessness that swept across China in the 1930s. Unfortunately, very little of the original Muli is left standing today. It was mostly destroyed in the 1950s. The king of Muli's modest palace is gone; his monasteries were razed. A few temples have been partly rebuilt, with a handful of monks in residence. It appears that the rocks and materials from many dismantled buildings were carted across the valley to build a new town called Wachang. A 16-metre-high Buddha statue was carted off and disappeared: it was later replaced with a very poor copy.

YUNNAN

The borderlands of Yunnan are home to many ethnic groups, some of Tibetan origin. Yunnan's wealth of flora has long attracted botanists, keen to discover new ornamental species and medicinal plants: the place is a wonderland of unusual species. In the early 20th century, that's why Joseph Rock was there, and British collectors George Forrest and Frank Kingdon-Ward, too. Rival plant collectors like these were fiercely territorial: Kingdon-Ward accused Rock of stealing his native assistants (Rock lured them with higher rates of pay). The modern territorial battles are over a cash crop called tourists.

ZHONGDIAN

As far as Beijing is concerned, Tibet does not exist on any map as a political entity – and nor does Taiwan, for that matter. But Beijing recognises Shangri-La as a real place that *does* exist on the map.

In 2002, by official decree from Beijing, three counties in upper Yunnan were officially renamed Shangri-La County. Due to this renaming, the largest town of the counties, Zhongdian, became Shangri-La Town by default. It is today referred to as Xiangerila, the Chinese transliteration of Shangri-La, or Xianggelila for the Chinese who can't pronounce that. Its old Tibetan name is Gyalthang and its old English name is Chungtien.

Zhongdian (elevation 3,275m) has a population of around 20,000, which makes it the largest town in this corner of Yunnan. Nobody with marbles intact would mistake Zhongdian for Shangri-La: it's a bland Chinese city full of concrete and karaoke, which doesn't fit the bill. But Zhongdian is being marketed as the gateway to Shangri-La County. A number of businesses in Zhongdian blithely use the Shangri-La logo without rhyme or reason: Shangri-La Online Tea Bar, Xiangerila Mini-mart, Shangri-La Bus Station, and so on. It's just another day in Shangri-La. There are even packets of Shangri-La-brand cigarettes on sale, made in Yunnan. You have to wonder about the marketing of those (the box says nothing) under the Shangri-La label – would the cigarettes prolong your life or shorten it? Well, James Hilton himself was a heavy smoker, and noted in *Lost Horizon* that a fine brand of tobacco was grown in the Valley of the Blue Moon – good news for Conway and

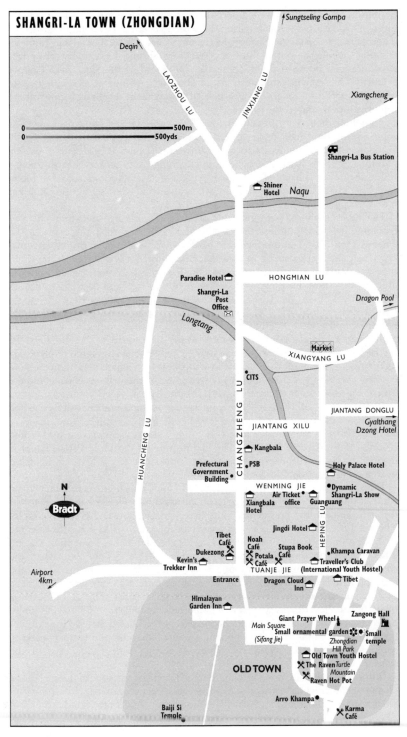

SHANGRI-LA TOWN (ZHONGDIAN)

Sungtseling Gompa

Deqin

LAOZHOU LU

JINXIANG LU

Xiangcheng

0 ——————— 500m
0 ——————— 500yds

Shangri-La Bus Station

Shiner Hotel   *Naqu*

Paradise Hotel   HONGMIAN LU

Shangri-La Post Office

Longtang   *Dragon Pool*

Market

XIANGYANG LU

CITS

CHANGZHENG LU

JIANTANG DONGLU

Gyalthang Dzong Hotel

JIANTANG XILU

Kangbala

PSB

Prefectural Government Building

Holy Palace Hotel

WENMING JIE   Dynamic Shangri-La Show

Air Ticket office   Guanguang
Xiangbala Hotel

HEPING LU

Jingdi Hotel

Tibet Café

Dukezong   Noah Café   Stupa Book Café   Khampa Caravan
Kevin's   Potala   Traveller's Club
Trekker Inn   Café   (International Youth Hostel)

TUANJE JIE

Entrance   Dragon Cloud Inn   Tibet

Airport 4km

Himalayan Garden Inn

Giant Prayer Wheel   Zangong Hall

Main Square   Small ornamental garden   Small
(Sifang Jie)   *Zhongdian*   temple
   Hill Park

Old Town Youth Hostel

OLD TOWN   The Raven   *Turtle Mountain*

Raven Hot Pot

Arro Khampa

Karma Café

Baiji Si Temple

HUANCHENG LU

N

Bradt

Southwest China YUNNAN

4

Mallinson, who both smoked. Interestingly, some signs in Shangri-La Town are given in Chinese, but not in English. Maybe that's because they don't fit the image. Thus there is a sign saying 'Shangri-La County Police Bureau' but only in Chinese. Another one bears only Chinese script for 'Shangri-La County Hospital'. Brochures and booklets about Zhongdian (produced by the Shangri-La County Publicity Department) studiously avoid showing anything to do with mobile phones or traffic or modern devices. Instead, photography dwells on happy smiling minority groups and scenic beauty.

To bolster their claim to paradise, in 2001 authorities in Zhongdian unveiled some irrefutable evidence: an ancient flush toilet – imported, used, and finally abandoned by foreign missionaries. The mythical Shangri-La had state-of-the-art plumbing, but it's hard to imagine tourists lining up to look at a flush toilet – unless the device is made of solid gold (there is such a bathroom of gold in Hong Kong, built by a gold-broker company, where mainland Chinese tourists come and have their photo taken on the solid-gold toilet seat).

Having been blessed with the name of Xiangerila, Zhongdian is trying hard to live up to it – actually, to recreate it. The place is being turned into a Shangri-La Theme Park. Local authorities are hard at work manufacturing sights that previously did not exist. In an area that once hosted a few dozen decrepit old mansions without plumbing, an entire Old Town has been constructed from the ground up – now bustling with boutique hotels, bars and souvenir shops. A Chinese booklet says the Tibetan name for this area translates as 'Blue Moonlight City', which is a load of hot air, but not a bad theme park name. The picture would not be complete without ethnic song and dance, so that too has been created: at night, there's a regular ethnic dance circle at the main square of the Old Town. At the back of the area is a massive ugly rotating prayer wheel monument, towering 23 metres – it was built in 2002. Nearby, a couple of Chinese-style temples were constructed. None of these temples is active: this is more about channelling the inner cash cow than anything to do with spirituality.

On the fringes of town, billboards for mobile phone companies show Tibetan women in full ethnic dress, or, worse still, ads for Shangeli-la Wine, made in Yunnan. Tibetan monstrosity hotels in gaudy colours have sprung up – some resemble mini Tibetan temples. The architecture of the Holy Palace Hotel is inspired by the Potala, except that the Potala does not have a karaoke-nightclub warren on the rooftop. Not yet, anyway.

Even steeper in price is the luxury Paradise Hotel, which boasts its own climate control: this five-star effort is completely enclosed by a Plexiglas dome. Rates go through the roof: the presidential suite here is priced at over US$1,000 a night. The hotel is ranked five-star, which means lots of guest facilities. In this case, the facilities do not mean tennis courts. The Paradise Hotel has something that no other hotel across the entire Tibetan plateau has. It has its very own hyperbaric chamber. These are sometimes found at high-end dive resorts in the West – the function here is to change the pressure for those suffering from altitude sickness. In case you are wondering who can afford a presidential suite of US$1,000 a night, researcher Rupert Hoogewerf reported in 2007 that China has more billionaires than any country in the world except the United States. He attributes the dramatic rise in the number of billionaires in China to booming stock markets, combined with surging property values – creating a new elite class of the super-rich.

Within the town of Zhongdian, there are a dozen text variants on the spelling of Shangri-La: ShangliLa, Shangeli-La, Xianggelila, Xiangerila, Shangbala (a mix of Shangri-La and Shambhala), Xiangbala, Xiongbala... And to the southern end of Zhongdian, I spotted a hotel with flags fluttering out front that bore the script

The awesome peak of Jambeyang
in Yading Nature Reserve, Sichuan

above   Tourist horse caravan heading for Jambeyang

left   Tibetan B&B in converted stone farmhouse, Daocheng

below   Chinese tourists at Yading revel in clean air

bottom   Gongaling gompa

The show goes on in Zhongdian, Yunnan, with a musical called 'Dynamic Shangri-La'

above Dancers in yak-suits perform a number that Gary Larson would love

right Women in nomad costume, kicking up like chorus girls

below Pathetic attempt at Tibetan sacred dance

The strange state of tourism in Zhongdian

top   Diqing Shangri-La Airport opened in 1999 in Zhongdian

above left   Lost in translation: a hotel in Zhongdian flies a special flag for 'Shag-Rila', although the Chinese characters for 'Shangri-La' are correct

above right   Billboard showing a mountaineer making a call from a Himalayan peak — an advance due to the spread of cellphone towers

below   Chinese 4x4 on the road to Shangri-La: the green signpost indicates a right turn to Shangri-La (Zhongdian Town)

The Paradise Market

top   Chinese tourists posing at Sungtseling Gompa, Zhongdian

above   Paradise Hotel in Zhongdian has an enclosed dome roof to prevent rain falling on a holiday parade

right   The Holy Grail of Shangri-La: a handful of Chinese caterpillar fungus, touted to be a miraculous cure-all

top   The iconic peak of Kawakarpo (Meili Shan), viewed near Deqin, pops up on most Yunnan literature about Shangri-La

above   Sungtseling Monastery in Zhongdian (compare this to the Chinese photo-montage depicted on colour page 5)

left   Big bend of the Yangtse, en route to Deqin

Song and dance in Shangri-La: an essential part of the image promoted by spin doctors is happy smiling ethnic folk

above   Tibetan dance performance near Deqin

below   Naxi traditional orchestra, which Xuan Ke claims to be the world's oldest orchestra, performing in Lijiang

LOST HORIZON LOST HORIZON

● （英）詹姆斯・希尔顿
● 和为含
● 海天出

消失 *De* 地平线

● 关于"香格里拉"最忠实于原著的译作
● 客观而切实地阐释"香格里拉"之谜

沿着洛克足迹
走进香格里拉

FOLLOW ROCKEB'STEPEP
TO SHANGRI-LA

Meet the mythmaker

above left　Xuan Ke, the man behind the re-discovery of Shangri-La in SW China, holding a copy of Hilton's *Lost Horizon*

above right　Xuan Ke was involved in launching the first Chinese translation of *Lost Horizon*, claiming it was inspired by Joseph Rock's travels

left　This sign points the way to Joseph Rock's old house, near Lijiang

below left　Xuan Ke signing copies of Joseph Rock's *The Ancient Na-Khi Kingdom of Southwest China*. Xuan Ke helped translate the mammoth academic work into Chinese.

opposite page　Two nomad women from eastern Tibet on pilgrimage in Lhasa, strolling around Barkor Bazaar

བོད་ལྗོངས་དང་རང་སྐྱོང་ལྗོངས་ཡུལ་སྐོར་ཅུས།

中国西藏自治区旅游局
CHINA TIBET TOURISM BUREAU

སྣ་ཚོགས་ངོ་མཚར་ཅན་བོད་ཡུལ་གངས་ལྗོངས་སོ་མཚར་ཡིད་འཕྲོག་ལ་བསུ་ལ།

带您进入神奇的雪域高原
Brings you to the mysterious snow-land

舌: 6834193 旅游咨询电话: 6834315　Tourist Complaint Telephone: 6834193　Tourist Information Telephone: 6834315

top	Chinese tourists pose in Tibetan dress for photographer at Potala Square
above	Tibet Tourism Bureau billboard in Lhasa promotes 'the mysterious snow-land'
below	What monks do — playing billiards in eastern Tibet

Dystopia in Lhasa

top left   Chinese architecture stands in complete contrast with Tibetan: here showing the 10-storey China Telecom building in Lhasa

top right   A poster showing modern Lhasa, undergoing rapid change from Chinese engineering plans, accelerated by the arrival of the Tibet railway

above left   Fake coconut palms, imported from China, decorate a street close to the Potala

above right   Paradise Chinese-style is depicted in this Maoist Utopian vision from China Post: the Potala appears at top left, the Great Wall at right

below   The architects of Tibet: poster in Lhasa showing Mao Zedong, Deng Xiaoping and Jiang Zemin

Despite restrictions, festivals still carry on in Tibet

above   Villagers preparing for horse-race festival

left   Cham dancing at a monastery courtyard in central Tibet

below   Monks with trumpets, Shigatse

Geomantic architecture is a unique feature of Tibet

top The imposing fortress of Gyantse

above left Pilgrims leave banknotes and pins (symbolic of sharpening the mind) at shrine in Gyantse

above right The Kumbum in Gyantse is a rare form of architecture based on mandalic principles

below The vast monastic citadel of Ganden, mostly rebuilt after great destruction in the Cultural Revolution

Mysteries of west Tibet

above left   Rare Kashmiri-style Tara mural, from ruined temple at Tsaparang

above right   Mt Kailash, the most sacred peak in all of Asia

below   The ruins of the Guge Kingdom, at Tsaparang

opposite page **Tibet's surprising landscapes**

top   Rongbuk gompa in foreground, with the north face of Everest looming in background

middle   Thermal landscape with bubbling sulphurous activity, central Tibet

bottom   Deep green valley and village, eastern Tibet

Rough roads in west Tibet

above left   Nomad woman travelling in open back of truck

above right   21st-century nomad with shiny new motorcycle — and snow lion carpet on the saddle

left   Truck crossing high snowbound pass near Guge region

below   Group of travellers admire views at Lake Paiku Tso

'Shag-ri-La'. Perhaps this is a species of hotel where local loose women are available with the blankets, and where karaoke is piped into the rooms.

The Holy Grail of Souvenirs

When the Old Town of Zhongdian suddenly surfaced, with brand-new buildings made to appear ancient with the clever laying down of moss on the roofs, it instantly laid claim to being the main nightlife area, playing host to dozens of small bars. But by day, a very different trade goes on – selling souvenirs to the Chinese tourists who traipse through.

And what, you wonder, could you possibly take home from Shangri-La? Well, the souvenir shops are packed with imported items that run the gamut from pashmina scarves to cowboy hats, from Tibetan trinkets to expensive jade pieces. You can find huge bricks of tea, stamped with Chinese characters – once used as a currency by Tibetan traders in these parts. And then, if you look closely, there are some curious local products on sale, claiming to only be from the highlands of this region – though more likely mass-produced in lowly Kunming. Aside from a slew of books, CDs and DVDs about Shangri-La, there are various yak-derived souvenirs on sale, including yak skulls engraved with sacred mantras. Outside Zhongdian, farmhouses display open-air racks where rows of yak-tails are drying out – these are sold to passing motorists as souvenir whisks (used to keep the flies away, or else for dusting around the house). And you can buy Shangri-La-brand dried yak meat to chew on (a strong set of teeth is required to deal with this yak jerky).

But the ultimate souvenir from Shangri-La may be the gift of long life and good health. Fungus would be a good start. Traditional-medicine fungus products are in abundance in the souvenir shops of Shangri-La, with a number processed at local factories. According to German mushroom expert Daniel Winkler, collecting mushrooms at the eastern side of the Tibetan plateau is of great importance to rural folk, as they can make more in a few weeks of foraging for fungi than they do in an entire year of farming or herding. While varieties like the cuckoo mushroom are exported to Europe and the matsutake mushroom is flown fresh to Japan, by far the biggest market is domestic – with huge demand from east coast China. The trade is dominated by a fungal variety endemic to the Tibetan Plateau called *Yartsa gunbu* (*cordyceps sinensis*, also known as Chinese caterpillar fungus). Cordyceps accounts for over 95% of the fungi market value, and in the Tibet Autonomous Region contributes to some 40% of rural cash income. According to Winkler, collection across the Tibetan plateau rakes in around 100 to 150 tonnes of this bizarre fungus each year. When you consider than a tonne is equivalent to roughly three million cordyceps specimens, that's an awful lot of fungal worms being traded.

The Zhongdian region lies at the crossroads of this intense fungal economy, a paradise for fungophiles – or a nightmare for fungophobes. The caterpillar fungus is the Holy Grail for Chinese tourists. Like something out of *The X-Files*, cordyceps is a parasitic fungus that grows on the larva (caterpillar) of the ghost moth over the winter season, and takes it over, killing it in the process. Thus cordyceps lies somewhere between insect and plant. The Tibetan *yartsa gunbu* means 'summer grass, winter worm', summing up the parasitic process. This thin worm-like 'plant' is hard to find – it must be dug up from surface soil in alpine grasslands above 4,000 metres in the spring. Can this fungus be the source of the fountain of youth? Are dead caterpillars the answer?

Little is known about this fungus or how it originates, but Tibetan medicinal texts list its remarkable properties as far back as the 15th century, claiming it to be highly efficacious against kidney, lung and heart problems. Chinese caterpillar fungus is reputed to possess not only anti-ageing properties but is also an aphrodisiac, prized as an energy booster that stimulates the circulation and the

4

immune system. It has been fed to racehorses in China to enhance speed and stamina – and used for the same reasons by Chinese athletes. The fungus was much sought-after in China during SARS epidemics. Modern Chinese takes on cordyceps claim it contains anti-cancer, anti-tumour, anti-oxidation, and anti-viral properties. Whatever the case, it certainly has remarkable inflationary properties: the cost of cordyceps has risen more than 200% over the last two decades in Lhasa, where top-grade specimens are worth close to their weight in gold. The miraculous fungus ranks high on the gift list, and is used for bribery (no money changed hands, just lots of caterpillar fungus). Packets of cordyceps are on sale in Zhongdian, and the worms are added to special dishes in restaurants. None of this is cheap: a rare fungal aphrodisiac with a long list of magical properties is going to cost.

Somewhat more affordable are other fungi on offer in Zhongdian. Yunnan Shangri-La Tibetan Dragon Bioengineering Development Company of Zhongdian produces Jizong Fungus – described as a wild edible fungus from the snowline, best enjoyed in soup or fried or steamed. Or you might like to indulge in Wild Edible Black Fungus (fry it up with pig stomach), or perhaps Gastrodia Elata, said to nourish the kidneys and brain, calm the liver and stop wind. This is best served with chicken, duck or pigeon, or soaked in wine. A good choice would be Herbal Wine, made in Zhongdian from fresh ginseng, centipede, whole worms, lotus flower – the list goes on. This one claims to be excellent for curing impotence, rheumatism, and a number of other dodgy ailments.

Zhongdian by Night

When the sun goes down, Chinese tourists head for fancy group-tour restaurants to view ethnic dance performances while they eat, or else drink themselves stupid

---

PLANE-SPOTTING IN SHANGRI-LA

It's hard to tell what tourist authorities have up their sleeves in the way of producing new sights in Shangri-La now that the name has been officially sanctioned. Here are some ideas under discussion.

PLANE SPOTTING Create an area with a few couches just past the end of the runway, where foreign enthusiasts can inhale the heady aroma of jet fuel as a departing Airbus passes overhead with a deafening roar.

MONASTIC KARAOKE Modify chanting at Sungtseling Gompa with more upbeat dirges in the karaoke vein, and choreograph new monastic dances with hip-hop moves.

FOUNTAIN-OF-YOUTH SPAS Not getting any younger? It's an old dilemma. Solution: promise a holding pattern on age – even a touch of longevity – at FOY spas through a regimen of yoga and a steady diet of Chinese wolfberries.

SACRED SOUND YOGA The special yoga of Shangri-La, where yogis go through their moves accompanied by a small ensemble of monks who provide sound effects with longhorns, singing bowls and throat-singing chants, thereby evoking a long-lost aural horizon.

SUN-AND-MOON-OF-THE-HEART CELLPHONE THERAPY In this short but brutal programme, addicts are surgically separated from their cellphones, Wifi, SMS and other handheld devices – to enable them to re-connect with real human beings.

THE RUNNING OF THE YAKS Take a leaf from Pamplona and let yaks loose in the narrow alleys of the Old Town. If tourists get gored, that's better than being bored.

in karaoke bars. Slightly more authentic is the free ethnic dance in the open-air square of the Old Town, where you can join in for circle dances. The Old Quarter, known in Tibetan as Dukezong, boasts more than 40 small bars. These include the Cow Bar, which was converted from a barn for cows. The Raven serves jazz and coffee in the afternoons, and martinis at night. Nearby is Hazel Bar, with a restaurant and attached guesthouse.

Meanwhile, back in Zhongdian, there could be a stage show in progress. This takes place near the Holy Palace Hotel, and costs an exorbitant Y180 and up a seat. Billed as 'Dynamic Shangri-La', the show features minority groups prancing around in garish costumes, making a lot of noise with drums and other instruments, and men in yak-suits jumping around in conga-lines. Some dance numbers are quasi-Tibetan. Others, like a dance with swirling paper umbrellas, and another featuring men covered from head to toe in chicken feathers, appear to be of Chinese choreographic origin. The ethnic song-and-dance hoopla lasts a bit over an hour. The programme notes are every bit as garbled as the concept: 'Dynamic Shangri-La is a scenic song and dance medley with the beauty of local minority tradition and the folk cultures of Shangri-La Diqing. It compromises the concept of postmodern arts and the fantastic creation of stage design, lighting, sound effects.'

SUNGTSELING MONASTERY
The main sight of Zhongdian is Sungtseling Monastery, 5km north of town, set in rolling farmland. If bicycling out this way, or arranging a driver, take your time along the way to drink in the scenery, making it a half-day trip or longer. To avoid the tourist hordes, time your visit for very early in the day, when monks are more likely to be at prayers, or linger around at sunset when the tour groups are winding down.

Sungtseling is a Geluk (Yellow Hat) monastery that was founded in the 17th century by the 5th Dalai Lama. The place was destroyed in the Cultural Revolution and completely rebuilt. Viewed from a distance, the monastic citadel is striking, with an entire hillside stacked with Tibetan housing for monks, and the gleaming rooftops of the uppermost temples. The gompa is the largest in Yunnan, and if you've never seen a Tibetan monastery before, the steep central staircase leading up to the main prayer hall will certainly impress. It will also knock the wind right out of you. But though ideal for a *Lost Horizon* movie set, the place is soulless when it comes to religious practices. Although there are supposed to be several hundred monks in residence, not much seems to be going on in the way of prayer-chanting or studies. The monastery is all show for bus-loads of Chinese tourists who descend on the place, vastly outnumbering the hapless Tibetan monks. There is a gaudy circus of souvenir shops lining the approach to the monastery gates.

The place may come to life for Losar (Tibetan new year, around February), or in a late-November festival, with sacred Cham dance performed by the monks in the uppermost courtyard. In these rituals, monks wear masks representing demons, spirits and mythical animals.

BAISHUITAI TERRACES
Located in a valley 108km southeast of Zhongdian, Baishuitai is the spiritual heart of the 300,000-strong Naxi people of Yunnan and Sichuan. Baishuitai is the birthplace of intriguing Dongba shamanism: the distinctive Naxi pictographic script originated here. Dongba script has more than 2,000 pictographs, including ferocious tigers and dagger-wielding demons. Dongba shamanism was severely suppressed during the Cultural Revolution, and thousands of ancient manuscripts were destroyed. It is debatable whether the pictographic script is still in use, since

Embarrassingly, there is no Tibetan word for Shangri-La. They have no need for one because they already have Shambhala. Even Shambhala is not a Tibetan word – it is Sanskrit in origin. In a Tibetan dictionary entry, Shangri-La is likely to be equated with Shambhala, or with *dechen shingkham* (Buddhist pure land or paradise) or *beilung* (a *beyul*). However, to make things look authentic, the Chinese spin doctors need the exact Tibetan script for Shangri-La.

One technique is to turn the Chinese characters into something that resembles Tibetan characters by using a customised Chinese font. The font looks Tibetan but is actually Chinese, and most foreigners can't tell the difference.

Another approach is simply to fudge it, by claiming that 'Shangri-La' in the obscure local Tibetan dialect means 'sun and moon of the heart'. However, 'Shangri-La' has no meaning in any Tibetan dialect. A Chinese-produced map of Zhongdian shows quite a different origin for that turn of phrase. On the map there are three scripts – English, Chinese, Tibetan. The Tibetan script, *senjinida*, means 'sun and moon of the heart' and the origin of this is given as a quote about Gyalthang (Zhongdian) being 'a jewel of the east, sun and moon of the heart'. In the fine print, this is attributed to Buddhist king Jigme Peicto. But the seal is that of Khenpo Jigme Phuntsok, a highly revered lama – considered a *terton* or treasure-revealer by Tibetans.

A charismatic teacher, Jigme Phuntsok founded Serthar Institute in Amdo as a religious school in 1987. The institute went on to attract more than 7,000 monks and nuns – both Tibetan and Chinese – who blanketed the hillside around the institute with simple meditation huts made of wood and mud. Monks and monasteries are fine as tourist attractions, but if there is any real religious teaching going on, Chinese authorities step in. They are nervous of any assembly of the size of Serthar: in summer 2001, work crews protected by the People's Liberation Army destroyed the homes of followers in an attempt to reduce their numbers to fewer than 1,400. The upheaval meant great anguish for the ageing Jigme Phuntsok – so frail that he could not walk unassisted. He later died under house arrest.

Welcome to Sun and Moon of the Heart Airport! *Senjinida* in Tibetan script appears everywhere around Zhongdian – on hotel signs, restaurants, government offices, local products. Jigme Phuntsok may have had the last laugh. There is a common Tibetan saying that in the sky there are the sun and moon, while on earth there are the Dalai Lama and the Panchen Lama – and those two are the sun and moon of the heart.

only shamans learn to read and write Donga script, and the shamans have died out – though there is talk of training more. According to some sources, Naxi wizards still practise the art of reading chicken entrails to tell the future in Baishuitai. In any case, Baishuitai's big attraction is its glorious creamy limestone terraces that cascade down the valley in surreal majesty – with snowy peaks looming in the distance and emerald rice paddies far below. From Baishuitai, preferably with a local guide, you can trek out to other Naxi villages affording spectacular vistas, like the 25km trail to Haba. It's about five hours by road from Zhongdian to Baishuitai.

DEQIN

While Zhongdian has the monastery, the peak you see in Shangri-La-type collages put out by Yunnan tourism lies 200km north at Deqin, the capital of Deqin County. Deqin County adjoins Shangri-La County: along with Weixi County,

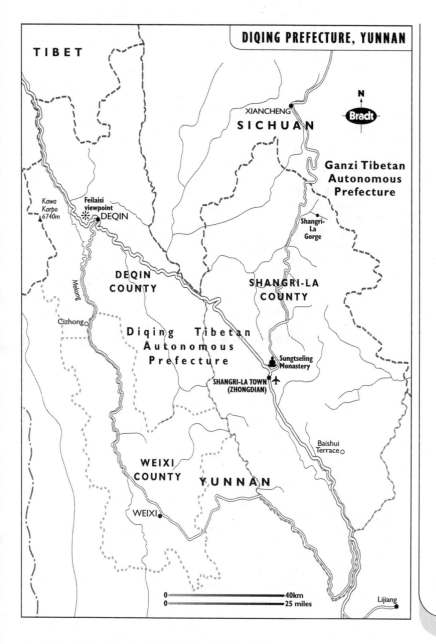

DIQING PREFECTURE, YUNNAN

TIBET

XIANCHENG

SICHUAN

N

Bradt

Ganzi Tibetan
Autonomous
Prefecture

Kawa
Karpo
6740m

Feilaisi
viewpoint
DEQIN

Shangri-
La
Gorge

DEQIN
COUNTY

SHANGRI-LA
COUNTY

Mekong

Cizhong

Diqing   Tibetan
Autonomous
Prefecture

Sungtseling
Monastery

SHANGRI-LA TOWN
(ZHONGDIAN)

Baishui
Terrace

WEIXI
COUNTY

YUNNAN

WEIXI

0   40km
0   25 miles

Lijiang

4

these three fall under the jurisdiction of Diqing Tibetan Autonomous Prefecture, comprising almost 24,000km² and a population of 330,000, with a number of ethnic groups.

Deqin is a frontier town of about 5,000 souls, and sits at 3,280 metres. It is reached by a spectacular 10-hour bus ride from Zhongdian. On the way in, just south of Deqin, is a brilliant viewpoint over a sweep of snowcapped peaks.

While there is guesthouse and hotel accommodation at Deqin, a better idea is to stay at Feilaisi viewpoint, 10km north of Deqin. Feilaisi has a handful of guesthouses and rooftop cafes. The mountain views from here are most spectacular at sunrise and sunset, so if you stay at a guesthouse overnight you will be in the right spot. If there is no cloud cover, the rising sun lights up a string of a dozen 6,000m peaks like candles. At centre-stage is Mount Kawakarpo (aka Kawagebo, or Meili Xueshan in Chinese), which at 6,740m is Yunnan's highest peak. At Feilaisi's white *chortens*, devout visitors murmur mantras, throw rice in the air at juniper hearths, and tie on prayer flags. And Chinese photographers (*Homo photographico siniensis*) gather in large numbers to capture a classic scene: a deep valley leading to the Mekong River, with the ethereal snowcap of Kawakarpo looming high above. It's a setting that could easily grace the cover of *Lost Horizon*.

Blue Moon Valley Hike

You can get much closer to the peak of Kawakarpo by crossing over the Mekong River to the other side of the valley. Allow the better part of a day for this excursion. You can stay in Tibetan-style guesthouses near the trailhead, or return to Feilaisi or Deqin to overnight. In hired transport, proceed from either Feilaisi or Deqin to the trailhead of Minyang glacier trail.

The trail winds up through splendid forest, host to a diverse range of flora and fauna. Minyang glacier, cascading down the flanks of Mount Kawakarpo, is unusual because it descends to a low altitude of 3,100m, providing meltwater for the Mekong River. A steep hike (or horseback ride) brings you past a tiny Tibetan temple and on to the toe of Minyang glacier, with a viewpoint. The glacier is 500m wide and almost 12km long. You can hear the occasional crunching and cracking of ice as it slowly advances. And this, according to the entry ticket, lies at the very heart of Shangri-La. Some sort of icy heart perhaps? Longer treks in the vicinity of these peaks are possible. You would need a guide to avoid getting lost.

BINZHONGLUO

The remote town of Binzhongluo, to the far northwest of Yunnan, is the northernmost town of spectacular Nujiang Gorge. The town sits close to a bend in the Nujiang (Salween) River. In the middle of town is a large piece of granite etched with Chinese characters that tout the village's claim to be Shangri-La. The origin of this claim is not clear (not that the other claims are, either). The town can be used as a base for great hiking to outlying spots. Although Binzhongluo can be reached by rough road from Kunming, there is no direct road link from Binzhongluo to Deqin, a distance of some 100km. However, you can trek from Binzhongluo to Deqin or vice-versa in about four days, crossing a pass of 4,000 metres. This is best done with a local guide.

Binzhongluo sits in a UNESCO World Heritage Site called Three Parallel Rivers, so named because the deep gorges of the Salween, Mekong and Yangtse rivers run close to each other here. The protected region, encompassing 1.7 million hectares, includes a swath of Deqin (Minyang glacier and Mount Kawakarpo), and is considered a treasure-house of biodiversity. But shortly after the World Heritage Site was announced by the UN in 2003, Chinese engineers also announced the building of a series of large-scale dams on the Salween – one of Asia's last wild rivers. If that seems to be a contradiction – damming a World Heritage site – it washed right over the Chinese planners, who are bent on using large-scale dams on this pristine river to generate hydropower to distant Chinese cities. The UN is doing little to counteract this, apart from raising a few eyebrows and muttering some stern rebukes.

CIZHONG

To the far west side of Yunnan, close to the Mekong in Deqin County, lies the town of Cizhong, set in a glorious green valley, with barley, corn and vineyards. Cizhong stakes its Shangri-La claim on the fact that it used to be a French Catholic missionary outpost.

The missionaries arrived in the late 19th century and built a church that blended French and Chinese architectural features. Seems like this was mission impossible. The French priests found the locals highly resistant to conversion, and encountered a backlash from militant Tibetan Buddhists, who counted brigands among their number. The church was destroyed in 1905 and two priests were murdered. Soldiering on, the missionaries rebuilt the church. There is a garbled story about a five-tonne bell for the church that was flown in on a plane that crash-landed – further details about the fate of the bell or the crash-landing are hard to come by, but the story is told to bolster the case for Shangri-La.

In 1952, the beleaguered priests of Cizhong were finally pushed out by the communists. The church remains – a mini cathedral with a squarish steeple. Inside is a fresco of Jesus above the altar and narrow banners of Chinese script to either side. The ceiling tiles and walls are decorated with Christian crosses, lotus blossoms from Buddhist iconography, and yin-yang symbols borrowed from Taoism. The church is still used for services by the local people who are of various minority groups. A somewhat more successful legacy of French priests are the extensive vineyards growing within and beyond the walled compound around the church. These vineyards are the source of one of China's best homegrown wines, bottled by Shangeli-La Winery, a Yunnan company run by a wealthy Hong Kong businessman. The Shangeli-La label on the bottle harps on about the fact that this wine has been around since the days of the French missionaries; some labels feature Cizhong church. The company prattles on about the harmonious blending of religions during the French era (the monastery of Shangri-La blended Catholic, Taoist and Buddhist elements). Wisely, the manufacturers have chosen to overlook the murder of priests and burning down of the church in their write-up about peace and harmony in this valley.

LIJIANG

In the 1940s, there were only two big-noses in Lijiang – the cantankerous Joseph Rock and Peter Goullart, a Russian refugee. They were both pushed out by the advancing Red Army in 1949. Rock never made reference to Shangri-La in any of his writings, but Goullart did. Goullart wrote a nostalgic book about Lijiang entitled *Forgotten Kingdom,* published in 1955, which he concluded with these words:

> I had always dreamed of finding, and living in that beautiful place, shut off from the world by its great mountains, which years later James Hilton conceived in his novel Lost Horizon. His hero found his 'Shangri-La' by accident. I found mine, by design and perseverance, in Likiang.

That might have held true in the 1940s, when the town was inhabited by ethnic Naxi people and there were no Chinese in sight. Today, the old town of Lijiang is completely overrun by Chinese tour groups on voracious shopping sprees, and rich Chinese patronise the KFC at the crossroads of the old town and new Chinese city.

If passing through, a few things are worth looking into. In contrast to a number of other Shangri-La contenders in this region, the ethnic group in Lijiang is not Tibetan. It is a Tibetan-related group known as the Naxi, whose exact origins are mysterious. This group was nearly decimated by the onslaught of the Cultural

Revolution, with its customs and traditions completely outlawed in the upheaval. Since then, the Naxi have returned full swing, with their customs and traditions revived as the main tourist attraction in Lijiang. Another group commonly seen is the Mosuo, whose heartland is Lugu Lake, several days from Lijiang. Tour guides in the Old Quarter are usually Naxi or Mosuo women, dressed in striking traditional costume. Naxi women dress in a maroon velvet top and ruffled white skirt; Mosuo women wear a white skirt, red brocade tunic and floral headpiece. Around the main squares of Lijiang, hordes of Chinese tourists form an even bigger group, posing for ethnic-style pictures. One of the dress-up photo-props is a whole red panda pelt, fashioned into a fur hat, with the ringed tail hanging down. A red panda fur hat is regarded as a traditional good-luck marriage charm in Yunnan – and very unlucky for the red panda itself, as it is being hunted to the brink of extinction because of this.

Both the Naxi and the Mosuo ethnic groups are matrilineal: lineage is traced on the female side of the family, not the male. The Naxi were once completely matrilineal, but those at Lijiang today practise a compromised version. Women make family decisions, control the finances, and do much of the labour in the house and the fields, while men idle their time away – possibly indulging in cultural life, like poetry and calligraphy, or music.

Wandering the Old Quarter, you can see women in Naxi dress running trendy bistros, cafés and boutique hotels. Here you can sample European, Chinese or Naxi cuisine – which is hot-and-sour with liberal use of chillies, vinegar, soy and onion. You can wash all this down with Naxi homemade wine, tasting similar to port. Shangri-La for the gourmet, if you're coming from Tibet.

The Naxi today number perhaps 300,000 people, living in Yunnan, Sichuan and Tibet. Rock became fascinated with the obscure origins of the Naxi and spent over a decade deciphering their ancient pictograph script, used by Naxi shamans – a project on a par to decoding the hieroglyphics of the Rosetta Stone. The Dongba script of Naxi shamans qualifies as the last pictographic script still surviving, though usage today is no longer practical – it is mostly the subject of scholarly study. The script was employed for a millennium to record and guide the religious traditions of the Naxi. The religious culture of Dongba shamans is described by scholars as being an amalgam of Tibetan Bon and Tibetan Buddhism – as well as elements of Taoism, Confucianism and local shamanism. That particular mix would match the spiritual blend found in James Hilton's Shangri-La.

Naxi is pronounced 'Na-shi', and should not be confused with Nazis (Joseph Rock transcribed the ethnic group as Na-khi). With the Japanese invasion of China in 1937, Rock, in the course of his travels, went to Berlin to see the Nazis for himself. Horrified by what he saw, he bid a hasty retreat back to Lijiang, which he figured was as good a place as any to sit out the war.

In early 1944, the ever-restless Rock took a short trip to India. He turned up in Calcutta, where the US Army Map Service took a sudden interest in him. Military officers hustled Rock onto a top-priority flight to Washington, promising that his voluminous belongings would follow. Rock's invaluable knowledge was needed by the US Army to draw maps for pilots flying 'the Hump' – the mountainous region lying between China and India. These supply flights departed India and flew over Burma to southwest China, landing at Kunming. With large parts of China and Burma occupied by the Japanese, the flights were a lifeline for southwest China. While Rock was flown to Washington, his precious Naxi research was packed into trunks in Calcutta and dispatched to the USA by ship. The trunks included all the research for his Naxi encyclopedia and dictionary – a project he had laboured on for the last decade – plus translations of Naxi religious ceremonies and notes on Muli. The ship was torpedoed by a Japanese submarine: a decade of research sank to the bottom of the sea. Rock went ballistic when he heard the news. For a few days, he was perilously close to suicide.

Once he got over this, he decided he would just have to go back and start the Naxi research all over again. There were a few hitches: Rock calculated he had invested US$18,000 of his own money into Naxi research, and he didn't have the funds to kick-start the project. At sixty, he was too old to lead expeditions. But Rock was stubborn, and he had good connections. He talked Harvard University Press into agreeing to publish a two-volume Naxi history, and secured guarantees that they would help finance his return to Yunnan to complete the rest of his Naxi research.

In late 1946 he was back in Lijiang again. He put in some productive years, reassembling his Naxi material – he found a good Naxi Dongba wizard, traced manuscripts, recorded religious ceremonies. This time he took no chances – in 1949, he personally loaded all his research onto a turboprop aircraft he chartered to fly out of Lijiang, with the Red Army hot on his heels. Harvard published Rock's two-volume work *The Ancient Na-Khi Kingdom of Southwest China* in 1947. The text ran to over 800 pages, with 256 plates as illustration. Rock died in 1962; he did not live to see the publication of his two-volume Naxi encyclopedic dictionary – this was published posthumously. Because of the destruction of the Cultural Revolution, Rock's work became invaluable as the only extensive record of Naxi culture and pictographs.

Lijiang by Night

Joseph Rock wrote several stories for *National Geographic* about the shamans of Yunnan, who made house calls for exorcism rituals and medicinal healing. The shamans have since disappeared, though a small downtown theatre purports to show some still surviving. These shaman shows are only for tourists: the 'shaman' performers speak in gibberish that resorts to insulting the tourist audience on occasion.

Across the way are nightly performances by the world's oldest orchestra, or so it is claimed by Xuan Ke – the prolific mythmaker who is behind the discovery of Shangri-La in southwest China (see page 49). Xuan Ke was instrumental in reviving Naxi traditional music. After spending 21 years in prison under the Chinese, Xuan Ke has made a fortune promoting Naxi music and selling his biography. Clad in an old Confucian gown, Xuan Ke acts as the orchestra conductor and speaker who explains the music. Breaking political taboos, in between numbers Xuan Ke cracks jokes about the visits of famed party leaders like Jiang Zemin to an audience of mainly Chinese tourists, who laugh and whistle. Veiled criticism of China's venerable leaders is considered to be sacrilege.

Xuan Ke claims the ancient Naxi music is inspired by masters of Taoist and Confucian works, dating back some 13 centuries. The authenticity of reviving music from centuries past is a dubious affair, but if not the world's oldest orchestra, this venue certainly features the world's oldest performers. They keep going till they drop. Some are in their eighties – several with long flowing white beards, or else wearing sunglasses (due to blindness). Longevity hints: keep the music going. Performers say this nightly musical get-together is what keeps them active. Pictures of orchestra musicians who have passed along to celestial realms (no longer with us) are displayed above the performing area. The music itself sounds like a cacophony to the Western ear, with frequent clashing of gongs and shrill sound of flutes.

In 2004, Xuan Ke sued the magazine *Yishu Pinglun* (Art Criticism) for libel after a Chinese writer claimed that 'Naxi Ancient Music' was just a commercial product packaged for tourists instead of a cultural legacy. The writer claimed that Xuan Ke

WHEN TO GO

Best times to visit are April–June and September–November. Roads can be impassable in the winter months, and heavy rain in summer can wash out bridges or cause landslides.

LOGISTICS

No permits are required to visit Tibetan areas of Sichuan or Yunnan, and there are no restrictions on your movements. These regions just require a regular Chinese visa. In embassies around Asia, a Chinese visa is often issued valid for a month, but better if you can obtain a two-month, three-month or longer visa to avoid the need for extensions if planning to stay longer. Visas like this are easily obtained in one or two days in Hong Kong SAR. Currency is the Chinese Yuan RMB (US$1 = 7.8 Yuan RMB); you can also use US dollars to settle larger bills.

Agents/guides: An excellent agent in Zhongdian is Khampa Caravan Adventure Travel Company, with lots of details on their website: www.khampacaravan.com/. They can arrange unusual camping trips – even homestays with nomads on the grasslands of Kham – and onward trips by Landcruiser to Lhasa.

Following up: For lots of detail on Yunnan, consult *China: Yunnan* (Bradt Guides, 2007). A good website with information on Kham is www.khamaid.org/.

ROUTES

Gateways to the region are Chengdu, Kunming and Zhongdian, with large airports. There is a flight Kunming-Zhongdian-Lhasa several times a week. If your time is short, use more aeroplanes. You could, for instance, fly from Kunming to Zhongdian, and travel overland from there to Chengdu, and then take a plane to Lhasa. Or, in the reverse direction, fly from Lhasa into Zhongdian, tour this area and head overland to Kunming.

Overlanding: put all this together and visit all the Shangri-La candidates in one wild long road trip. This is the Shangri-La Grand Tour. The full route goes from Chengdu to Kunming, or the reverse. You could go by bus from Chengdu via Litang to Daocheng (and possibly Muli). The overland section from Daocheng to Zhongdian and on to Deqin must rank as one of the most beautiful road trips in southwest China, winding and switchbacking on rough roads past stone farmhouses and dipping through dense forest. From Deqin, backtrack all the way to Lijiang, take a stop there, and complete the journey to Kunming on a deluxe bus. The complete overland journey described could take two to four weeks or longer. A shorter variant is to go from Chengdu overland via Daocheng to Zhongdian and Deqin, back to Zhongdian and fly to Lhasa. A longer variant is to take a rented Landcruiser from Zhongdian via Deqin all the way to Lhasa. That would take at least a week from Zhongdian.

YADING NATURE RESERVE

The Konkaling range is only accessible about six months a year. Best times to visit are April–June and September–November. You can rule out the winter, when the area is snowed in, and write off the summer monsoon period (July–August), when heavy rains reduce the trails and access roads to mud.

The gateway to Yading is the town of Daocheng. Until an airport is completed at Daocheng, the only way to get there is by road from Zhongdian or Chengdu. From Zhongdian, it is a day overland to Daocheng. From Chengdu, it takes several days by bus to reach Daocheng, via Kangding and Litang. Litang (elevation 4,200m) is a drab town, but comes alive in August, with a five-day horse-racing festival, held on nearby grasslands. Daocheng is the transport hub for the southern border region of Sichuan province. It's a small town with a number of guesthouses, including the Blue Moon Valley Hotel, which offers hot showers (there are also some hotsprings near Daocheng). You might also be able to find a Tibetan B&B, run by a Tibetan family. There are some castle-like Tibetan structures around Daocheng that offer guesthouse rooms.

From Daocheng, it's a round trip to Yading Nature Reserve. The sole access route into Yading snakes in over some high passes – it's about 90km from Daocheng to Yading village, at the trailhead. There are basic guesthouses here, and tent accommodation. The road is exceedingly rough and best attempted in a hired jeep, taking about six hours. On the way in, make a point of stopping at Gongaling Monastery, the largest in southern Sichuan, with over 300 monks. In the morning, they're all seated in the lofty main prayer hall, which reverberates with the sound of chanting.

Your return point for Yading will be Daocheng. From Daocheng there is an alpine route leading to Shangri-La (Zhongdian, read on) in upper Sichuan. A stupendous winding high-alpine route leads over a pass of 4,700m, heading for the town of Xiangcheng (elevation 3,000m). Transport may be scarce between Daocheng and Xiangcheng (might have to hire a jeep for this leg), but Xiangcheng to Zhongdian presents no problem. From Xiangcheng, the road dips through dense forest – a rare sight in China today.

MULI
Muli is a tough destination to reach. Try the Joseph Rock approach: hire some horses from the village at Gongaling and set out for a few days. The only real drivable 'road' to Muli comes in from the east from the town of Xichang, which lies on the the the Chengdu–Kunming railway line.

ZHONGDIAN
By air Diqing Shangri-La Airport is the official name of Zhongdian's airport, opened in 1999, on the outskirts of town, with flights to Chengdu, Kunming and Lhasa. The Kunming–Zhongdian–Lhasa flights are not likely to run in winter (December to May), but the Kunming–Zhongdian flights probably will.
Overland A smooth ride by road coming from the south via Lijiang, or rough ride from the north via Daocheng. The Daocheng–Zhongdian road switchbacks over several high passes, one being 4,700m, complete with hairy yaks roaming the high pastures, and then plunges back into thick forest – an unusual sight in China.

Basics
A good travel agent, able to supply guides and transport, is Khampa Caravan, on Biemen Jie, tel. 887-828-8648, www.khampacaravan.com/. The office is located near the entrance to the Old Town.

For air tickets, touring information, bus tickets, food, jeep rentals, bicycle rentals and accommodation, your one-stop shop is Tibet Café, on Changzheng Rd, tel. 887-823-0019. This has comfortable double-rooms with bath for $20, and cheaper dorm rooms. The Tibet Café runs an excellent restaurant. In the Old Town, there are lots of 'rustic' guesthouses, such as the Potala Log Cabin, or Tibet Lucky Home.

Zhongdian has some B&Bs that lodge guests in converted Tibetan manors.

Continued overleaf

Several are located along the road to Sungtseling Monastery. Right near the gates of Sungtseling is the mid-range Songtsam Hotel, tel. 887-828-8889, www.songtsam.com, a finely designed boutique hotel with lots of atmosphere. There are 22 rooms for US$40–70. You will need a bicycle or car and driver to commute back to town.

On the outskirts of Zhongdian is Gyalthang Dzong Hotel, tel. 887-822-3646, www.coloursofansana.com/gyalthang, with 45 rooms and two suites for US$60–120 apiece. Though there is an attempt at Tibetan design and décor, this place is somewhat lacking in atmosphere. The Singaporean-managed hotel offers its own spa, with menu items like the Matahari Massage or another called the Crown Chakras. And five-star Tibetan-retro style arrives in Shangri-La with a series of lodges at the Banyan Tree Ringha, tel. 887-828-8822, www.banyantree.com/ringha/. There are 32 spacious lodges and suites in converted Tibetan manors – most have a wooden hot tub in the room, and the Spa Suite has a spa treatment room within. There is a separate Banyan Tree Spa too. Is that the phone number or the price? The lodges go for US$350 single, US$560 double, or US$740 for three to four persons.

LIJIANG

Lijiang is easily reached by deluxe bus rides from Kunming. The town is divided into the Old Quarter, with cobblestones, boutique hotels and bistros, and the newer Chinese city with concrete and karaoke.

No motorised transport is allowed in the Old Quarter – heavy luggage is moved around on hand-carts. Naxi-run hotels in the Old Quarter would be the best choice for a place to stay. It's hard to recommend one as they are small and tend to fill up fast, especially on weekends. Your best bet is to drop your bags somewhere and venture into the cobblestone alleys to find a suitable place.

had blended three different musical genres into a single entity and then labelled it 'Nakhi Ancient Music'. Xuan Ke sued for damages: in a landmark case, he was awarded 1.2 million RMB by the county court of Lijiang. However, the court refused to accept as evidence the arguments in the article itself, ruling that these were scholarly matters for experts.

Outskirts of Town

Shades of Shangri-La: according to Xuan Ke, Lijiang was a model for the utopia because of imposing Jade Dragon Snow Mountain, visible from town on a clear day. An Italian-made cable-car runs almost 3km up the flanks of the peak, ascending from 2,600m at the base to 4,500m at the top of the lift. This is the longest cable-car in Asia. Chinese tourists in suits and platform shoes slip and slide around in the summit snows, though the more sensible ones hire down jackets and oxygen canisters to deal with the sudden shift in altitude.

Out in this direction is Joseph Rock's courtyard-style mansion, which was once heralded as *National Geographic* Yunnan expedition headquarters. The mansion is small, and is now an on-site museum with Rock's pictures and some of his gear on display, including hunting rifles. The Spartan upstairs bedroom is preserved as in Rock's day. The mansion is located in the village of Yuhu. At the crossroads near the village is a sign etched in stone with Chinese calligraphy and English writing, giving the directions to Rock's house. The Chinese reads properly, but the English is rendered as: Follow Rocker's Step to Shangri-La.

5

Tibet

RED SUN ON LOST HORIZON – IN SEARCH OF OLD TIBET

Shangri-La's great vision, and its primary purpose, is the preservation of precious wisdom and culture for impending times of great destruction. *Lost Horizon* leaves the reader with a profound sense of loss too, because the main character, Hugh Conway, loses the valley of his dreams. Indeed, the title *Lost Horizon* could be interpreted as Lost Dreams or Lost Idealism.

Lost Horizon hints that Shangri-La is located near the borders of Tibet, and combines Chinese and Tibetan features in its lamasery. Today, many realms of mixed Chinese and Tibetan features exist within Tibet – for reasons that James Hilton could not have imagined. When *Lost Horizon* was first published in 1933, Tibet was an independent theocracy, free to follow its path of Tibetan Buddhism.

In early 1933, shortly before his death, the ailing 13th Dalai Lama wrote a brief tract about the welfare of Tibet, noting that it was happy and prosperous, and that he had done everything to protect its religion. But he warned about what was happening in Mongolia, where the Russian Communists had seized monasteries and outlawed religious practices. He warned that this could happen in Tibet too – that Tibet could be broken down and left without a name, that monasteries would be destroyed:

> The officers of the State, ecclesiastical and regular, will find their lands seized and their other property confiscated, and they themselves made to serve their enemies, or wander about the country as beggars do. All beings will be sunk in great hardship and overpowering fear; the days and the nights will drag on slowly in suffering.

Through World War II, Tibet remained neutral and avoided the horrors of war and aerial bombings. For Heinrich Harrer and Peter Aufschnaiter, escaped German POWs, Tibet was the ultimate sanctuary (see pages 92–3). But in 1950, with the Chinese invasion of Tibet, the 13th Dalai Lama's dire predictions were coming to pass. In a steady decline since 1950, Chinese occupation of Tibet has seen 5,000 years of Tibetan culture go down the tubes.

In today's Tibet, Buddhism is no longer free – and the suffering that results is great. The Tibetans have lost much: lost their revered spiritual leaders (the Dalai Lama, Karmapa, and other sect leaders are all in exile), seen their temples destroyed, their sacred art plundered and sold to collectors, their culture downgraded, seen their wildlife decimated, and their rivers and sacred lakes exploited for hydropower. With the arrival in 2006 of a rail link to Lhasa, Tibet stands to lose a lot more. The far cheaper transport cost of the train will most likely result in a large influx of Chinese settlers and tourists. For the first time in its long history, a way has been found to export resources cheaply from Tibet; the train can economically export resources like minerals, which Tibet has large reserves of – and spring water, freighted to water starved Chinese cities in the east.

Tibet's great losses are reflected in book titles like *Lost Tibet* or *Lost Lhasa*. The books create nostalgia for old pre-1950 Tibet under the Dalai Lamas – a kind of Shangri-La lost in time, isolated from the rest of the world, devoid of modern technology. To find that, you would have to be a temponaut – a traveller in time – transporting yourself back to the pre-1950 period, when the sacred city of Lhasa was one of the most difficult destinations on earth to get to, and much-coveted by explorers. Pre-1950 Tibet was not paradise: there was little in the way of plumbing, or sewage, or health care. It was a medieval society that was out of synch with the rest of the world, and which paid dearly for its isolationist policies and its failure to keep abreast of the times. The invading Chinese declared Tibet feudalistic and backward, and claimed their goal was to liberate the place by introducing new technology, and health care and roads. But the Tibetans have always cared more about independence than electricity, and more about freedom than sewers.

Communist China claims that the socialist transformation of Tibet has been a complete success, and that the Tibetans are living in a Maoist socialist paradise – a kind of Maotopia. But the new technology, health care and roads, it turns out, have largely benefited the Chinese occupiers of Tibet. The main Chinese imports into Tibet are military bases, and loads of military and paramilitary forces. There are loose women from Sichuan to keep them happy, karaoke bars to keep them happy, and beer factories to keep everyone oblivious. A concrete factory in Lhasa provides the favourite building material to modify the environment – for the worse. Advertising billboards for mobile phone companies pepper the landscape. Concrete and karaoke: this dystopia is being blithely marketed to well-heeled Chinese tourists from the east coast as mysterious Tibet, an exotic realm. Although army bases are discretely located (even camouflaged) to keep them out of public view, there is no way that the Chinese military and paramilitary presence can be completely hidden. This is Shangri-La with machine guns.

Technology has come to Tibet, but Tibetans cannot access that technology freely. News on television and other media is heavily censored, and spews out official propaganda. There is a complete blackout on foreign news media. Internet use is heavily restricted and monitored. Tibetan language is ignored or downplayed. The Tibetans are treated like third-class citizens in their own domain – the prisoners of Shangri-La.

March 2008 saw the biggest protests in Lhasa for 20 years. Chinese response was swift and brutal, with hundreds of Tibetans killed, and thousands more arrested. By this time, in an extraordinary show of bravery, Tibetans all over the plateau rose up in spontaneous demonstrations against Chinese rule. Behind these protests lies immense Tibetan frustration with Chinese policies and governance of Tibet – the arrival of the train has seen large numbers of Chinese settlers flood in, and has enabled large-scale exploitation of Tibet's mineral and other resources. Nomads have been pushed off traditional lands to make way for mining operations or dam-building projects. Chinese response to Tibetan protest has not been to deal with the causes of discontent, but to undertake mass patriotic re-education campaigns where Tibetans must denounce the Dalai Lama and show their love of the Chinese Motherland. These campaigns are on a scale of a second Cultural Revolution.

The Tibetans are amazing resilient in the face of extreme adversity. Within Chinese-occupied Tibet there are pockets where the Tibetan pulse runs strong. These remote valleys offer glimpses of Tibet's once-great culture, of its free and independent spirit. They are like a lamp in the darkness – the darkness of terrific loss under Chinese occupation. This chapter looks at a handful of remote valleys where Tibetan culture still thrives, where the smell of yak-butter lamps permeates the air.

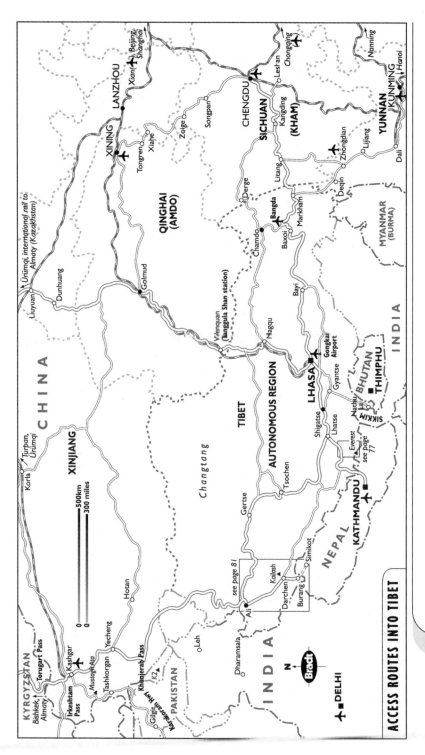

ACCESS ROUTES INTO TIBET

In March 2006, the world's most unlikely song-and-dance show opened in Seoul, South Korea. It was set in Yoduk Re-education Camp 15, the biggest of North Korea's extensive gulag of labour camps for political prisoners. The director of the musical defected from the north. A musical set in a concentration camp? That sounds like a tough sell, but the controversial play hit a nerve with its South Korean audience. The story tells the fate of a leading state troupe dancer, sent to Yoduk with her family after her father is accused of spying. There she is raped by the prison governor and becomes pregnant. While emaciated political prisoners prance across the stage, in the background is a chorus line of goose-stepping soldiers. In other scenes, young male dancers pirouette with bayonetted Kalashnikovs.

Sounds ground-breaking and controversial, but in today's Tibet 'military theatre' is nothing unusual. The place is ruled by the military, who like to get their share of military entertainment on the TV. In their free time, the soldiers practise revolutionary dance moves and platoon karaoke numbers. Which all end up on state-run television in Lhasa and beyond – minus the emaciated political prisoners, of course. This kind of 'revolutionary ballet' first surfaced as entertainment for Mao's troops. Around the time of military celebrations in Lhasa, such as the anniversary of the Liberation of Tibet, the anniversary of the founding of the Tibet Autonomous Region, or National Day, the song-and-dance routines performed by the People's Liberation Army on TV hit fever pitch. Soldiers in camouflage fatigues dance around the stage chasing beautiful Tibetan maidens, with the Potala Palace as a backdrop. In other TV extravaganzas, large chorus lines of PLA troops belt out patriotic numbers with synchronised movements.

The Democratic People's Republic of North Korea has its own unique version of 'military theatre'. In a regimented society that brooks no dissent, and has a standing army over one million strong, North Korea believes it is building a socialist utopia. Every so often, the regime stages Mass Games – a choreographed extravaganza of singing, dancing and gymnastics, with backdrops of guns, missiles and other military hardware. The Mass Games show a heroic struggle for a prosperous and independent 'people's paradise' where harvests are abundant. The reality is somewhat different: an estimated two million citizens in North Korea died of famine in the 1990s.

A TEMPONAUT IN TIBET

It comes as a shock to see Lhasa with so many ghastly Chinese trappings. But you can still find a strong Tibetan pulse at sites within day-trip range of Lhasa. This is the pulse of Old Tibet, and you become a temponaut – a traveller in time.

An easy site to get to is the back of Sera monastery, to the northeast side of Lhasa, with a circuitous hiking path winding past Pabonka, a small temple. The caves, hermitages and shrines dotted in the vicinity are among the oldest in Lhasa. There are superb views along the way. Hiking here can be strenuous, but will help you acclimatise for further trips on the plateau. For something totally different, try rafting on the Drigung River – you can arrange the trip with a group of four or more from Lhasa.

By hired Landcruiser (assemble your own small group of three or four), there are several sites (below) within daytrip range that evoke an older Tibetan presence. You might consider staying overnight to savour the experience – a two-day excursion for each destination. Travellers tend to include these destinations with longer road-trips, taking in a number of spots.

Tidrom Hotsprings A spa run by nuns, you say? Yes, it's true – about 110km northeast of Lhasa, Tidrom Nunnery is set in a beautiful valley with numerous hermitages and caves in the surrounding hills. Miraculously, there's hardly a Chinese building in sight. A charming aspect of Tidrom is that it is a walking zone: no vehicles can enter the village. Pilgrims and visitors come to Tidrom for the sulphur hotsprings, also frequented by the nuns. The hotsprings are said to have magical healing powers – or at the very least, to be good for the treatment of arthritis, gastritis and other ailments. It's a detox for the soul, anyway, to be in such a purely Tibetan atmosphere. These have to be the finest hotsprings in central Tibet. But beware of the heat at this altitude (4,320m) – it can make you dizzy. The springs are located right near a river, where the water bubbles under a great rock and disappears. There are three hotspring pools with attractive stone-laid enclosures surrounded by wooden fencing (no concrete!). One pool is for men, another for women, and the third pool is mixed: it is extra-hot and lies across a small bridge. You can get a hot stone treatment, of sorts – there are hot stones below your feet if you step into a pool. Locals rub smooth hot submerged stone as

FREEDOM FROM FEAR

There is no fire like greed,
No crime like hatred,
No sorrow like separation,
No sickness like hunger of heart,
And no joy like the joy of freedom.
Look within. Be still.
Free from fear and attachment,
Know the sweet joy of living in the way.
– from the Dhammapada

In old Tibet, the goal was freedom from attachment – a major tenet of Tibetan Buddhism. In new Tibet, the goal is more likely to be freedom from fear. A pervasive climate of fear has been generated in Tibet by Chinese overseers, with stooges in monasteries, and spies all over. Foreigners travelling in Tibet for short periods may well be insulated from this climate of fear, but for Tibetans it is very real. As a foreigner, you have a far greater degree of freedom than Tibetans.

The concept of happiness in Tibetan is very much linked to the concept of freedom. Tibetans use the terms *rangwang* and *shenwang* for 'happiness' and 'unhappiness'. A rough translation of *rangwang* would be 'self-power', which denotes freedom, being in control of one's situation, full rights, no obstacles, no leash. On the other hand, *shenwang* is best translated as 'others-holding-power'. In Tibet, the Chinese occupiers hold a tight leash. With all the important lineage leaders in exile, monks in Tibet are without direction – and they have no freedom to pursue their beliefs. Monks do not even have the freedom to look at a photograph of their own spiritual leader, the 14th Dalai Lama. His image is banned by Chinese authorities. Nomads are being forcibly taken away from their traditional grazing grounds, told to sell their animals, and resettled in shoddy Chinese housing in towns, where they are essentially unemployed. Going from horse-riding herdsmen – free to roam the great grasslands of Tibet – to a small house packed in among many others, is a stark transition. And one that does not sit well with the nomads.

One of the strangest Shangri-La-like collages shows the Potala Palace in Lhasa backed by the imposing north face of Everest. It appears on the cover for a Chinese-made CD-ROM about Tibet. The Potala and Everest: two Shangri-Las for the price of one.

Winter shots of the Potala with snow-dusted peaks behind it have an enchanting mythic look – as long as you don't show the ugly Chinese concrete or Chinese flags close by. For Westerners, getting to Lhasa back in the 1930s was the Holy Grail of travel – it was one of the most elusive destinations on earth. But that Shangri-La is locked in time. For Chinese tourists, however, Lhasa is still very much on the paradise programme. Lhasa is regarded as an exotic corner of the far-flung Chinese empire. The Potala is the number one touring attraction in Tibet: over half a million Chinese tourists a year traipse through the former Dalai Lama's palace. Few of them have any idea about the current Dalai Lama (whose image is banned) or about Tibet's tragic history since the Chinese invasion in 1950. So convincing is the Communist Party's propaganda about the Chinese 'liberation' of Tibet that few Chinese question it. They know nothing of the destruction wreaked in Tibet, or of the scores of Tibetans who have died at the hands of the Chinese.

Large-scale Chinese tourism to Tibetan regions is a fairly recent phenomenon. In the 1990s, there were few Chinese tourists because Tibet was viewed as primitive, backward and dirty. But today, Tibet is seen as a coveted trophy destination – it is cool to go there. Chinese tourists are now by far the largest contingent in Tibet, accounting for more than 90% of visitors. With the speed and lower cost of using the railway to reach Lhasa, there could be a lot more Chinese tourists; in the first year of the train's operation, from July 2006 to June 2007, the railway alone transported 1.5 million visitors into Tibet – an average of more than 4,000 a day. According to Chinese figures, over four million tourists visited Tibet in 2007 – an increase of 64% over the previous year. Those figures are warped because they count all those entering Lhasa – even if twice or more on a single journey – and the figures include Chinese businesspeople and military.

Some foreign tour agencies have christened the train 'The Shangri-La Express' to hype it up. China has been in the grip of a fad for all things Tibetan since the

a kind of massage. No yak-yoghurt scrubs or *tsampa* rubs on the menu, but then again, you're not subjected to flaky New Age music, either. It's all very low-key. The bubbling thermal activity sometimes attracts small black snakes, but don't worry, they're harmless: nuns and snakes have co-existed for centuries. If you stay overnight, you can indulge in a moonlit soak with candles, and – if the skies are clear – a magnificent canopy of stars overhead. There is basic accommodation in guesthouses at Tidrom; some are run by the nuns. Hiking above Tidrom is rewarding, in terms of views and photography. You can hike up to several small gompas, and there are nomad tents in the vicinity.

Samye Temple Complex About 170km southeast of Lhasa lies Samye. You can get there directly by hired Landcruiser, driving past Tsedang to reach a bridge over the Tsangpo. Or you could drive to a ferry crossing opposite Samye, which means leaving the Landcruiser on the south bank. You can also get to the ferry crossing by taxi or bus from Lhasa. Samye was probably founded in the 8th century by King Trisong Detsen, in consultation with Indian sage Padmasambhava. The temple, destroyed and rebuilt a number of times over the centuries, was designed according to the principles of geomancy, a concept derived from India. The layout

opening of the railway. There is brisk shopping for Tibetan products – from *dzi* stones to ginseng-berry juice – most of which are actually not made in Tibet. Chinese women get their hair braided Tibetan-style with small chunks of turquoise tied in, and drape their arms in Tibetan-style bracelets. Chinese tourists crowd the top of the Jokang Temple in Lhasa, making cellphone calls to Shanghai or Shenzhen. And the latest must-have accessory for China's wealthy elite is...a Tibetan mastiff. These large nomad guard dogs are special to Tibet, thought to be the oldest domestic dog with a known history. They are fearless, extremely loyal, and superbly adapted to harsh conditions. A grown male can fetch up to 300,000 yuan (US40,000), while a pure-bred dog with a strong bloodline could be worth ten times that.

Although China is officially atheist, Buddhism is resurfacing, with some high-profile figures openly practising the religion to fill a spiritual void. At some pilgrimage sites around Tibet and in Kham and Amdo, you can see Chinese participating in rituals like tying on prayer-flags, burning juniper, and chanting *Om Mani Padme Hum*. But some who come to Tibet have been deeply shocked by what they see. Arriving in 1985, writer Ma Jian was at the vanguard of Chinese 'hippies' who come to Lhasa hoping to find refuge from the soulless society that China has become, to escape into a different landscape and culture, and to gain deeper insight into the Buddhist faith. And though he found hypnotic beauty in Tibet, he also found poverty worse than anything he'd seen in China. He later wrote: 'My hope of gaining some religious revelation also came to nothing. Tibet was a land whose spiritual heart had been ripped out. Thousands of temples lay in ruins… Most of the monks who'd returned to the monasteries seemed to have done so for economic rather than spiritual reasons.'

Ma Jian's short work about Tibet, *Stick Out Your Tongue*, was published in a Beijing journal in 1987. It caused a furore because of its raw descriptions of life in Tibet – contradicting the official party line that communism fostered the building of a united, prosperous and civilised Socialist Tibet. Copies of the offending journal were confiscated and destroyed, but ironically resulted in copies being sold on the black market for ten times the issue price. Ma Jian was in Hong Kong at the time: these events set him on the road to exile.

is based on Buddhist cosmology: it is a mandalic 3-D replica of the Tibetan Buddhist universe. The main temple represents Mount Meru, while colour-coded *chortens* represent the four island-continents and eight sub-continents. The complex is bounded by an oval wall topped with 1,008 small *chortens* that represent Chakravala, a ring of mountains that surrounds the universe. Inside the main temple is a statue of Padmasambhava; on the second floor is a gallery with a long string of murals – one of which shows the fabled land of Shambhala. There is good hiking around Samye; further afield is Chimphu, which is riddled with hermitage caves where monks and nuns come for retreats.

Gyantse Fort Some 240km southwest of Lhasa lies Gyantse, with a Tibetan old quarter and a brooding fort and monastery. This is one of the very few sites in Tibet where you can get an idea of old Tibetan town architecture. A hike to the top of the fort is exhausting, but it gives you a bird's-eye view over the whole area. Bits within the fort were blown up by the Nepalese, then the British, and again by the Chinese – who blame it all on the British in a special on-site Anti-British Museum. Getting to Gyantse is a brilliant ride if you take the south route, passing Khamba La, with ethereal views over the sacred lake of Yamdrok Tso.

QOMOLANGMA NATURE PRESERVE

It is eminently possible that James Hilton, a keen mountaineer, drew inspiration from the 1920s British expedition attempts on Mount Everest, about which there was a lot of press at the time. Some think that Hilton based the character of Conway on George Mallory, who discovered a place called Chang La on the Kharta (east) approach to Everest. The juxtaposition of the world's highest monastery, Rongbuk Gompa (4,950m), with the snowcapped north face of the world's highest peak, Everest (8,848m), is a definite Shangri-La setting. Rongbuk Gompa was established some time in the early part of the 20th century, razed during the 1960s, and rebuilt in the 1980s and 1990s. The monastery is small but imposing.

When Everest was identified as the world's highest peak in 1856, it became the Holy Grail of mountaineering. British expeditions to the Tibetan side of Everest were mounted in 1921, 1922 and, disastrously, in 1924. Due to their special relations with the Tibetan government, the British held a monopoly on access to Everest. On the 1921 reconnaissance, expedition leaders managed to convince the monks at Rongbuk that the British were on a pilgrimage to the sacred peak. In 1922, General Bruce told the Tibetans that it was the religion of the white men – the tribe called mountaineers – to climb to the tops of high mountains in order to reach near heaven. On Everest, they would reach nearer to heaven than any man on earth. But the High Lama of Rongbuk wised up, saying that the Goddess of Snows would cast down anyone who dared to climb her flanks. A fresco shortly appeared on the walls of Rongbuk Monastery, showing the body of a white man being cast down. Jolmo Lungma, the Goddess of Snows, is the wrathful deity believed by the Tibetans to reside on top of Everest. Tibetan belief holds that high peaks are the abodes of gods, goddesses, demons, ghosts and yetis.

Unable to fathom why the British wanted to climb the peak, the monks at Rongbuk suspected they were after sacred relics. Apart from the dwelling place of the Goddess of Snows, the summit was thought to be the site of the magical Sacred Chair of Padmasambhava – the great tantric master given to jetting around the Himalaya on a flying tiger. Another legend held that the mythical Snow Lion lived there. And the peak was said to be the lair of the hairy Sukpa (yeti), who could gaze down from this perch and choose which yak herd he would dine on next.

Captain John Noel, cinematographer with the British expeditions, made a movie, *The Ascent of Everest*, which was widely shown in Europe in the 1920s. This was the silent-movie era: sound effects for this film were, incredibly, provided by seven Tibetan monks who had been somehow spirited out of Tibet by Noel. At the Scala Theatre in London, a scene painter had built and painted a spectacular Himalayan set, with temple doors and a monastery courtyard in the foreground, and snowy peaks in the background. The Tibetan monks played longhorns, drums and cymbals in the foreground, while lighting illuminated the mountain peaks behind. Then the lights dimmed, and the temple doors swung slowly open to reveal a movie screen – and *The Ascent of Everest* started to roll. When word of this reached the 13th Dalai Lama, he refused permission for further Everest expeditions, offended by the smuggling of the monk musicians, and by the showing of sacred masked dance and other ceremonies to all and sundry in foreign lands, especially with Noel's frivolous captioning.

Shegar Gompa

On the route in or out of Rongbuk, you should consider a hike to Shegar Gompa, which is perched partway up a mountainside above the town of Shegar, with sweeping views over the fertile valley below. That fulfills two Shangri-La parameters – large monastery grafted onto mountainside overlooking verdant valley – but there's no snowcap. British expeditions of the 1920s passed through here and marvelled at Shining Crystal Dzong, built on top of the peak above Shegar Gompa. This castle was completely razed during the Cultural Revolution. You can hike up through the ruins and get views of Everest in the distance, assuming clear visibility.

Trekking in the Everest Region

Qomolangma Nature Preserve is the highest profile conservation area in Tibet, with a 34,000km² zone under protection, although it is a mixed-use zone, with herders and villagers living within the boundaries. There are a number of trekking

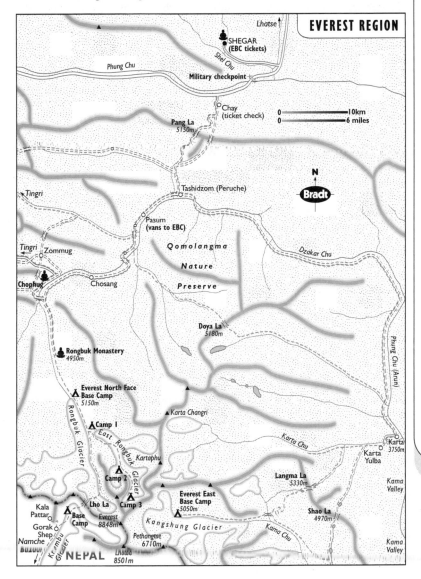

EVEREST REGION

possibilities. The first is to trek from Rongbuk to Everest north face base camp, a distance of around 12km. The 'base camp' is actually more of a tourist viewpoint, with tented tea-houses out this way (where you can stay), plus the world's highest post office (5,150m). Horse-carts are allowed along this route to transport tourists to the base camp area, but you might consider hiking the route at least one-way. From the 'tourist base camp' area, you can sign up for a four-day trek at US$100 a person to go further toward Everest, to the climbers' base camp and back. You would need your own trekking and sleeping gear for this.

Other treks in the Everest region require more in the way of equipment, planning and logistics. There's a hike of three or four days from Tingri to Rongbuk (or the reverse route). And to the east side of Everest is the Karta approach: a ten-day trekking loop is possible, passing through the beautiful Kama Valley, with meadows of wildflowers and rhododendrons.

KAILASH

To the far west of Tibet lies Asia's most sacred peak, Mount Kailash. Kailash is the centre of the universe – or at least, the Tibetan view of the universe. The peak is thought to be an earthly manifestation of mythical Mount Meru, abode of the gods. The traditional Tibetan cosmology model places Mount Meru at dead centre. On the summit of Meru is the celestial city of Sudarsana; above Meru float 25 more heavens of the gods, while under the mountain lie the hell realms. Mount Meru is surrounded by seven rings of golden mountains and seven oceans. Beyond all this are the paths of planets, with the mandalic model enclosed by massive rings of fire.

Kailash is sacred to Tibetan Buddhist and Bon adherents, and the Hindus and Jains of India. At 6,714m, the mountain is modest by Himalayan standards, but stunning to view. As a sacred peak, it is off-limits to climbers.

Though Kailash has no direct connection with Shangri-La, a number of book covers for Shangri-La-type titles show Mount Kailash with Chiu Gompa in the foreground, suggestive of the utopia. That's because this photographic composition has two key Shangri-La facets in the same frame, though the peak is a still a long way off from the monastery (long lenses compress the perspective). In any case, Kailash has strong elements of what you might call the 'mythic journey'. For Tibetan pilgrims, this is the top *kora* in Tibet. For Western trekkers, Kailash is a very challenging trek, due to the altitude.

Kailash is bursting at the seams with mythical lore – and not just for Tibetans. And in the late 19th century and early 20th century, Kailash assumed mythical dimensions among Western geographers and explorers. For a long time there was reputed to be a high mountain that was the source of the great rivers of India. But Tibet was inaccessible, so geographers were unsure if this was myth or fact. Finding the source of India's great rivers was a prime geographer's puzzle, on a par to finding the source of the Nile. The British employed Indian pundits, who, disguised as pilgrims, measured distances with prayer beads, and tossed marked logs into rivers to find out where they would pop up further down the line in India. Eventually, it was discovered that the headwaters of four of Asia's mightiest rivers lay within 100km of Kailash – the Indus, the Yarlung Tsangpo (which later emerges in India as the Brahmaputra), the Karnali (a major tributary of the Ganges) and the Sutlej. Remarkably, the mouths of the same rivers end up as far as 3,000km apart.

KAILASH *KORA*
Gateway to the *kora* is the town of Darchen (start and end point), a dismal place of tents and shanty housing. A complete walking circuit of the sacred peak generally

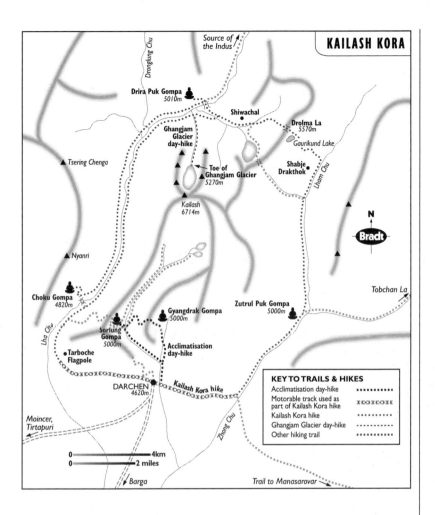

Within the map:

Source of the Indus

Dronglung Chu

Drira Puk Gompa
5010m

Shiwachal

Drolma La
5570m

Gaurikund Lake

Ghangjam
Glacier
day-hike

Tsering Chenga

Toe of
Ghangjam Glacier
5270m

Shabje
Drakthok

Lham Chu

Kailash
6714m

N

Bradt

Nyanri

Tobchan La

Choku Gompa
4820m

Gyangdrak Gompa
5000m

Zutrul Puk Gompa
5000m

Lha Chu

Sorlung
Gompa
5000m

Acclimatisation
day-hike

Tarboche
Flagpole

Kailash Kora hike

DARCHEN
4620m

KEY TO TRAILS & HIKES
Acclimatisation day-hike
Motorable track used as
part of Kailash Kora hike
Kailash Kora hike
Ghangjam Glacier day-hike
Other hiking trail

Moincer,
Tirtapuri

Zhong Chu

0   4km
0   2 miles

Barga

Trail to Manasarovar

takes two to five days, depending on your pace. You can head out of Darchen at the trailhead carrying your own backpack and food supplies, or you can hire a porter in Darchen to carry gear. There are some rudimentary guesthouses along the *kora* – you will need to bring your own sleeping bag. If you bring your own tent, you can camp out where you want – offering a greater degree of freedom. Group tours often hire yaks in Darchen to carry camping gear and duffle bags on the *kora*.

Kailash is a trek for Westerners, but a pilgrimage for Tibetans and Indians. The pilgrims are a major part of the Kailash experience. They come from all over Tibet, so you will see some unusual ethnic groups. Indians come in for the trip of a lifetime. Part of their journey is ritual bathing in the icy waters of sacred Lake Manasarovar; they pick up pebbles from the lakeside and fill containers with holy water when returning home.

One of the most embarrassing aspects of the Kailash *kora* is being overtaken on steep inclines by Tibetan grandmothers. Of course, Tibetans are fully acclimatised to the extreme elevation, but even so. Tibetan pilgrims proceed at a brisk pace because they often aim to complete the whole *kora* in a single day, starting before sunrise and finishing after sunset. And then there are the hardy pilgrims who aim to do not just one, but three, five or even 13 circuits of the peak. Others may prostrate the full length of the circuit – through rain, snow, ice, whatever – which could take several weeks. Bon adherents complete the *kora* in an anti-clockwise direction. The following itinerary is clockwise, which is the direction most Tibetan pilgrims take.

Day 1 Near the start of the route, high on a ridge, is Choku Gompa, originally set up in the 13th century as a shrine. Shiny-eyed pilgrims crowd in to see the monastery's treasures – a white stone statue of the Buddha Opame, and a sacred silver-embossed conch shell, said to have been Milarepa's. The target of the first day's hike is Drira Phuk Gompa (5,010m), which is about 8 to 10 hours from Darchen. That's because the gompa offers basic accommodation. If you bring your own tent, however, you have more flexibility for the night's camp.

Day 2 It's a good idea to build in a rest day, with a half-day hike up to Ghangjam Glacier and back. If you've come all this way to see Kailash, then you might as well take the time to savour it. And a rest day helps acclimatise for the hike over Drolma La. From Drira Phuk Gompa, hiking up to 5,270m, at the toe of Ghangjam Glacier, there are awesome views of the glistening icy walls of the north face of Kailash, assuming clear conditions. It is said that a wish made in front of the north face will definitely be granted.

Day 3 From Drira Phuk there is a tough ascent to Drolma La (Pass of Tara), which at 5,570m is the focus of the entire *kora*. Tibetans tie on prayer-flags, and leave coins, pins or locks of hair as proof of their passage. They fling windhorse squares into the air and shout *Tso tso tso, Lha Gyalo!* (Victory to the gods!). On the other

THE WISDOM OF MILAREPA

Tibetan sage Milarepa is credited with these words: 'All worldly pursuits have but one unavoidable and inevitable end, which is sorrow: acquisitions end in dispersion; buildings, in destruction; meetings in separation; births, in death. Knowing this, one should, from the very first, renounce acquisitions and heaping up, and building, and meeting, and…set about realising the truth.'

Easy for Milarepa to say: he dined on nettle soup, lived in caves, and sat on an antelope skin, composing songs all day. And in the 12th century, when Milarepa was around, there weren't a whole lot of possessions to get attached to anyway. Those were the days long before the invention of the sleeping bag, the ballpoint pen or the chocolate bar. But there's a certain resonance to his philosophy: in the West, mindless consumerism is a distraction from living, from seeking real experience. The Tibetans view life from a very different perspective; the attainment of spiritual well-being is a prime priority. The Kailash *kora* is one of those raw experiences that Tibetans thrive on: pilgrimage as a kind of truth-seeking, a source of inner strength.

Around the Kailash *kora* are relics of Milarepa, founder of the Kagyu sect, who engaged in fierce competition with the Bon sorcerer Naro Bonchung. A legendary showdown between Milarepa and Naro Bonchung took place on the peak of Kailash. Milarepa reached the peak through his magical power of alighting sunbeams. In the ensuing duel, Naro Bonchung fell and, in doing so, is said to have carved a long vertical cleft in the mountain's south face. The duel established the supremacy of Tibetan Buddhism at Kailash. Monasteries around Kailash are mostly associated with the Drukpa Kagyu sect, but Milarepa allowed Bon adherents to continue circumambulating the peak in anti-clockwise circuits.

side of the pass is a tiny greenish tarn, the sacred Gaurikund Lake. There is a long descent – and after a very long day (10 to 12 hours) you reach Zutrul Phuk Gompa, which has a basic guesthouse attached.

Day 4 Into the magician's lair. The reconstructed monastery at Zutrul Phuk encloses a cave that the great sage Milarepa is rumoured to have fashioned with his bare hands: there's a statue of him within. Fortunately, it's a level or downhill walk to Darchen, and it doesn't take that long to dribble back into town, where hot noodles await.

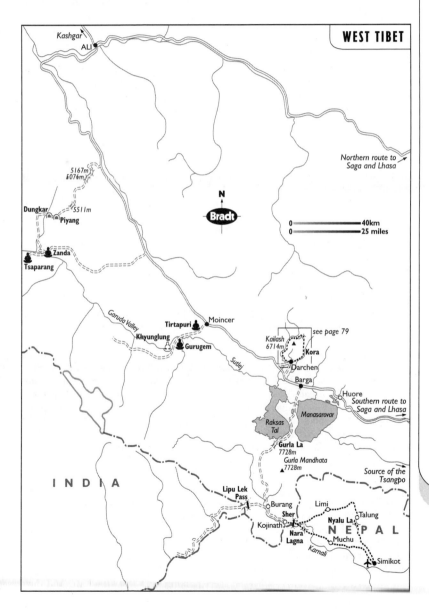

TIRTAPURI'S HEALING WATERS

While Kailash is the major sacred site of western Tibet, there are others high on the pilgrim wish-list. Lake Manasarovar presents some stunning vistas, and the drive past Manasarovar to the border town of Burang is well worth it.

An easy target from Darchen is Tirtapuri, a short drive to the northwest of Darchen and 10km from Moincer. Pilgrims come to Tirtapuri after circling Kailash and Manasarovar for a relaxing circuit – the *kora* here is only an hour, and there are grassy meadows for picnicking as well as hotsprings for soothing tired limbs. Although the entire Tirtapuri circuit only takes an hour, you could allow several hours to stop and drink in the atmosphere and the landscape. Pilgrims walk past elaborate *mani* walls, and sacred caves set in red and white clay cliffs, and pay their respects at a small monastery to a shrine of Guru Rinpoche. They bathe – or dip their feet – in several sulphurous hotspring pools, which can accommodate three or four people. The hotsprings are reputed to have healing powers, and Tibetans search the waters for pellets of lime, for medicinal purposes. Just being able to feel hot water is therapeutic enough for Western visitors. There are plans for a bathhouse, supplied by the milky-white steaming pools, along with a small guesthouse at the gompa.

VALLEY OF THE BEEB

In 1998, British writer Charles Allen took a BBC film crew on a wild chase through western Tibet, looking for evidence of Shangri-La, which he claimed was a watered-down version of Shambhala. Or was he looking for Shangshung, the lost Bon kingdom? Maybe a bit of each. In any case, he ended up in the valley of Khyunglung. Charles Allen concluded he came close to the origins of whatever kingdom he was seeking, but needed more time to find it. Khyunglung is a dry rocky place with no snowcaps visible, nor verdant valleys. He wrote a book about it, called *The Search for Shangri-La*.

A few years later, British presenter Michael Wood took a BBC film crew on another wild goose chase through western Tibet, on a similar trajectory. In search of Shangri-La, of course. After passing through Limi Valley and Mount Kailash, he ended up at the Guge kingdom, practically on the doorstep of Khyunglung. In a book about a handful of mythical journeys, he wrote a chapter entitled 'The Search for Shangri-La'. The BBC programme on this mythic journey was broadcast in 2005. If you find Khyunglung a tongue twister, just call it the Valley of the Beeb.

In 2002, along came Oxford lecturer Charles Ramble, following a similar route up from Nepal, with an entourage that included Bon practitioner Gelek Jinpa. He was not looking for Shangri-La at all: he was looking for the lost kingdom of Zhangzhung, the ancient Bon centre. He says in his book, *Sacred Landscape and Pilgrimage in Tibet*, that in the valley of Khyunglung he came close to finding Zhangzhung, but the civilisation had returned to dust. That would be closer to the mark: Khyunglung is an ancient Bon site.

THE LOST KINGDOM OF GUGE

Located 26km west of the town of Zanda are the imposing ruins of Tsaparang, the once-powerful capital of the Guge kingdom, dating from the 10th century. Your journey getting to Zanda may be dusty and difficult, but think of this: it will be a hell of a lot easier than it was in 1642. The earliest Western accounts of this hidden valley were by two Jesuits, who'd heard rumours of a lost Christian-like sect. The first Westerners known to enter Tibet were looking for a lost kingdom. And they may have contributed to the total collapse of the Guge kingdom in the process.

In March 1624, two Portuguese Jesuits, Father Andrade and Father Marques, set out from India disguised as Hindu pilgrims. They were on foot with pack animals, crossing passes that were 5,000 metres or more. At times, they sank into snow up to their chests. They complained of frozen feet, of blindness and of suffocating 'poisonous vapours', probably the first Western accounts of altitude sickness.

Arriving in Tsaparang, the centre of the Guge kingdom, the Jesuits were surprised to be warmly received. They puzzled over how people in such a barren wasteland could survive – all the food had to be imported from fertile valleys that were two weeks away on foot. But part of the jigsaw fell into place when they witnessed a caravan of 200 Chinese traders passing through, carrying silk and porcelain. Tsaparang was an important trading centre, and flocks of goats and sheep kept the royal court supplied with basics. Father Andrade wrote of being invited by the king to Toling Gompa to celebrate a special occasion. There were over 2,000 monks in attendance. The Jesuits found that the temple rituals bore superficial similarities to the Christian ones – monks in robes spent hours chanting – but drinking from human skull-cap vessels and playing trumpets from human thighbones were definitely a bit different. Andrade was the first to publish to the world the sacred chanting mantra *Om Mani Padme Hum*, but could not determine its meaning (which experts still debate today). Andrade returned to Tsaparang in 1625 with fellow missionaries, and the Jesuits eventually built a small church there. Andrade died in India in 1634, poisoned by a colleague who evidently did not share his enthusiasm for the Inquisition.

Guge was quite special to the survival of Tibetan Buddhism. In the 9th century, Buddhism was snuffed out in central Tibet by King Langdarma, a staunch supporter of the rival Bon faith. Upon the assassination of King Langdarma, Tibet was broken up into lay and monastic pockets of influence. The Guge kingdom became an enclave that was vital for the survival of Buddhism. The king of Guge promoted cultural exchanges with Indians Buddhists, and Guge became an important centre of Buddhist studies, a reputation that grew with the arrival of the 11th-century scholar Atisha, from India.

The Guge kingdom probably lasted over 500 years. In several sources, it has been described as a cultural citadel far greater than Lhasa at the time. But around 1650 (some sources give 1630 or 1685), Tsaparang was suddenly abandoned. It is said that the king angered his lamas by favouring Father Andrade, and that factional fighting ensued, tearing the kingdom apart. Other sources claim that a two-year siege by Ladakhis led to the fall of Guge. The reason: the king rejected a bride who happened to be the sister of the king of Ladakh, who was supremely insulted. Although well entrenched in his citadel, the king of Guge decided to cut a deal and surrender, but this backfired because the treacherous Ladakhis had no intention of honouring the deal. The king and royal family were carted off into exile (some sources say they were killed on the spot), and his followers reduced to slavery. Guge fell into obscurity – and ruins. Not only that: successive waves of invaders went to great lengths to wipe out all traces of the kings of Guge, making it near-impossible to recount the history of the place.

Touches of Shangri-La abound in the Guge kingdom: Jesuits stumble into an unknown kingdom, a remote sanctuary that is an important centre of learning with many Buddhist lamas. Andrade's book about the adventure is found on the library shelf at Shangri-La in *Lost Horizon*. Filmmaker Michael Wood, who retraced the footsteps of Andrade, coming up through the Limi region of Nepal, writes in his 2002 book, *In Search of Myths and Heroes*:

by Bradley Rowe

Until Paul Pelliot unearthed the Dunhuang documents in a hidden Silk Road cave in 1908, the name Khyunglung Ngulkar (Silver Palace of the Garuda Valley) was unknown to the West. As the capital of an ancient Bonpo kingdom in west Tibet called Zhangzhung, Khyunglung appealed to the imagination immediately because of accounts of a queen installed in a richly adorned palace – who betrayed her husband and caused his downfall.

It was not until the 1930s that the general area was identified – and not until half a century later that visitors began to arrive in small numbers. But the location of the Silver Palace remained elusive. As the number of visitors swelled, so did the legends, building on centuries of spin-doctor work about Zhangzhung in more recently translated Bonpo texts. Zhangzhung became a Bonpo empire of mythic age and proportions, only finally conquered by the Buddhist king in an epic battle beneath the palace. However, closer examination of Bon sources and Chinese accounts of the Yang Tung reveals little evidence that Zhangzhung was ever more than a small principality. It could only conclusively be dated back to a couple of centuries before the reign of Songtsen Gampo AD618-649). The connection to earlier inhabitants on this part of the plateau could not be proven. The supposed mighty 'empire' had left few traces.

The area where Zhangzhung vanished is extremely rugged, based in the mountainous knot between the Pamirs, the Kunlun and the western Himalaya. The Indus and Sutlej rivers lead west from here, and the Yarlung Tsangpo east, separated by Mount Kailash and Lake Manasarovar. Some 70km west of Kailash, the infant Sutlej broadens into a wide valley with Tirtapuri, an ancient hotsprings and gompa associated with Guru Rinpoche to the south, Gurugem Bonpo gompa to the west, and the modern county town of Moincer to the north.

Gurugem, built very late for a monastery in Tibet, was founded in the 1930s by Khyungtrul Rinpoche beside a cliff housing an ancient Bonpo cave. After Khyungtrul Rinpoche passed away in 1955, the monastery continued to be inhabited by his disciple Tenzin Wangdrak Rinpoche, until his death in 2007.

Khyungtrul, originally from Kham, had come here from his base in Kinnaur in north India to reveal elements of Zhangzhung. Also there in 1935 was Tucci, an eminent Italian Tibetologist. Tucci was told Khyunglung lay 15km downstream through a treacherous gorge, only reached by horse along a tortuous backtrack through high canyons at over 5,000 metres.

Tucci found a small isolated valley with a sulphurous hotspring and a few houses with a small Gelukpa temple. Two kilometres away lay the remarkable cave-complex referred to by the locals as Khyunglung Ngulkar. The caves spread over the wings of an enormous array of multi-coloured cliffs, but show few of the features associated with a permanent settlement. There is no obvious water supply, and the nearby Sutlej is downstream of some sulphurous springs – making its water unsuitable for constant usage. Bones, feathers and furs have been found in these caves, instead of broken pottery and other artefacts found in abandoned caves elsewhere. Whatever its origins, it is a unique and mysterious site well worth a visit.

Down the central spine of the crumbly slopes there are ruined temples, the grandest of which is accessible only by a dangerous narrow ledge. It probably dates from the 10th-century absorption of Khyunglung by the neighbouring Buddhist kingdom of Guge. The caves themselves are simple – almost beehive or troglodyte in form, with a raised shrine for fires at the rear and no chimney. The blackened ceilings make it clear that smoke would have filled the caves when in use. Sleeping places are pokey at best – quite unlike the quarters at Tsaparang, the cave city of Guge.

It would appear that rather than a city, this place acted more as a hidden retreat, or occasional gathering place. It was certainly not the vast palace described by Queen Sadmarkar, the wife of the Zhangzhung king; parts of the palace were said to have walls of gold encrusted with agate. She had been sent to him by Songtsen Gampo to cement an alliance with central Tibet but ended up leading the king to his death – and sounding the death knell of Zhangzhung.

In 2001, a team of archaeologists from China and the USA (Huo Mei and Mark Aldenderfer) started survey work on a group of small mesas behind Gurugem called Khardong. By 2004, they had uncovered a series of walled foundations with outbuildings and a cemetery with standing stones. Some finds were carbon-dated back at least two millennia. By 2005, Tenzin Wangdrak Rinpoche was no longer sending people to the cave complex of Khyunglung on a two-day high-canyon trek (this was just about to be replaced by a 20-minute drive through a new road in the gorge anyway). Instead, he was identifying Khardong as the more likely location for the Silver Palace, known to him and Khyungtrul from 19th-century Bon texts, and the presence of a stone statue of the Bon sage Dranpa Namkha.

Khyungtrul Rinpoche and his disciple may have kept the location of Khardong secret from Tucci and Lama Govinda in the 1930s. This confusion continued half a century later, sidetracking Namkhai Norbu's team of Dzogchen scholars, as well as assorted Tibetologists and eminent travel writers such as John Bellezza, Charles Allen and Bruno Baumann. But with the re-discovery of Khardong, the hidden land of Khyunglung in Zhangzhung is beginning to open. In a curious twist of fate, it was Tucci who bought the young Namkhai Norbu to Italy, where he developed a world-renowned Dzogchen Buddhist practice – which shows close parallels with Bonpo Dzogchen.

The threads of Zhangzhung are spread long and thin in distance and time. In *Acta Orientalia*, Vol 68 (Havniae: Munksgaard, 2007), Blezer discusses the construction of sacred Bon landscape in the area, sketches the lineage of knowledge about the site, and concludes that evidence for the Silver Palace suggests a location much further east. The first faint patterns of this ancient Bon principality are starting to appear. And the search for the lost kingdom of Zhangzhung and the Silver Palace is still very much on the radar.

Bradley Rowe first visited Kailash in 1984 and Khyunglung three years later. He has ranged widely over Tibet since then, in recent years taking special interest group tours to some of the least-visited parts of the plateau. His particular interest is in environmental concerns and pilgrimage routes. His photographs appear in several books under the name Stone Routes.

The first aeroplanes to enter Tibetan airspace were two British biplanes. They were on a mission to photograph the summit of Everest so that a climbing route could be identified from aerial pictures. In April 1933, the date that Hilton completed his draft of *Lost Horizon*, two Westland PV3 Bombers took off from an airfield near Purnea in India, 240km south of Everest – and headed north into the Himalayan massif. The biplanes were specially modified for high-altitude flying, powered by supercharged Bristol Pegasus engines. Each biplane had two seats – the forward one with the pilot, the rear one with the observer (photographer). They had flying suits that were electrically heated, and carried oxygen masks.

At the time, it was rare for an aircraft to fly much above 3,000m, though the altitude flying record was around 12,000m. In the early 1930s, with both poles flown over, pilots started looking at an overflight of the Himalaya. Everest would require clearance of over 9,100m, but dealing with severe winds.

Approaching Everest, the biplanes were waylaid by ferocious winds. One pilot was caught in downdrafts. And then the glorious summit of Everest was glimpsed for the first time – from less than 40 metres away – by a photographer named Blacker, who wondered if that wasn't a bit too close to be filming. He was looking down a hatch in the back-seat floor of the biplane. The pilot pulled the biplane out at the last minute.

As for the other plane, it cleared the summit of Everest by a slim margin. On a second circuit of the peak, McIntyre, the pilot, noticed that his observer, Bonnett, was no longer visible. His oxygen apparatus was malfunctioning: he'd blacked out and slumped to the floor. On the trip back to India, dropping to lower elevations, the unconscious photographer revived and struggled to rip off his oxygen mask: his face, according to the pilot, was 'a nasty dark green shade' – but he survived. And the planes came back with the first aerial pictures of the Holy Grail of mountaineering: the summit of Everest.

In December 1943, the first aeroplane landed in Tibet – or rather, crashed in Tibet. Just like James Hilton predicted. After America entered the war in 1942, President Roosevelt made a commitment to supply China's Nationalist forces based in Kunming. His strategy in doing so was to keep the Japanese Army preoccupied in China. Since approaches to Kunming were mostly in Japanese hands, Allied pilots found a way to ferry strategic supplies from India to southwest China by flying over the Himalaya, a route called 'the Hump'. That meant everything from medicine and fuel to ammunition and guns. Tibet did not allow overland passage of these goods through its territory; despite pressure from the British and the Chinese, the Tibetans wished to remain neutral. Besides which, the Tibetans were not exactly thrilled by Chiang Kai-shek's declaration that his

Tsaparang and the great mother monastery of Toling are surely what Hilton had in mind when creating his fictional Shangri-La. The first photographs of the two places, published by Tucci in 1932, excited the world just as Hilton was planning his book… here, if anywhere, I tend to think, is the source of the Shangri-La story.

AT THE RUINS

The main building material at Guge is not stone, but clay, with walls, buildings, secret tunnels and escape exits all fashioned from this material. Thousands of people lived here in cave-dwellings in this kingdom of clay. Tsaparang is built tier-on-tier up a clay ridge. The best-preserved parts are the temples in the lower section, with

Nationalist forces would 'liberate' Tibet – after they settled a few other wars. The air-route over the Hump operated from 1942 to 1945; at its height, the operation used 13 launch bases in India and six in China. It was considered one of the most treacherous routes of World War II because of the high peaks traversed and the associated rough weather. Over a thousand men were killed flying the Hump, and over 600 planes were lost – a number shot down by Japanese planes.

Tibet did not allow flights over its territory, but that was hard to police, given the limited technology at its disposal. In December 1943, five American airmen in a C-87 (a modified version of a B-24 bomber) took off from Kunming for India. They got blown off course at night in a severe storm with high winds. When the clouds started to clear, the airmen were startled to see huge snowcaps looming. The plane was running out of fuel, and they circled Lhasa, believing it to be an Indian town. With no radio response from the town – and no obvious airstrip – they decided to bail out.

Regrouping on the ground next morning, the airmen were confused. Seeing what he took to be 'swastika' shapes painted on some houses, the pilot thought he'd somehow stumbled into German-controlled territory. Reception from the villagers of Tsedang at first seemed enthusiastic, with a crowd of onlookers clapping – but then drawing knives from their belts, which did not appear so friendly. The crew later learned that clapping in Tibet is used to drive away evil spirits. More mixed signals arose when some villagers stuck out their tongues at the airmen – actually a sign of respect. The villagers of Tsedang clothed and fed them; eventually the wide-eyed airmen were escorted to Lhasa, by now wearing fur-lined boots and fur coats.

Here, at the British Mission, the reception was quite different, as they faced angry mobs of Tibetans. It transpired that the airmen had committed great sacrilege by flying over the Dalai Lama's palace. As further proof of this, Tibetan priests had long predicted that any aircraft flying over the Holy City and daring to look down on the Dalai Lama would be doomed. This is exactly what happened to the C-87: it had crashed into a mountainside near Tsedang and exploded. Eventually, Tibetan villagers salvaged usable parts of the plane.

The airmen never got a tour of Lhasa: they were quickly hustled out of Tibet by the Sikkim border for their own safety, and because Tibet wished to maintain its neutrality in the war-theatre. The airmen's escapade was recounted in a book called *Jump to the Land of God* (1965), and more recently retold in *Lost in Tibet* by Richard Starks and Miriam Murcutt, published in 2004.

After the Americans, the next planes to land in Tibet were war planes, of a kind: Russian turboprops – the standard Chinese military aircraft in the 1960s. Most airfields in Tibet are military. Gongkar Airport doubles as a military and commercial airfield, as does Bangda Airfield, to the south of Chamdo.

stunning murals showing tantric deities locked in poses with their consorts.

From the top are excellent views of the area from Tsaparang Dzong – the king's simple summer palace. There are several temples at the top; the most important is tiny Demchok Mandala Chapel. This is the *gonkhang* or protector temple, and the former site of initiation rites. It was heavily damaged during the Cultural Revolution. If you can manage to get in (the chapel is locked), fascinating tantric murals are visible (you need a torch to see them). Depicted are rows of dancing *dakinis*, the naked female goddesses who personify the wisdom of enlightenment; below these are gory scenes of disembodiment from hell realms.

The artwork of the Guge kingdom, while much of it was destroyed by the

by Bradley Rowe

In Tibet, jewellery is a form of portable wealth, usable in barter. But Tibetans would be reluctant to part with prize pieces because of their strong belief in amulets and talismans. This combination of wealth and talisman comes in many forms on the Tibetan plateau – jewellery of turquoise, coral, amber, gold and silver. An unusual form of jewellery for women is the wearing of a cowrie shell around the wrist, still seen in parts of Tibet.

The two items that Tibetans prize above all else are *dzi* and *thogcha*. *Dzi* beads are a distinct variety of Chalcedony, an agate-rich quartz, which has geometric designs bleached into the stone by potash or soda and dyed possibly with copper nitrate or wood ash before re-firing. They resemble the 2,000-year-old Carnelian patterned stones found across Iran and the Indus valley regions, and similar stones have been found in Tang tombs.

The time and place of manufacture and the secrets of the process are lost but most reported finds are scattered on the grasslands of Tibet. The ancient Tibetans, painted in red ochre, raided trading caravans on the Silk Road, their plunder ending up in the burial tombs of the kings and nobles. *Dzi* beads, however, seldom appear in archaeological sites outside Tibet. Despite many attempts to copy them in stone, glass or plastic, there are a handful of experts who can distinguish the genuine article from the fakes, which are now omnipresent and have vastly outnumbered the real stones for many decades.

The Tibetans revere them as powerful protective charms, cast off by the gods when they chip or crack which must be covered with dust to stop them moving away. Some claim them to be snake bones or to have fallen from the sky but the protection offered is personal and sales are inauspicious. Some *dzi* stones are with 'eyes' – black circles in the white stone. The most powerful nine-eyed *dzi*, which can be seen on the Jowo in Lhasa and in the Potala, is very rare. An authenticated example was reputedly available in 2006 for over $100,000. Even genuine five-, three-, or single-eyed *dzi* stones would fetch thousands.

Yet you can now find them all over tourist Tibet for a few dollars to a few hundred. Collectors bought the few available *dzi* stones in the 1980s and all you can find on sale in Tibet today are a variety of fakes and imitations. The most obvious are of plastic or glass, worth no more than a few yuan, but the best are real agate – etched, dyed and even chipped to resemble the genuine article. They are manufactured all over Asia from Taiwan to Thailand and should properly be called 'etched agate in the *dzi* style'. Even Tibetans find them difficult to identify and almost all on sale around the Barkor are new. So if you intend to buy one of these strange beads, be aware that it is without doubt a modern product and should be priced as such.

Thogcha, a powerful talisman worn around the neck on a cord, is larger than a

Chinese, has one thing going for it: the dry desert air has preserved murals that would have disappeared over time elsewhere. Caves bearing this artwork are still being discovered in the region. The Guge kingdom was wealthy – those who made the murals are thought to have been master painters brought in from India and Nepal. Murals at Guge are in early Newari and Kashmiri styles, both rarely seen in other parts of Tibet. Back in Zanda, at Toling Gompa, you can see a number of fine murals that have survived destruction by Red Guards, who trashed these temples in the 1960s.

ring and comes in a great variety of designs. A strangely shaped mix of copper alloy, the *thogcha* has one of the most obscure and exotic histories in Tibetan culture. The high Changtang plateau 3,000 years ago began to be used for grazing yaks and sheep while to the east and west civilisations arose that had contact with Persia and China. The earliest rock carvings had animal motifs and abstract design dating back to the Zhangzhung era when bronze, copper and ironwork were renowned. *Thogchas* reflect and expand on these designs and were cast using metals from unknown mines in unknown production centres over many centuries. However, like *dzi* beads, they were distinct enough to be identified by the connoisseur.

The Tibetans call them 'thunderbolt iron' or 'sky metal' and some examples are of the renowned five-metal mix, where traces of silver and gold give a particular lustre to the copper. They have found them, again like *dzi* stones, in the fields and in tombs all over Tibet, discarded perhaps when the wearer had used the protection it offered or simply worn a hole in the support. They were worn for protection as an amulet, attached to horse tackle, or placed on a shrine. They range in size from a single centimetre to thirty or so, and the weights vary greatly.

In his 1973 book *Transhimalaya*, Giuseppe Tucci started systematically classifying *thogchas*, but this has proved a near-impossible task. It has been made even more difficult by the huge numbers of fakes that appeared on the markets once it was realised that they were valued by tourists. Many are crude copies; however, in some, the wear and patina are copied in convincing style and are difficult to detect.

Domestic and wild animals are depicted on the early pieces, from the frog to the deer and the crouching lion. Rather than a simple flange, *thogchas* are three-dimensional and very tactile. Worn around the neck, they may be sought out from other jewellery and rubbed in times of danger to invoke protection. Bonpo designs (such as the ladder or ruler pattern, the triangle inside a triangle on legs, the circular pieces with a horseshoe/vase centre crowned by bird heads) are known to be early, but highly valued (and most faked) is the Khyung or mythical bird and the Dorje (Vajra or thunderbolt), some of which were made as rings. Buckles, buttons and arrowheads are also found, mostly with worn-out eyeholes.

Nestorian crosses from the Mongol Yuan dynasty and Buddhist icons are also found as *thogchas*, showing that they continued to be produced until a few hundred years ago. Genuine items have now disappeared from the market stalls, but one or two family pieces are still worn by Tibetans – which is your best chance of seeing one outside a collection.

Bradley Rowe has been exploring the Tibetan region for three decades. His photographs appear in several books under the name Stone Routes. He lives in Glastonbury, England, with his wife Wendy Teasdill (author of a book on Kailash) and their three children.

CANYONS TO ZANDA

Although Zanda can be reached from the southern approach via Moincer, the more spectacular route is the northern approach, from Ali. From this direction you traverse an entire mountain range – a breathtaking trip, with snowy passes as high as 5,200m and 5,500m – before dropping down into a canyon with ghostly shapes. You drive through this canyon along a dry riverbed to reach Zanda. As you enter the multi-coloured gorges, a side road leads to newly discovered caves at Dungkar and Piyang, which are said to have murals rivalling those at Guge. Permits to see

WHEN TO GO

June–July is the period when nomad horse-racing festivals are in progress on the grasslands (exact dates are hard to pin down as they are based on the lunar calendar). Weather-wise, April to October is the best time to visit Tibet. April can be very windy, and there's a rainy season around July and August, but this is not as severe as in Nepal, because Tibet is on the northern side of the Himalaya. Because Tibet is so large, climate conditions vary considerably from east to west, and with the elevation. For reaching the Mount Kailash region, the optimum season is short: June and July are good months to go, and September is fine too. August is not good – rains can wash away bridges and roads leading in. Winters are long: the rest of the year may be snowed in at Kailash.

LOGISTICS

Tibet has always been a difficult place to get to. Depending on which way the political winds blow, access is sometimes completely off-limits to foreigners, and at other times relaxed. Your chances of getting in are far better if you approach from Chengdu, taking a flight to Lhasa. To enter Tibet you need a Chinese visa. Do not depend on visa extensions – make sure you get a visa valid for the intended length of stay (you can get Chinese visas valid for three months or longer in Hong Kong SAR). As well as a visa, there may be a requirement for a 'Tibet permit', which is mostly an exercise is raking in more money. In Chengdu, you can arrange this paperwork and air ticket to Lhasa through agents in the lobby of the Traffic Hotel (Jiaotong Binguan). Currency is the Chinese yuan RMB; US cash dollars will work too. Tibet runs on Beijing time, which can throw your Circadian rhythms off. The time zone in Nepal is two and a quarter hours behind Beijing time. That means if you fly from Lhasa to Kathmandu, you will actually arrive before you left.

Agents and Guides When dealing with agents in Tibet, you must make arrangements well before your trip. Once in Tibet, you will probably not be allowed to work with them and will be forced to deal with the official agencies. Deal with agencies that have Tibetan staff and guides, otherwise you'll end up with Chinese guides who know nothing about the culture and cannot speak Tibetan. Recommended are the following two agents. Windhorse Adventure, North Minzu Lu, Lhasa, tel. 683-3009, email: wha@public.ls.xz.cn, www.tibetwindhorse. com, is a high-end outfitter specialising in adventure touring, including rafting, trekking and mountaineering. A much smaller company, but attentive to detail and using all-Tibetan staff, is Shangrila Tours, office in the Ohdan Hotel, tel. 656-3009, email: ttinfo@public.ls.xz.cn, www.shangrilatours.com/.

Following up For high detail on Tibet, consult *Tibet: The Bradt Travel Guide* (2006). An excellent resource for hikers is *Trekking in Tibet* by Gary McCue (1999). Other inspirational reading: *Heartlands: Travels in the Tibetan World* by Michael Buckley (Summersdale, UK, 2002), and *The Hotel on the Roof of the World* by Alec Le Sueur (Summersdale, UK, 2001).

ROUTES

Lhasa is the gateway to most trips in the so-called Tibet Autonomous Region. The main air entry point is Chengdu, with daily flights to Lhasa. Chengdu is very well-connected to the rest of China, and to international destinations like Bangkok. You can also fly from Kunming via Zhongdian to Lhasa. The only international flight into Lhasa is from Kathmandu.

Overland By Landcruiser, you can make the run from Lhasa to Kathmandu, or Lhasa to Kailash and back south to Kathmandu. Another overland route to consider is Zhongdian to Lhasa.

LHASA

All loads lead to Lhasa. One way or another, if you visit Tibet, you will pass through dystopic Lhasa, the largest city in the Tibetan world. For atmosphere and character, highly recommended are the following two hotels, both Nepalese-managed, but with Tibetan staff and Tibetan-style décor. The Kyichu, at 149 Beijing Donglu, tel. 6338824, has wings arrayed around a central garden, with rooms going for US$60. The Gorkha Hotel, at 45 Jiangsu Lu, tel. 6271991, is a solid castle-like structure originally built as the old Nepalese consulate: it is arrayed around several courtyard gardens, with double rooms for US$50.

The Shangri-La Hotel group hasn't got round to Lhasa yet, but they have cast a spell over others in the capital – who studiously avoid incurring the wrath of the hotel chain. The Shangri-La Hotel group operates around 20 luxury hotels in major Chinese cities, with plans to open a dozen more – and is hanging on tight to its brand name through powerful connections in Beijing. Instead, some hotels have gone for the Shambhala legend. Here's a sneaky name: the Shangbala Hotel. That's a cross between Shangri-La and Shambhala. Another hotel is named Xiong Bala. And a third is the House of Shambhala. This boutique hotel was set up by Lawrence Brahm, a former New York lawyer who lives in Beijing (see page 36). His boutique hotel runs Tibetan Secret Spa, which claims to use soothing balms distilled from high-plateau herbs.

For food, Norling Restaurant inside the Kyichu Hotel is an upmarket place serving great Indian, Nepalese and Western fare with a fine atmosphere. At the back of the Barkor, Makye Ame has lot of things going for it: for starters, an excellent viewpoint over the Barkor to watch the pilgrims streaming past. The tented rooftop affords even better views. The eclectic menu runs from *thukpa* (noodle soup) to pizza. This place is steeped in legend. Makye Ame is thought to be the name of a beautiful woman that the licentious 6th Dalai Lama pursued while in disguise. The original tavern on this site was said to be the trysting place, and was thus allowed the honour of having its exterior painted in royal yellow.

Shangri-La Restaurant, in the courtyard of the Kirey Hotel, stages a regular dinner-dance show at night. The food is nothing special, but the traditional song-and-dance performances are good, with patrons quaffing Snow Beer or Lhasa Beer. Highlight of the night is the Yak Attack. This is a traditional yak welcome dance, performed by two men inside a yak-skin. The beast lunges into the audience with hilarious results.

RONGBUK

Rongbuk Monastery runs a small guesthouse: it's best to bring your own sleeping bag as nights can be freezing. You've heard of the abominable snowman: at Rongbuk there is the abominable *binguan* – an ugly pink concrete structure called Drufung Binguan, with rooms for US$40 apiece. The Chinese cellphone crowd stays here.

It takes several days by Landcruiser from Lhasa to reach the Everest region. Landcruisers must stop short of Rongbuk at the village of Pasum, where passengers transfer to a shuttle van service for the final run to Rongbuk. Groups may include Rongbuk and Everest on the Lhasa-to-Kathmandu overland route. A longer trip is to combine it with the epic drive to Mount Kailash.

Continued overleaf

KAILASH

Getting to Kailash is an epic overland journey by Landcruiser. Permits and paperwork must be in order to get past checkpoints. On the south route from Lhasa, it is 1,200km one-way to Darchen, and on the north route via Ali it's around 1,900km to Darchen. Small groups heading out of Lhasa can opt for a 12- to 15-day round-trip tour, or 16- to 20-day round-trip tour. Another option is not to return to Lhasa but head for Nepal overland. You could drive from Lhasa to Kailash and Guge, and then backtrack down past the beautiful lake Paiku Tso to cross the border into Nepal at Zhangmu. Some do approach Kailash entirely from Kathmandu, with Landcruisers heading up from Zhangmu. One more route in, requiring lots of advance paperwork, is to fly to Simikot in far-west Nepal, and trek five days up to the Tibetan border, transferring to Landcruisers for the ride to Darchen. For details on trekking through the Limi Valley on the Nepalese side, check the Nepal section of this book (page 136).

VALLEY OF KHYUNGLUNG

Since this region is less than 100km from Darchen, it is possible to visit Khyunglung, Gurugem and Tirtapuri on a day trip from Kailash, but remember to get permits in Darchen if you do not already have them. A minimum of two days is needed if you want to visit Khardong, the caves, and the bathhouse at Tirtapuri. You can camp nearby or stay at a basic guesthouse in Moincer. Beyond Tirtapuri, the side-road bends west down the Sutlej, past the important Bonpo gompa of Gurugem.

In Gurugem you can pick up a local guide and hike up to the mesas at Khardong. Back on the road, after passing through a small gorge, you reach the village of Khyunglung, about 30km from Moincer. A further 3km onward, reached by a footbridge, is the remarkable cave complex called Khyunglung Ngulkar. A short visit of 3 hours or so, with a picnic, would allow you to poke around in several of the caves and climb up to the highest temple (by some accounts, the purported site of the Silver Palace), although the final approach is extremely precarious. The Khyunglung road does continue over the mountains to Toling, but this road runs close to the Indian border and is not open. In any case, the road is said to be exceedingly dangerous, especially when wet. It is best to return to the main road if carrying on to Toling and Guge.

ZANDA AND GUGE REGION

The town of Zanda is the gateway to the Guge region, with guesthouses and restaurants. Visiting Zanda and Tsaparang requires a string of paperwork that starts in Lhasa, continues in west Tibet, and is still ongoing in Zanda. Zanda can be reached by Landcruiser from the northern approach through Ali, or by coming up from the south from Darchen. There are basic guesthouses and restaurants in Zanda.

these might be hard to come by, however. With such a spectacular route, allow a full day to motor by Landcruiser from Ali to Zanda (or the reverse route), with frequent stops along the way. The canyons, with hues of yellow, red and copper, are extraordinary for their phantasmagoric sculpted forms, which appear at times to be like the outlines of dream castles or cathedrals, at other times like gigantic guardian statues or mythical animals. The imagination could run riot here.

Lowell Thomas' book, *Out of This World* (published in 1949), has a chapter entitled 'Escape to Shangri-La'. Lowell Thomas and his father, an American radio broadcaster, were officially invited to Tibet: they were among the last foreigners to witness a free and independent Tibet before it fell to the Chinese. The chapter 'Escape to Shangri-La' details the adventures of two German prisoners-of-war, climbers Peter Aufschnaiter and Heinrich Harrer, who escaped a British camp in northwest India in 1944 and crossed into Tibet near the Guge kingdom.

Against incredible odds, after crossing into Tibet they made their way eastward to a valley called Kyirong, where Tibetan officials allowed them to stay, pending a decision on where they would go. Permission to move on to Lhasa was refused. Local officials wanted them to go to Nepal. Aufschnaiter and Harrer played along with this, but they knew if they went to Nepal they would be handed over to British authorities and sent back to a POW camp. After a blissful stay of ten months in Kyirong, Aufschnaiter and Harrer bid the villagers goodbye, saying they were heading south for Nepal. Instead, they turned north to the bleak Changtang – in a bold move to cross this wilderness on foot and loop around to reach Lhasa.

In Kyirong, the two escapees were in limbo, but felt perfectly at home with the beautiful mountain setting. The place gave them a chance to learn Tibetan, to rest up, and to plot for the road ahead. A safe haven during times of world war and holocaust? If anyone could claim to have stumbled into the realm of Shangri-La, these two POWs came close. Peter Aufschnaiter explains in his book, *Eight Years in Tibet*:

> When we reached Kyirong in January 1945, we felt as if we were in paradise. After months spent in a highland landscape devoid of trees and shrubs, we were suddenly transported into a region that could compare with the most beautiful parts of the Alps.... The idyllic rhythm of olden times, by which this village lived, had a magical fascination that we felt deeply again and again.... one felt nothing of the haste of our modern world, from which it was separated by the narrow but well-guarded cordon of Nepal. Nor did we feel anything of the world-shattering events of the war, which many here knew little about, although by now it had been going on for five years.

Aufschnaiter has described exactly why you would come to Kyirong valley – to experience the rhythm of Tibetan village life. If you are heading from Kailash to Nepal via a back-route that runs past Pelku Tso and Saga, then you should consider trying to get to Kyirong, though technically you need a permit for both Dzongka and Kyirong.

Between Pelku Tso and Saga a road heads 35km east over a pass into the Kyirong valley, one of the few rivers that cuts through the Himalaya. If you can spare three or four days, this is a beautiful excursion. Dzongka, the county town, possesses a gompa ruined by invading Nepalese in the 18th century – the gompa is located in the upper plateau-like part of the valley. Downstream, high above the river gorge, is Milarepa's cave hermitage of Drakar Taso, but after 70km the valley opens with rich forest (the first real trees you will have seen since setting out for Kailash) and agriculture around Kyirong village. The oldest of the ancient temples here dates back to Songtsen Gampo but it is the village life of this remote corner of Tibet that is the most attractive. Not that it will remain remote for much longer. The road down to the border with Nepal has been finished to a high standard and with Chinese help, and with the completion by the Nepalese of a stretch north from Trisuli and Kathmandu, this is likely to become a major trading route. It will probably open to tourist traffic.

6

Bhutan

ONE GREAT SANCTUARY

In the Himalaya, of the vast area that was once the spirited domain of the Tibetan religion and culture – stretching from Ladakh to Yunnan – only the tiny enclave of Bhutan survives as a self-governing entity, with Tibetan Buddhism as its state religion. Outer Mongolia, far to the north, and the republic of Tuva, are also independent and follow Tibetan Buddhism, but the people and language are Mongolian.

Stalwart preservation of flora and fauna, and of Tibetan Buddhist practices, make Bhutan a prime contender for the mantle of the real Shangri-La. And that refers to the entire country, not just a few locations. This is fitting when you consider that Bhutan is a tiny nation sandwiched between the giants of India and China – both implicated in large-scale environmental degradation. It has managed to pull itself out of poverty without exploiting its natural resources – except for hydropower, which is sold to India as Bhutan's main source of foreign funds.

With an area of 47,000km^2, Bhutan is roughly the size of Switzerland, and seeks to be as neutral. It allows India to control its foreign policy in exchange for military protection from China. To protect itself from a take-over by India, Bhutan has held a seat at the UN since 1971.

Bhutan's great draw is its pristine environment. It boasts more than 65% forest cover, compared with less than 20% forest cover in neighbouring India. Wildlife is well-protected, with a complete ban on hunting of rare species like the snow leopard. Bird-watchers love Bhutan, with over 700 bird species recorded. And botanists are thrilled by Bhutan's range of unusual flowering species.

In a system adopted since medieval times, Bhutan is ruled from a series of fortresses by men in robes and Argyle socks. The system dates back to the 17th century, when a revered high lama, the Shabdrung, started a lineage of incarnate lamas. In the early 20th century, there was a change of rulers: the Shabdrung lineage was superseded by the rise of a new dynasty of kings. Ugyen Wangchuck, previously the governor of Bhutan, was crowned hereditary monarch of Bhutan in 1907 with British support, after his role as intermediary between the British and the Tibetans during the Younghusband expedition of 1903. The Shabdrung lineage continued, but the sixth Shabdrung, Jigme Dorje, died under mysterious circumstances in 1930 at the age of 26. Much later, it was revealed that he had been suffocated by royalist soldiers.

King Jigme Singye Wangchuck, the fourth king in the Wangchuck dynasty, came to power in 1972 and proved highly influential. Through his efforts, Bhutan entered the international community, establishing diplomatic relations with many countries. However, King Jigme Wangchuck fostered the traditional culture of Bhutan to the point of strong-arming other ethnic cultures. The predominant ethnic groups in Bhutan – the Drukpas and Monbas – migrated from Tibet centuries ago. Bhutan, however, is not a safe haven for refugee Tibetans, whom the

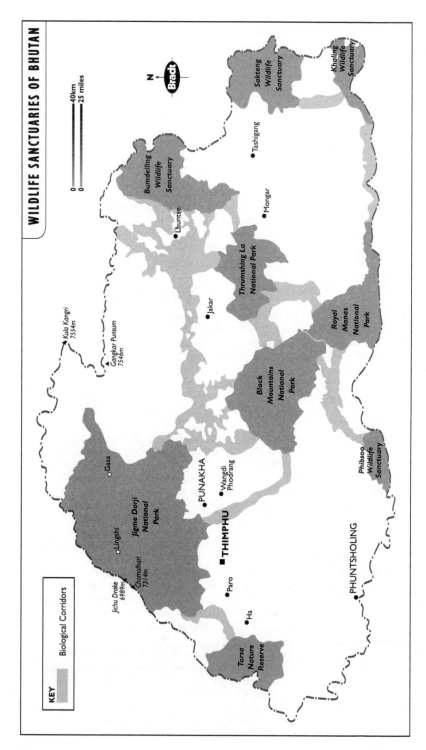

WILDLIFE SANCTUARIES OF BHUTAN

KEY

Biological Corridors

N

Bradt

0   40km
0   25 miles

Jichu Drake
6989m

Chomolhari
7314m

Lingshi

Gasa

Jigme Dorji
National
Park

Kula Kangri
7554m

Gangkar Punsum
7540m

Bumdelling
Wildlife
Sanctuary

Lhuntse

Jakar

Thrumshing La
National Park

Tashigang

Mongar

Sakteng
Wildlife
Sanctuary

Khaling
Wildlife
Sanctuary

Royal
Manas
National
Park

Black
Mountains
National Park

PUNAKHA

Wangdi
Phodrang

THIMPHU

Paro

Ha

Phibsoo
Wildlife
Sanctuary

PHUNTSHOLING

Torsa
Nature
Reserve

Bhutanese fear will build up in greater numbers and power (there are several thousand currently living in Bhutan). Nor are they keen on a large Nepalese presence. The southern lowlands are mostly occupied by people of Nepali origin.

Figures on population in Bhutan vary wildly from 600,000 to over a million. How you can lose so many people on a census is hard to fathom, but it seems that in a 1988 census, ethnic Nepalis were somehow overlooked for inclusion. With ethnic Nepali numbers approaching perhaps 250,000 within Bhutan at the time, this was seen as a threat by the Drukpa majority. The government banned the speaking of Nepalese, and has an on-going programme to return as many ethnic Nepalis as possible back to Nepal, citing their failure to assimilate into Bhutanese culture and learn the language as the reason for their marching orders. Over 110,000 of these people languish in UN refugee camps in eastern Nepal, while an estimated 150,000 ethnic Nepalis still live in Bhutan.

On the heels of this came a campaign to enforce Bhutanese culture – the compulsory wearing of national dress, compulsory building codes, and compulsory use of Dzongkha, the national language. Dzongkha is related to Tibetan but is quite different from the Lhasa dialect. The language is a compulsory subject at school, although the medium of instruction is English.

Bhutan is the best place in the Tibetan world to see traditional-style architecture – such as the parliament buildings of Thimphu and the numerous *dzongs* (forts) across the country. Although Bhutan has strong links with Tibetan culture, the two have historically been at odds with each other. Bhutan has long fought with Tibet to maintain itself as a separate entity. The royal families of Tibet, Bhutan and Sikkim used to mingle in marriage matches, but this has been altered by changing politics. In 1972, the third king of Bhutan, Jigme Dorje Wangchuck, died while on safari in Nairobi, apparently of a heart attack. It appears that the king's Tibetan mistress, Yanki, attempted to usurp the role of the king's legal son and heir by placing her own (illegitimate) son on the throne. Reaction was swift: after the Tibetan mistress fled to India, all the Tibetans in Bhutan were given the third degree, including the Dalai Lama's representative. Some were thrown into jail, others booted out of the country. Since then, contacts with the Tibetan government-in-exile have soured. The Dalai Lama has never been invited to visit Bhutan.

The official faith of Bhutan is Drukpa Kagyu, a tantric form of Tibetan Buddhism (and a sub-sect of the Kagyu order). Also practised is Buddhism of the Nyingma school. In Nepali areas, the faith is Indian and Nepali-influenced Hinduism. In Tibetan lore, Bhutan is said to harbour many *beyuls* or hidden valleys. That's because the originator of the idea, Padmasambhava (Guru Rinpoche), lived for many years in Bhutan. He is the patron deity of Bhutan. The mythical logo of the kingdom – the symbol of monarchy that appears on the Bhutanese flag, on the aeroplanes, on products made in Bhutan – is the dragon. The local people refer to their nation as Druk Yul, or the Land of the Thunder Dragon, because of its sometimes-violent storms. However, in tourist literature, this may be modified to 'Land of the Peaceful Dragon'.

In 2007, marking the centenary anniversary of the monarchy in Bhutan, the fourth king stepped down in favour of his son, King Jigme Khesar Namgyel Wangchuck. It was also decreed that there would be a transition from Buddhist monarchy to parliamentary democracy.

The March 2008 parliamentary elections were contested by only two parties: the People's Democratic Party (headed by a relative of the king) and the Bhutan Harmony Party (pitching itself as representing ordinary Bhutanese). The voters returned a strong 'no' to nepotism: the populist Bhutan Harmony Party won a landslide victory, taking 44 of the 47 seats up for grabs.

Amazing Thailand, Incredible India – these slogans have been highly successful in ad marketing campaigns that have drawn large numbers of tourists. North Korea doesn't exactly pursue the mass tourist market, but perhaps something like *Go Ballistic!* would suit. For Burma, the catch-phrase might be: *Just Plain Barbaric!* While for Tibet, a logo of a big iron fist coming down like a hammer might be appropriate.

Bhutan is lucky: the country doesn't need to advertise much. The tourist clientele is small (those that can afford the high tariff of visiting) and foreign media generally projects a very positive image. *The Last Shangri-La* is the most common tagline appearing in stories about Bhutan, but a number of other taglines would suit: *Bhutan – Land of No Plastic! Bhutan – A Land without MTV!* Or perhaps: *Bhutan – Carbon-neutral Holidays for Everyone.*

Bhutan was lucky because it learned from the mistakes of nearby Nepal. Like Bhutan, Nepal used to be a highly reclusive kingdom that was vigilant at keeping foreigners out. But when Nepal finally opened its doors in the 1950s, cultural chaos ensued as overlanders, backpackers and dope-smoking hippies invaded the place – generating a host of problems. Bhutan is like an exclusive club – the nation is in tune with what wealthy tourists want and are willing to pay high prices for. Bhutan attracts the super-rich, who view it as a trophy destination.

The nation is low-tech – no traffic lights, no traffic jams (compared to next-door India). Enforcing traditional dress and architecture has given Bhutan a distinct culture and look that is very different from its neighbours. Reinforcing this is a range of traditional festivals, and Bhutan's distinct brand of Tibetan Buddhism. Bhutan went green – and stayed green – long before that became the trend in the West. With strong conservation policies and wildlife protection laws in place, Bhutan is ahead of the game in promoting its great natural beauty. These factors all contribute to very strong place-branding concepts. This is the mystique of Brand Bhutan.

Another big transition under way: in 2006, a nationwide census conducted in Bhutan revealed a surprise statistic: that only 44% of Bhutanese were farmers. It was previously thought that 80% of the population still worked on farms, but there has been a demographic shift to the towns.

Bhutan is slowly modernising – greeting the innovation of television at the dawn of the 21st century. The nation is slowly opening up to the outside world, but official policy on tourism is to restrict it: if you have a capital city (Thimphu) with only 100,000 people, you do not want the locals outnumbered by visitors. In 2006, Bhutan saw a big jump in foreign tourism – well, a big jump for Bhutan, anyway. The nation recorded around 17,000 foreign arrivals, and upward of 40,000 Indian tourists (Indian tourists are allowed to visit without visas or paying statutory charges). Keeping the foreign tourist masses at bay is the crippling cost of getting into Bhutan. The handful of treks detailed in this chapter will reveal Bhutan's mountain majesty, and highlight a few mysteries as well – in this nation that often refers to itself in brochures as 'the Last Shangri-La'.

BLISSOLOGY IN BHUTAN

In the 1970s, the fourth king of Bhutan made a remark to a reporter from *Newsweek* that he cared more about Gross National Happiness than about Gross National Product. What he meant at the time was that economic growth alone does not bring contentment, and well-being does not have to be linked to high levels of consumption. The term Gross National Happiness (GNH) took hold in Bhutan, and the term went on to officially become the centre of the country's development policy. This cites 'the four pillars' of GNH as being: sustainable and equitable development, conservation of the environment, preservation of Bhutan's cultural values, and good governance. GNH has developed into a small academic industry: an international conference on GNH a few years back resulted in 60 papers being tabled.

Bhutan has no GNP to speak of – per capita income is low, and Bhutan's exports, all of which go to India, are tiny. Given these facts, critics say that pushing GNH is an empty slogan, one that includes everything and ends up meaning nothing. Bhutan's rulers find GNH a handy excuse for some of their wackier policies.

How does Bhutan rank on the scale of happiness? According to the colour-coded Map of World Happiness, produced by researcher Adrian White of the University of Leicester, Bhutan is a red zone, meaning very happy. In Adrian White's survey, judging the degree of well-being around the globe, Bhutan ranked 8th out of 178 countries. That sounds very impressive – until you learn that the UN Development Programme's human-development index places Bhutan right at the other end of the scale, ranking the nation 134th out of 177 countries.

Finding your own Shangri-La, finding your inner Shangri-La. Shangri-La is itself a kind of metaphor for happiness. Trouble is, it depends what you mean by 'happiness' – what thrills some can scare others, or totally bore them. And happiness can come at a high price. One of the hidden costs of material prosperity attained by high-achievers is stress – which in the West has spawned a huge wellness industry devoted to pampering those with disposable incomes.

Seeking answers on the slippery subject of happiness is the upstart science of happiness, which mixes psychology with economics. Dr Edward Diener, professor of psychology at the University of Illinois, has conducted research on happiness and SWB (subjective well-being) for over 25 years, including surveys across many cultures. He has developed a Satisfaction with Life Scale. According to Diener, many think that once they get everything just right, and achieve their goals, they will be happy. But Diener says that once we have attained certain dreams, we still need new goals and activities. Happiness is really about working and striving to reach those goals. In 2006, Diener wrote:

> In recent years I have proposed that governments need to create national accounts of well-being to supplement economic indicators in guiding policy formation. Like the DOW Jones Industrial Average or the Gross-Domestic-Product, the national accounts of well-being can signify how nations are progressing – but in non-monetary ways.

The New Economics Foundation, a think-tank in the UK, is calling for a 'global manifesto for a happier planet that will list ways nations can live within their environmental limits and increase people's quality of life.' If clean environment is a factor in happiness, then Bhutan would be right at the top of the list. Maybe Bhutan's Gross National Happiness spiel is ahead of the game after all.

PARO

Arriving by air in Paro, you step into an entirely different world. The indicators of which way the wind blows are prayer flag banners, flapping in the breeze. What immediately strikes the eye is the traditional architecture. You encounter a 'traditional' airport. Well, traditional-style terminal buildings. This falls into line

Nations agonise over the loss of traditional culture when faced with the onslaught of modern technology, particularly the power of Hollywood. Bhutan has come up with a novel way of dealing with the problem – the government simply enforces its culture. In Bhutan, it is compulsory to wear national dress in public, to follow guidelines for traditional architecture when building, and to teach the official language (Dzongkha) in schools. Fines are levied for not following these practices, and for repeat offenders there is even provision for prison sentences.

That means that blue jeans are banned, at least in public – although foreign visitors do not have to follow this fashion policing. This is a nation of people in robes. The men wear a knee-length robe called the *gho*, combined with knee-length Argyle socks, while the women wear a graceful ankle-length robe called the *kira*, which is complemented by a bolero jacket. An exception to robe-wearing is army personnel – probably for the reason that nobody would take them seriously if they dressed in robes.

Some other campaigns in this quixotic kingdom: plastic bags are banned, and there is a crusade to prohibit smoking. Traffic lights are not banned, but after seeing them in operation for a few hours in Thimphu, people decided they didn't like them. There are no traffic lights anywhere in Bhutan.

Structures in Bhutan have a four-storey limit, and must have squarish windows, a Bhutan-style roof, and specific exterior decoration. The building code applies to everything, including humble petrol stations. Cars themselves cannot be made to look traditional, or can they? Some have snow lions painted on the front. And while a television is definitely non-traditional, it can be set into a hand-crafted Bhutanese cabinet or box. Planes are definitely not traditional, but there are several features that set the Druk Air fleet apart. In the seat pockets are copies of *Tashi Delek*, the inflight magazine devoted solely to Bhutan. Planes in the Druk Air fleet are painted on the exterior with the dragon logo that appears on the Bhutanese flag. This is the Dragon Kingdom, after all.

Television and internet are latecomers to Bhutan – which for many years was wary of the damage that these can inflict on traditional culture. These weapons

with Bhutan's architectural code, which limits the style of building, the height of building, and exterior and interior decoration. All must be done in Bhutanese style.

Ancient architectural and engineering skills have been lost in Tibet itself as Chinese engineers take over all the construction. An example is bridges. Once, Tibetans had the know-how to build iron suspension bridges. This technology is attributed to Drubtob Tangton Gyelpo (the Iron Bridge Lama, who lived 1385–1464), who is thought to have originated the use of heavy iron chains in the making of suspension bridges. He is said to have built 108 iron suspension bridges in Tibet, including one that spanned the Tsangpo at Chaksam, 65km from Lhasa. The bridges are now all gone – the one at Chaksam was replaced by a modern Chinese bridge. Coming to Bhutan in search of iron ore, the Iron Bridge Lama built half a dozen bridges, including one in Paro. The traditional skill of bridge-building lives on in Bhutan, with arched wooden bridges used for human and animal passage over rivers in remote areas. Some ornate covered wooden bridges can be found in Paro.

Paro is a small town, but worth a few days. If you are permitted entry, try to access the inner courtyard of Rinpung Dzong, which has stunning artwork and frescoes.

Above the town sits a circular structure that was once a castle and has been

of mass distraction were held at bay – such powerful and evil influences as miniskirts and tank-tops (MTV), assorted flesh (Indian movies) and strange ideas (The Simpsons). Richer folk in Thimphu could access some foreign movies through video rentals in the capital, and also via satellite dish, pirating Indian programming.

The big turnaround came in 1998, when the fourth king of Bhutan permitted football-crazed residents to watch the World Cup final and dishes sprouted everywhere. The king himself used to play goalie in local matches, until he realised that none of his subjects dared score against him. The 1998 World Cup proved to be the point of no return: domestic programming was introduced the following year, as the BBS (Bhutan Broadcasting Service).

Suddenly viewers had access to nearly 50 channels through cable operators, offering everything from wrestling to near-naked fashion models. According to a media impact study for the communications ministry, Indian soap operas are spreading fast, with people adjusting meal times to watch them. Family life has changed considerably as a result, and television is blamed for rising crime rates. To stem the tide, some satellite programmes have been taken off the air: these include the sports channel Ten Sports, whose wrestling programmes were so popular that boys across Bhutan were mimicking them. MTV was quietly taken off the air, too – who knows what damage Britney Spears could do to the minds of Bhutanese girls?

There's something depressing about seeing a society cast aside its unique character in favour of programmes on a Californian beach, or reality TV shows that feature minor celebrities fighting in the jungle.

The Bhutanese are mesmerised by the box. A recent survey revealed that one-third of girls want to look more American (whiter skin, blonde hair). More than 35% of parents prefer to watch TV than talk to their children. And farmers' wives ogle ads for 'furniture you've always desired' or 'shoes you've always dreamed of'.

converted into a museum, with displays on Bhutanese history and culture. Among the displays is a section on natural history, with stuffed species – stuffed in both senses of the word (taxidermy and highly endangered). These will introduce Bhutan's unusual wildlife. And then there is the wild man; in the display on Bhutanese postage stamps, you can find some triangular ones featuring the yeti.

TIGER LAIR HERMITAGE

Before you set out for a trek of a week or longer, consider a day hike to Taktsang, or Tiger Lair Hermitage. This is part of the high-altitude mantra: hike high, sleep low, and to get your body attuned to becoming a ruthless walking machine. Taktsang is a steady upward hike, about 1,000m up, to a ridge where a hermitage has been grafted onto a sheer rock face. It is a fantastic and strange building. The site is thought to date from the 8th century, set up as one of 13 tiger lairs frequented by Guru Rinpoche (Padmasambhava). Guru Rinpoche had a fleet of flying tigers at his disposal, enabling him to ride around Tibet and the Himalaya to subdue hostile forces, most often in the form of demonesses.

The current structures at Tiger Lair Hermitage do not date back centuries, however. In April 1998, the entire complex burned down. It had to be rebuilt from

The early history of Tibet is filled with tales of high lamas subduing or exorcising demons and demonesses, or turning them into benign protector deities. Guru Rinpoche, the creator of the *beyuls*, was an important figure brought from India into Tibet by the king to quash troublesome demons. He later came to Bhutan on a similar mission. While Guru Rinpoche is the patron deity of Bhutan, it is another demon slayer who has captured the heart of the people. In central Bhutan is Chime Lakhang, a small temple built in 1499 and dedicated to the Divine Madman, Drukpa Kunley, who lived from 1455 to 1529.

Born in Tibet, Drukpa Kunley was trained as a monk, but veered away from traditional Buddhism in a rather shocking manner. He was an oversexed libertine. He drank a lot, he swore, he broke wind like a dragon – and he developed some highly unorthodox methods of exorcising demons. Drukpa Kunley's mission in Bhutan was to destroy or enslave troublesome demons, or turn them into something more positive. People in 16th-century Bhutan lived under the spell of animist superstition; it was Drukpa Kunley's duty – and pleasure – to battle the demons that cowed the Bhutanese. Sometimes he took on demons by using his penis as a battle weapon. And sometimes he exorcised demons from women using his penis.

In frescoes, he is portrayed as a portly man with a beard and a leer, who travelled everywhere with his dog Shachi. He wrote reams of pornographic verse – his songs had lyrics like: 'My meditation practice is girls and wine, I do whatever I feel like, strolling the Void.' And so Drukpa Kunley wandered around Bhutan, fathering children and happily blending the sacred and profane: he had children by nuns, who claimed they broke no vows because they had made love to a mad saint.

Stories about the irreverent exploits of Drukpa Kunley abound in the folklore of Bhutan, and his ribald songs live on. Kunley's favourite pastime – archery – has been adopted as the national sport of Bhutan. And the national animal of Bhutan, the takin, is attributed to a miracle by Drukpa Kunley. The takin looks like a bizarre mix of moose, musk-ox and wildebeest. As the legend goes, when a feast was thrown by villagers for Drukpa Kunley, he was asked perform a miracle. Looking around, Kunley seized upon the bones of animals eaten during the feast – and grafted the head of a goat onto the body of a cow. And that, when fleshed out, became the takin. The beast is also linked to the Greek legend of the Golden Fleece: some think that the takin's shaggy yellow coat is the source of that legend.

The Bhutanese love Drukpa Kunley for his irreverent humour, and his satirical and earthy approach in exposing corruption and hypocrisy among officialdom and the clergy. In his honour, to ward off evil, and to bring good luck and ensure fertility (in more than just the agricultural sense), large stylised phalluses are painted on exteriors of Bhutanese farmhouses. And wooden penises hang at the eaves.

Drukpa Kunley is very much part of fertility blessing rituals. Chime Lakhang is Bhutan's top pilgrimage spot for those who want to conceive. Female pilgrims are blessed with Kunley's old bow and arrow, or tapped on the head with an ivory phallus, then a wooden one, symbolic of Drukpa Kunley's prowess. They sip holy water and offer gifts of butter, wine, incense and small ngultrim notes. And Western women have also come for the fertility blessing. A fertility tour for women who have trouble conceiving? It has happened. Tovya Wager, an American tour operator, came to Chime Lakhang in 1996 to seek a fertility blessing. At the time she was 46 years old: within several months of the blessing, she became pregnant. When she returned to Bhutan with her ten-month-old daughter to give thanks for this miraculous conception, she brought along a few couples who, as it happens, were very interested in the special blessing. She advertised the trip as 'Fertility Blessing: Spiritual Bhutan'.

Hidden away at the back of the Great Sutra Chanting Hall of Sakya Gompa in western Tibet is a library that runs the entire length of the north–south wall, with shelves of sacred texts reaching from floor to ceiling. The entrance to the library is a small locked door hidden behind statuary. Lying in one corner is a huge manuscript illuminated in gold called the *Prajnaparamita Sutra*, setting forth the bodhisattva path to enlightenment. The book is so large it requires its own special rack: the pages, in traditional single leaf format, are 1.75m wide by 0.75m deep by 0.5m thick.

This ancient text was the prime candidate for the world's biggest book, but in 2003 along came another heavyweight that eclipsed it. *Bhutan: A Visual Odyssey Across the Last Himalayan Kingdom* has been certified by the *Guinness Book of Records* as being the world's largest published book. With pages open, this dazzling photo book measures 2m across by 1.5m high, weighs 60kg, and is so big it needs its own Sherpa to move it around. Portraits of Bhutanese people in the book are life-size or bigger; panoramas convey the sweeping mountain ranges and awesome ancient architecture of Bhutan. The 114-page book costs US$10,000 to purchase, although it only costs US$1,000 to produce (the remaining US$9,000 benefits the Bhutanese ministry of education as a charitable donation). For that price, you get a rack to stand the book on so you can turn the gargantuan pages. Behind the book is MIT professor Michael Hawley, who assembled a team of photographers and digital experts to take part in four extensive expeditions across Bhutan to get the photos for this colossus.

If you don't have the funds to get this mega-book shipped from Amazon, you can still catch up with it in Bhutan. A copy is on display at the National Library in Thimphu, but the pages are only turned once a month. The Uma Paro Hotel in Paro has a copy on a display rack in its business centre.

the base up. Suspicion arose that the fire was started to cover the tracks of art thieves, who made off with precious statuary from Taktsang. Bhutan has been targeted by art thieves, attempting to smuggle rare pieces out and reap large profits by selling to collectors. To stymie this, foreigners may be told that they cannot enter temples in Bhutan. If they are allowed in, interior photography is usually not permitted.

CHOMOLHARI TREK

This is one of the most popular treks in Bhutan, on account of stunning alpine vistas seen *en route*. Starting in Paro, you drive to the trailhead 15km north at the ruins of Drukyel Dzong (2,580m). The 17th-century fort is famed as being the scene of a major battle between Bhutanese and Tibetan forces where the latter were repulsed. Here your crew of horses and horsemen, cook and guide will assemble.

It takes three or four days to reach Chomolhari base camp. The stops *en route* are campsites, which can be varied to suit. What is important is the pacing. For the first day, it is advisable to keep the trek distance short. Drukyel Dzong to Rochi Dasa campsite (2,700m) is a hike of just four hours. This way you can adjust to longer marches, and acclimatise to the elevation. The second day, ascend to a campsite at 3,200m. Third day, move up to a campsite at 3,600m. On the fourth day, a morning hike brings you into Jangothang, elevation 4,070m.

You have reached one of the finest campsites in the Himalaya: a splendid setting with the ruins of a fortress in view. Pitch your tent at Jangothang for a front-row seat to see sunrise at Chomolhari, among the top sacred peaks of Bhutan. The 7,314m peak is thought to be the abode of goddess Jomo Lhari, one of the five Tsering sisters (another sister dwells on top of Everest). Chomolhari was first climbed in 1937 by Spencer Chapman and Sherpa Pasang. The locals believed this climb brought bad luck, and from the Bhutanese side a ban on climbing was eventually imposed. In fact, in 1994, the Bhutanese banned the climbing of peaks higher than 6,000 metres out of respect for local spiritual beliefs. However, climbers still attempt the peak of Chomolhari from the Tibetan side, with permits issued by the Chinese, who have zero respect for local spiritual beliefs.

Even more imposing than Chomolhari is the pyramidal classic Jichu Drake, 6,989m, just around the corner. You can get great views of this breathtaking peak on a day-hike out of Chomolhari base camp to Tshophu Lake (4,350m), which has excellent wildlife and birdlife viewing potential.

From Chomolhari base camp there are several route variations to reach Thimphu. A five-day route would be to head north to Lingshi, then trek south over the Yeli La, continuing via Shodu, Barshong and Dolam Kencho to Dodina, where you reach the road (with a short drive from here to Thimphu). For a much longer loop, taking 14 days, proceed to the Blue Poppy Trek description that follows.

BLUE POPPY TREK

JIGME DORJI NATIONAL PARK

The following trek describes a long loop from Paro through Laya to Gaza. This is the longest trek possible through Jigme Dorji National Park, which at 4,349km^2 is the largest protected area in Bhutan. Within the confines of the park, elevations range from 1,000 metres (tropical lowlands) to more than 7,000 metres (snowcaps

HUNTING THE BLUE POPPY

The blue poppy is the national flower of Bhutan. Five blue poppy species grow in Bhutan, but the national flower is *Meconopsis grandis*, the tallest one. Growing to about a metre in height, this brilliant blue poppy is found in alpine scree at altitudes over 4,000m. It is such a hardy species that the hairs growing on its stem have been observed coated in ice. Shorter blue poppy species are found in high meadows. In addition to the blue poppy, Bhutan hosts white poppies, yellow poppies, red poppies and purple varieties.

Although reports of the blue poppy surfaced in the 1850s from missionary activity in eastern Tibet, it was not until 1913 that British explorer and butterfly collector Frederic Bailey plucked one in the Tsangpo region, carrying it home pressed between the pages of a notebook. The specimen was named *Meconopsis baileyi* after him, and it aroused considerable interest in England. A decade later, retracing his countryman's route, botanist Frank Kingdon-Ward collected seeds from the plant and is credited with introducing the blue poppy to European gardens. It was Bailey again who discovered a huge white poppy (*Meconopsis superba*) while riding into Bhutan through the Ha district in 1922. But the blue poppy's presence in Bhutan was not confirmed until 1933, when botanist George Sherriff collected specimens in the mountains of Sakteng, along the kingdom's eastern borders. This variety became known as *Meconopsis grandis*. The seeds that Sherriff sent back to Britain flowered in cultivation, and not only that – they cross-fertilised with other species, producing new blue poppy hybrids. In the wilds of Bhutan, the different poppy species rarely 'meet', so natural hybrids are rare.

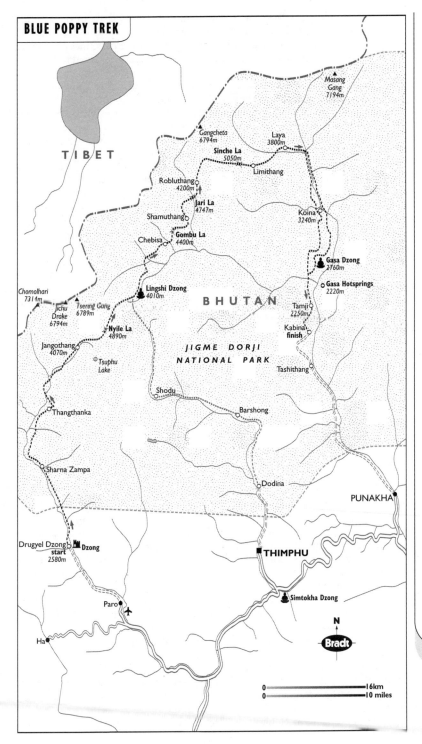

BLUE POPPY TREK

TIBET

Masang
Gang
7194m

▲ Gangcheta
6794m

Laya
3800m

Sinche La
5050m

Limithang

Robluthang
4200m

Jari La
4747m

Koina
3240m

Shamuthang

Chebisa

Gombu La
4400m

Gasa Dzong
2760m

Chomolhari
7314m

Jichu
Drake
6794m

Tsering Gang
6789m

Lingshi Dzong
4010m

BHUTAN

Gasa Hotsprings
2220m

Nyile La
4890m

JIGME DORJI
NATIONAL PARK

Tamji
2250m

Kabina
finish

Jangothang
4070m

Tsuphu
Lake

Tashithang

Thangthanka

Shodu

Barshong

Sharna Zampa

Dodina

PUNAKHA

Drugyel Dzong
start
2580m

Dzong

THIMPHU

Paro

Simtokha Dzong

Ha

N

Bradt

0 —————— 16km
0 —————— 10 miles

such at Chomolhari). Glaciers and glacial lakes are interspersed in the forested mountain zones, forming important headwaters for major rivers in Bhutan. The change in elevation results in great biodiversity within the park, including more than 320 species of birds (out of an astonishing 700-plus species listed in Bhutan). There are more than 30 mammal species found in the park, including takins, wild dogs, leopards, tigers, snow leopards, musk deer, Sambar deer and Himalayan black bears. Because tigers have been roaming higher and higher in search of prey, this is the one place in the Himalaya where two top predators may cross paths: the tiger and the snow leopard.

Normally trekkers attempt this trek in spring (March–May) or the autumn (September–October), when there are no blue poppies in sight. But if you want to lose the crowds, consider a trek in the early monsoon season, around June, to see the fabulous blue poppy – as this is the only time it flowers (May to July are the outer limits). Rhododendrons are blooming in April.

Spring in Bhutan brings out lots of other plant life – with a huge range of rhododendrons flowering in April. The Holy Grail for medicinal plant collectors is the Chinese caterpillar fungus (*cordyceps sinensis*), which is a kind of worm that is taken over and killed by a fungus, and is found in surface soil at high altitudes in the early monsoon. Chinese caterpillar fungus is eagerly sought after by Bhutanese nomads and farmers in the high country as a good source of extra income. Its therapeutic values are highly prized in traditional medicine cures in Tibet and China – a general energy booster that is reputed to possess aphrodisiac and anti-ageing properties. Bands of smugglers make frequent cross-border sorties from Tibet into Bhutan intent on poaching this unusual fungus.

There are downsides to trekking in the monsoon season. Snowcaps can be obscured by cloud, and trails can be slippery. At lower elevations, the biting bugs are fierce. But altitude is your friend here: once you get above 3,000m, the bugs will disappear. Leeches are encountered on this trek in the monsoon, but only at the end of the trek, descending from Gaza. There's nothing like leeches nipping at your heels to speed things up on the home run.

Days 1–4 Trek from Drukyel Dzong to Jangothang (Chomolhari base camp).

Day 5 Take a day-hike up to Tshophu Lake and back. The lake is a prime area for sighting the blue poppy because of the higher elevation: blue poppies often grow in alpine scree above 4,000m. Tshophu Lake is excellent for spotting wildlife and birdlife. You might spot ruddy shelducks up this way, or blue sheep. There are trout in the lake, but fishing is not allowed.

Day 6 Jangothang to Lingshi Dzong. This leg takes about 6 hours, and involves some strenuous climbing up to Nyile La. On leaving Jangothang, there are excellent views of Jichu Drake and later Tsering Gang, and in the right season the hills are carpeted in rhododendrons. The route climbs over Nyile La (4,890m). Once over the pass, an easier walk brings you into Lingshi (4,010m), which is dominated by Lingshi Dzong – the administrative centre, although it may appear rundown. Lingshi is famed for its mountain flowers and herbs – Bhutanese collectors come here looking for medicinal herbs, too. You may be able to find blue poppies close to Lingshi Dzong. It's worthwhile dropping into Lingshi school; the staff would be keen to show you around.

Day 7 Lingshi Dzong to Chebisa. There are no passes on this leg, but some brisk uphills. It takes about 4 hours to reach Chebisa, at 3,990m.

Day 8 Chebisa to Shomuthang. Trek over Gombu La (4,400m). On the approach to this pass, it is barren and windswept; once over the pass, there is a sudden carpet of rhododendrons, and the route drops down to 3,980m through beautiful forest, with the smell of spruce, larch and hemlock in the air.

Day 9 Shomuthang to Robluthang. Trek over 4,700m Jari La, and descend to

4,200m at Robluthang. Robluthang, also known as Tsarijathang, is a pristine valley with a few nomad herders around. Takins may be sighted here, but only in monsoon season when they gather in herds to mate. You might also see musk deer. **Day 10** Robluthang to Limithang. On this leg, you crest the highest pass of the route, 5,050m Sinche La. The prayer flags at the pass are a welcome sight for weary legs. New prayer flags are continually tied on by Bhutanese to ensure safe passage. Limithang lies at 4,160m, and in this part you might glimpse Gangcheta (Great Tiger Mountain) looming on the horizon at 6,794m.

Day 11 Limithang to Laya. This sector, taking about 5 hours, passes through a sci-fi landscape of fir trees bulging with lichen. Bhutanese bridge-building skills are evident when you cross a wooden cantilever bridge. At Laya (3,800m), you reach the first village since leaving Lingshi. Laya has a large school, a hospital and even a few tiny shops. The Laya are an ethnic group with distinctive dress. Laya women wear conical bamboo hats with elaborate decoration – for what reason, it's hard to fathom, since these hats are not practical to keep sun or rain off the head. The hat appears to be associated with fertility, and since the women of Laya are the yak-herders, wearing the hat ensures the herds remain healthy.

Build in a rest day at Laya if you can – take time to explore the village, and drop into the school. And drink in the wonderful views around Laya – the last high country you will see if you are descending to Gaza.

Day 12 Laya to Koina. The route starts some steeper descents, which can place a big strain on leg muscles not used to such exercise. Along the way, you cross 3,300m Kohi La. If visibility is good, you can sight the imposing snowcap of Masang Gang. The bugs are back at Koina (3,240m), along with leeches if trekking in monsoon season.

Day 13 Koina to Gaza. An up-and-down day: there is a long ascent up over Bari La (3,900m), and a long descent on muddy trails through forests of bamboo to Gaza. Closer to Gaza, there are fabulous views of Gaza Dzong in the distance, rising out of forest. Gaza (2,760m) is not much of a town, but the *dzong* is an unusual rounded castle enclosing internal gardens – an exquisite structure that combines monastery and administrative centre. With maroon-robed monks walking around, it has a definite Shangri-La touch. How long that charm will remain is debatable, as electricity from Kabina arrives (there is also a roadway under construction from Kabina).

Day 14 Explore Gaza, and make a steep descent of several hours to the hotsprings, where there is lodging here in wooden farmhouses. After trekking for weeks and pounding your feet, a visit to Gaza hotsprings (2,220m) is a heavenly experience. You slide into piping-hot stone-laid baths, where natural sulphurous hot water is fed in. There are baths of varying temperature – some big enough to hold a dozen people. One set of baths (off-limits) is reserved for use by the royal family, who maintain a residence close by.

Days 15–17 From the hotsprings, you move down through sub-tropical terrain and bamboo thickets to a campsite at Tamji (2,250m), which lies in an amphitheatre of terraced rice fields. The next day, there's a morning hike from Tamji to Kabina. Heading into lower elevations, the flora changes dramatically to forest zones. And you may notice large marijuana plants, some towering over two metres. Marijuana grows wild in central Bhutan; farmers feed the leaves to the pigs. At Kabina, you join a road suitable for jeeps: drive from here to Punakha and tour the town. See if you can get permission to visit the *dzong*, with impressive murals of the Tibetan universe. Then head by road to Thimphu.

Some scientists theorise that the yeti may be a missing link – an undiscovered descendant of *Gigantopithecus*, a large hominid that roamed Asia about 300,000 years ago. Although talk of yetis goes back a long way in Himalayan lore, the myth was not widely known in the West until British climbers returned from expeditions to Tibet in the 1920s.

The search for the yeti intensified in the 1950s and '60s, with some strange expeditions under way – just as strange as the expedition drawn up by Belgian cartoonist Hergé in the comic *Tintin in Tibet* (1958). This yarn is about a young Chinese called Chang who is rescued from the clutches of a King Kong-sized yeti in Tibet.

In 1960, Sir Edmund Hillary, the New Zealander who conquered Everest in 1953, mounted a full-scale expedition to find the yeti. After ten months of fruitless searching, he concluded the yeti was all fabrication, compounded by superstition – and that this myth had been enthusiastically embraced by Western expeditions. What he probably meant was that mountaineers like Eric Shipton were notoriously fond of hoaxes, like planting giant footprints in the snow. Mysterious tracks in snow were located by Hillary's expedition – he concluded these were made by a Himalayan bear. A 'yeti skull' held in a Tibetan monastery turned out to be that of a goat. In 2000, another conqueror of Everest, Reinhold Messner, mounted an extensive expedition in the Himalaya and eastern Tibet. Back in the 1980s, Messner claimed to have sighted the legendary yeti while climbing at altitude: he was convinced it was an animal unknown to zoology. But Messner has also acknowledged having hallucinations at extreme altitude, a side-effect of climbing an 8,000-metre peak without oxygen. A decade later, Messner modified his claim, telling *Outside* magazine that the creature was a rare Tibetan bear that whistled and smelled of garlic. *Outside* editors later came up with their own

SNOWMAN TREK

Until the 1960s there were no roads in Bhutan: everything proceeded on the backs of horses or yaks, including postal deliveries. In the northern part of Bhutan, that is still the case – trails for bipeds or quadrupeds, but no wheeled transport. And due to snow, some parts are only accessible to pack-yaks, not to pack-horses.

Arcing right across the north of Bhutan, from Paro all the way to Jakar, is the toughest walk in the Himalaya, the Snowman Trek. The trek is rough, but the rewards are great. Here, in the remote north, the romance of the Tibetan world – the yaks, the hardy nomads, the snow, the high passes – all comes together. This is a chance to witness a nomadic lifestyle that has disappeared in other part of the Tibetan world.

This trek requires great stamina, and deep pockets due to the longer period required to complete it (at US$200 a night levied). Costs are likely to snowball (pardon the pun) if you get stranded in Lunana due to heavy snow and have to helicoptered out. Timing is critical on this route due to snowfalls in Lunana; the best season for trekking is late September to mid-October. There are several variations on the eastern side of the route for the exit. The entire trek can take between 25 and 30 days. If you build in more rest stops, it can take even longer.

Days 1–12 Paro to Laya (see Blue Poppy Trek), with a rest day in Laya.

Days 13–19 Laya to Thanza. East of Laya, the Snowman Trek begins in earnest, traversing a series of high passes in the Lunana region. Everything in Lunana is carried in by yak caravans. That means your entourage will have to shift to pack-

theory: that Old Reinhold and the yeti are one and the same creature.

The chances of encountering the elusive yeti are more successful in fiction. In his novel *Escape from Kathmandu*, Kim Stanley Robinson relates the hilarious story of the liberation of a yeti from the clutches of scientists. The rescuers dress the yeti up as a guide, with a Free Tibet T-shirt, jacket and other garb, and are heading across the lobby of a Kathmandu hotel when they encounter the entourage of former president Jimmy Carter. Somehow, Jimmy Carter ends up shaking hands with the yeti. Carter has shaken hands with millions, but as soon as he shakes hands with the yeti, he knows that something is very different. The yeti squeaks 'Namaste' in a hoarse voice, and the president smiles and moves on, but remains perplexed by that long skinny hand.

In her book *Kingdom of the Golden Dragon*, Isabelle Allende introduces yeti warriors, galvanised into action to help defeat the forces of evil. They are smelly and slimy, like animals. The code of the Golden Dragon is based on four sounds representing one of 840 ideograms of the lost language of the Yetis. This code was once written on parchment but was stolen by the Chinese when they invaded Tibet. The code is written in Sanskrit, but, when moistened with yak milk, a dictionary appears in a different colour, with each ideogram translated into the four sounds that it represents. Are you still with us? In Allende's story, the Yetis used to have a civilisation of sorts, with a language, but now are like animals and only use a few words and grunts. Yetis are particularly useful to the monk hero of Allende's story because they are bloodthirsty warriors who enjoy a good battle – once their aggression has been awakened, they lose what little reason they have.

And a final footnote in the Lost and Found department: the yeti has not been found, but a deep-sea denizen that is completely white and has long hairy claws has been discovered. It has been christened the Yeti-crab.

yaks instead of pack-horses, because horses are useless in snowy conditions. The yak drivers from Laya will go as far as Thanza. The route goes from Laya via Rodophu, Narethang, Tarina, Oche and Lhedi to Thanza, with arduous ascents over a series of high passes that eclipse 5,000m.

Days 20–28 From Thanza, the third leg of the Snowman Trek gets under way: the exit route. There is a change of pack animals here, as the Laya yak-drivers turn around and head back. The trail diverges from Thanza: there are basically two options. The shorter option from Thanza takes 6 days south via Jichu Dramo, Chukarpo and Maurothang to Nikka Chu, which lies to the west of Tongsa on the main road to Thimphu. A longer exit takes 8 days from Thanza east to Danji, Tsorim, Saram, Dur Tsachu, Tsochen and Thankao, where you join the road to Jakar in the Bumthang region.

ABOMINABLE SNOWMAN TREK

To the far east of Bhutan, past Tashigang, lies Sakteng Wildlife Sanctuary. It is also known as Migoi National Park: in the Bhutanese language, 'migoi' means yeti. Here you can indulge in the extreme sport of cryptozoology, which means chasing cryptids – creatures that are rumoured to exist, but whose presence has not yet been confirmed by science. The 650km^2 park was set up to take care of the yeti, and may not be open to trekkers. If you manage to access this region, the trailhead lies at Phongme, which is about 35km east of Tashigang. Phongme is the start and

WHEN TO GO

You may want to look at the festival calendar for Bhutan when planning. Bhutan is famed for its traditional festivals – elaborate affairs with parades, Cham sacred dances and archery contests. The archery teams trade verbal insults to try and throw the concentration required to hit the target, and the winning archers perform jigs with their hands in the air, like Morris dancers. Arrayed in their robes and Argyle socks, the archers offer further proof that the Bhutanese are descended from a lost clan of Scots.

Best seasons for trekking are autumn (September–November) or spring (March–May). For very good reasons (slippery trails and leeches), trekkers studiously avoid the June–August monsoon period. However, if you are looking for flora, May and June are the months when glorious rhododendrons and blue poppies are in bloom. Trekking is closed in the winter months of December–February due to snow, but tourism authorities are attempting to bring in winter itineraries that do not involve trekking.

LOGISTICS

Though the policy may change in future, access to Bhutan is highly restricted – visitors are allowed only in a group-tour, unless you can wrangle an invitation visa or have royal friends. Because Bhutan does not have many embassies abroad, the Bhutanese visa is usually issued on arrival (at Paro or Phuntsholing) for US$20. The currency in Bhutan is the ngultrim, but you can use Indian rupees at par with the ngultrim – they are interchangeable (US$1 = 44 rupees, or 44 ngultrims). US dollars in cash are useful too, with smaller denominations advisable for tips. For group tours, a set fee of US$170–240 a day is levied on each visitor, depending on the kind of trip and the season. A surcharge is levied for smaller groups. This may sound very high, but it includes all the bills (accommodation, food, trekking equipment, guide, staff and ground transport). All expenses, including air fare, must be paid up front by wiring money to the Bhutan tourism authorities in New York. Paperwork can take several months to complete if going through an agent outside Asia; in Kathmandu, the red tape can be completed in a week.

Agents and guides Because of all-inclusive packaged deals, hotels and food are arranged by your agent. Depending on the fees paid, the agent determines whether moderate or high-end hotels will be used. There are scores of officially sanctioned agencies, like Etho-Metho, or Shangri-La Bhutan Tours, but these tend to be large and forgetful. If you have a small group, consider going with a small operator. Recommended is Blue Poppy Tours, at: www.bluepoppybhutan.com/.

Following up *Bhutan: a Trekker's Guide*, by Bart Jordans (Cicerone, UK, 2005),

end point; you trek around a loop via Sakteng and Merak. This takes about five days to complete, including stops in villages along the way. The people of this region are Brokpas, semi-nomadic herders who have a dark complexion and wear a distinctive felt hat made of yak hair, with parts woven into extensions that act to drain off rainwater. The women wear red dresses.

Should you be privileged enough to gain entry to this park, and should you be lucky enough to sight a yeti, be aware that the abominable snowman can be exceedingly dangerous if cornered or provoked. To distract a yeti, wave this guidebook in a rapid circular motion. This should confuse the yeti sufficiently for you to make your escape. If all else fails, throw the book directly at the yeti's conical

gives great detail on 27 trekking routes with excellent maps. For a broader view, the *Footprint Guide to Bhutan* (2004), by Gyurme Dorje (a Scotsman), is good. Check www.kuenselonline.com, for *Kuensel*, the national English newsaper of Bhutan.

ROUTES

Gateway points are Paro, Phuntsholing and Thimphu. The only airport in Bhutan is at Paro, and the only airline flying into Paro is Druk Air. For airline schedules and air pricing, check www.drukair.com.bt/. The national airline, Druk Air, operates a fleet of four planes, flying on the Bangkok–Paro–Calcutta–Kathmandu–Delhi route, and occasionally from Paro to Dhaka. That means you could carry on to Kathmandu after visiting Bhutan. If you are moving on to Sikkim, however, you might want to consider an overland exit from Thimphu to Phuntsholing, where you leave Bhutan and enter India. From this point, by hired taxi, you can make the run from Phuntsholing to Darjeeling in a day, winding up through tea plantations. Another possible exit from Bhutan by road is to the eastern side through Manas into Assam.

PARO

Tucked into the hills above Paro are pleasant mid-range hotels with separate lodges. The single street downtown has some good upstairs dining spots, offering Western and Bhutanese dishes. Watch out for the chillies. Bhutanese-style dishes tend to be heavy on these: a popular one is *ema datsi* (chillies and cheese).

While the Bhutanese are trying to get their hands on television sets to find out what is happening around the world, TV is banished from the grounds of the deluxe Uma Paro, where the idea is to keep the world at bay, and cultivate the Shangri-La image. The Uma Paro (www.comohotelsandresorts.com) is a deluxe retreat, offering meditation, yoga and spa treatments in a quiet rural setting. One of the spa treatments is the Hot Stone Bath, which is the traditional Bhutanese way of soaking. This consists of a wooden box partly buried in the ground and filled with water: large stones are heated on a fire and dropped into the water to heat it. The ones at Uma Paro are, of course, deluxe models, more sauna-like. Rooms at the Uma Paro go for around US$250 a night.

The last word in luxury must be the Amankora, 17km out of Paro, run by the Aman Resorts group (www.amanresorts.com). Each of the 24 rooms has its own woodburning stove. If you have money to burn, this is the place – rooms go for over US$1,000 a night. They attract high-end clients like Hollywood stars Uma Thurman and Cameron Diaz.

forehead and scream at the top of your lungs. If a book is lost in this fashion, the present author guarantees to replace it – provided that a picture of the yeti is first sent along as proof of the encounter.

Despite the government of Bhutan employing yeti-watchers at this location and also in Bumthang and Lhuntshi, no concrete evidence of yetis has emerged. But that could well be because the Bhutanese believe the yeti has the power to render itself invisible – sort of like the Invisible Man and the Planet of the Apes rolled into one. Kunzang Choden explains more about this highly reclusive ape in his book, *Bhutanese Tales of the Yeti*. The book reveals that yetis have a rank smell, probably due to their fondness for garlic. The males stand over 2.5m tall – about the height of a polar bear rearing up. Females have long drooping breasts (no sports bras). Although the face of the yeti is nearly hairless, the rest of the body is covered in dark shaggy hair. Yetis completely avoid all contact with humans, and are said to devour yaks and sheep, which are sometimes found torn to pieces by herdsmen. A couple of special adaptations: the yeti's skull is conical, with an air cavity within that provides immunity to altitude sickness. And the yeti's huge feet are thought by some to face backwards, which would make it difficult to track.

That said, the yeti could not possibly hide all evidence of its passage, such as droppings. Different species of animals can be identified and tracked from droppings, but no-one has come up with yeti droppings. The main evidence is large footprints, left in snow or mud, and a piercing call – a mournful shriek, usually heard at night. In remote parts of the Himalaya, odd howling sounds are sometimes heard at night. Nomad parents are prone to warning their children about yetis when these sounds are heard. But it appears that the howling is simply the mating call of the snow leopard.

There are many fanciful stories told about encounters with yetis – but none based on verified facts. Despite this, Bhutanese belief in yetis is so strong that they appear on a handful of Bhutanese postage stamps, including a triangular series of five stamps, and another series that shows the legends of Bhutan.

7

Himalayan India

PRESERVING THE TEACHINGS OF BUDDHISM

Thus far, this guidebook has made little mention of connection to the driving force of Shangri-La – its harmonious spiritual community. The snowcaps may be there in Tibet and southwest China, along with the imposing monasteries, but where have all the spiritual masters gone? Answer: moved to the other side of Tibet border – into exile in India.

Arriving in India in 1959, exiled Tibetans did not fare well in the hot and humid conditions, and were susceptible to diseases and viruses not found on the Tibetan plateau. Where they could, Tibetans gravitated to mountain zones with cooler climates – to places like Manali, Mussoorie, Bir and Dehra Dun – which are all located in the mountain regions north of Delhi. There is a cluster of Tibetan settlements scattered throughout this area.

Until the mid-20th century, there was little motivation for Tibetans to leave the sanctuary of Tibet; some Buddhist masters travelled back and forth to India, and certain groups like the Sherpas migrated southward over the Himalaya. The exodus of Tibetans from their homeland really began in earnest with the escape of the Dalai Lama in 1959, who was soon followed by some 60,000 of his people. Today, Tibetan refugees continue to escape, dodging Chinese bullets and biting snowstorms to negotiate high passes when crossing from Tibet into Nepal.

In exile, the Dalai Lama has established nearly 200 monasteries, with over 15,000 monks. There are estimated to be about 140,000 Tibetan refugees living in exile, mostly in India (100,000) and Nepal (perhaps 20,000). The West has been very reluctant to accept Tibetan refugees, although occasionally the doors have opened a crack, allowing 2,000 to settle in Switzerland, 2,500 in the USA, and 700 in Canada. In pockets of the Himalaya in India and Nepal, you can see Tibetan culture in a more pristine environment, without Chinese troops and police. Traditions disrupted in Tibet, or festivals that are no longer permitted in the Tibet Autonomous Region, can be seen in places like Dharamsala. The main Tibetan exile location is India. A rough breakdown of where they live is as follows: in northwest India, about 21,000 in Himachal Pradesh, 6,500 in Uttar Pradesh, and 5,000 in Ladakh; in northeast India, an estimated 8,000; while 14,300 live in West Bengal and Sikkim. Like neighbouring countries, the Indians are not keen on large groups of Tibetans amassing, which explains scattered settlements in central India (8,000 Tibetans) and south India (30,000 Tibetans) where frontier-type settlements were hacked out of humid jungle, and the temples of Sera, Ganden, Drepung and Tashilhunpo were built anew at Mundgod, Mysore and Bylakuppe.

If you think of the spiritual community as being at the heart of Shangri-La, then India would be the place to find that heart – in Dharamsala, Dehra Dun, Musoorie, Ladakh and Sikkim. These centres are like Bodhisattva bootcamps, offering courses in meditation and Tibetan Buddhism, retreats, Tibetan language, and so on. Dharamsala offers much more – a kind of mystical smorgasbord where spiritual shoppers can choose between courses ranging from reiki to yoga to magnetic healing.

Due to Mughal (Muslim) invasion, Buddhism was snuffed out in the land of its birth, India. The cradle of Buddhism became Tibet, which for thousands of years preserved the teachings. This is no longer the case: Chinese authorities in the region of ethnic Tibet have cracked down on teachers of the dharma because of their supposed associations with sect leaders in exile. Coming full circle, Buddhism has been forced out of Tibet and has returned to the embrace of India. Apart from exiled Tibetan Buddhists, there are over six million 'New Buddhists' in India. These are Dalits, of the caste previously known as the 'untouchables'. Finding themselves severely discriminated against under Hindu tenets, the Dalits have converted to Buddhism as a faith that promises equality. The movement was started in 1956 by Dr Bhim Ambedkar, in the city of Nagpur.

Bodhgaya, in Bihar state (in north-central India, due south of Kathmandu, and 15km from the town of Gaya), is the place where the Buddha attained enlightenment under a Bodhi tree. The original Bodhi tree was destroyed, but a sapling taken from it was introduced back from Sri Lanka and this exercise was then repeated half a dozen times. The present tree is part of the grounds of Mahabodhi Temple. Bodhgaya is today a site of special significance because the Dalai Lama has conducted Kalachakra initiations there. These esoteric initiations were once highly secret and exclusive, and were only conducted in Tibet. They are said to have derived from Shambhala. In the ceremony, the initiator would harmonise inner elements of the body and mind to bring about harmony and peace in the outer world. In an attempt to counter humankind's destructive forces, the Dalai Lama has dispensed with exclusivity, conducting Kalachakra initiations around the world: up to 150,000 devotees have attended initiations in Bodhgaya.

Another Kalachakra empowerment site and Indian pilgrimage site visited by the Dalai Lama is Sarnath, 10km from Varanasi. Sarnath is the site of the Buddha's first sermon at Deer Park, 'Setting in Motion the Wheel of the Law'. Symbolising this sermon is the golden sculpture of the wheel with two deer that sits over the entrance of most temples in Tibet and is the national emblem of Tibet.

DHARAMSALA

Dharamsala is the lifeline for Tibetan culture. The Dalai Lama resides here, along with the ministers and cabinet of the government-in-exile, and the oracle of Tibet. Dharamsala is a former British hill station in Himachal Pradesh, 495km north of Delhi. India tolerates the Tibetan government-in-exile, but does not officially recognise it. India does not allow Tibetans to engage in political work, but as one exile put it, 'everything we do here is political'.

At Gangchen Kyishong are the offices of the Central Tibetan Administration, with various ministries and information centres, as well as the Tibetan Computer Resource Centre and the Library of Tibetan Works and Archives (LTWA). The LTWA acts as a repository for ancient books and manuscripts from Tibet; a team of Tibetan scholars is engaged in translation, research, and publication of books. Among other educational centres around Dharamsala is the Amnye Machen Institute, a small centre for advanced Tibetan studies. The institute also endeavours to expose Tibetans to Western literature and culture through translations. Educated Tibetans say not enough steps have been taken for ushering the Tibetan community into the modern world – by translating modern literature into the Tibetan language, for instance.

Knowledge of Tibetan medicine is continued through the Tibetan Medical and Astro Institute, the only one of its kind in the world. It dispenses herbal medicines

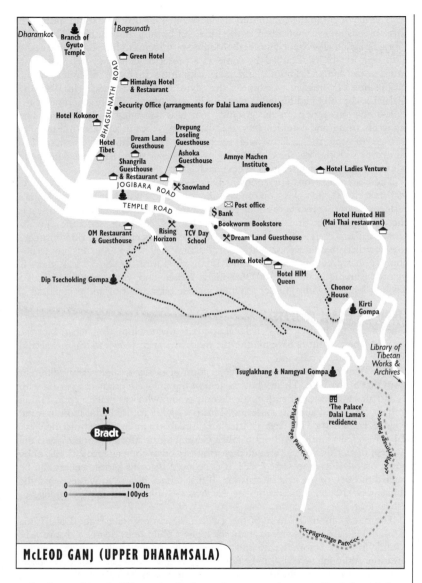

McLEOD GANJ (UPPER DHARAMSALA)

and trains students in Tibetan medical practices; research on new herbal medicines is also carried out here. The Tibetan arts have been revived through the Norbulingka Institute (for Tibetan artisans) and TIPA (Tibetan Institute of Performing Arts). The Tibetan Children's Village, mainly looking after orphans, is run by the Dalai Lama's sister, Jetsun Pema.

In Dharamsala you can see festivals celebrated in full fashion, and Tibetan Buddhist ceremonies that carry real meaning (since they're not restricted, as they are in Tibet itself). The biggest celebration is Losar (Tibetan new year, around late February), which coincides with Monlam (Tibetan prayer festival).

The practices of Tibetan Buddhism are not always harmonious. Apart from the four main schools of Tibetan Buddhism, there are a number of offshoots or subsects. A major rift in the community developed in 1997 over a wrathful spirit with three bloodshot eyes, wreathed in the smoke of burning human flesh. Known as Dorje Shugden (Powerful Thunderbolt), this spirit seems to have originated in the 17th century: he is regarded by some as a protector deity, but by others as a murderous demon. The Dalai Lama, beginning in 1976, discouraged the propitiation of Shugden worship on the advice of the state oracle. In 1996, the Dalai Lama prohibited Shugden worship in state offices and in government-in-exile-run monasteries, on the grounds that it is damaging to Buddhism. The subject is arcane and complex: several Dalai Lamas – the 5th and 13th in particular – tried to stop the practice and teaching of Dorje Shugden worship. The controversy is ongoing: the Chinese, happy at any exile strife, have seized upon the rift to restore Shugden temples in occupied Tibet.

There are numerous attractions in Dharamsala related to Tibetan culture. As well as seeing the temples, you can visit the Tibet Museum, near the Dalai Lama's residence, offering two floors of displays. But the main attraction in Dharamsala is the teaching. To find out the Dalai Lama's teaching schedule, go to www.dalailama.com/. To find out about other teachings on Tibetan Buddhism, go to www.dharamsalanet.com (click on 'Teaching'). The LTWA runs numerous courses on aspects of Tibetan culture. If you need fresh air and a break, there is plenty of hiking in the hills of Dharamsala and beyond, with camping trips of a week or longer possible. Other activities include biking, rafting and paragliding.

FINDING A MORAL COMPASS

One of the main attractions in Dharamsala is the teaching, but what does the ancient Tibetan culture have to offer the modern world? How can this arcane and obscure culture be relevant?

The Tibetan Buddhist view and perception of reality is significantly different from that of the West. Their whole system of training is to produce a person with heightened awareness of empathy and compassion, who can make a contribution to help others and alleviate suffering. This is a highly focused education in mind science. High in the Himalaya, isolated for more than a millennium from the West, Tibet fostered a culture without parallel. Central to the Tibetan world-view is the concept of accruing merit through performing good or compassionate deeds, or by going on pilgrimage to sacred sites. It is believed that this karmic energy can be carried through to the next incarnation. If that sounds bizarre to Western ears, the concept of shopping to accumulate Air Miles would sound mighty strange to Tibetan ears.

The most famous graduate of the Tibetan monastic system is the Dalai Lama himself. He debated his way to attain the highest philosophy degree – that of *geshe* – while in Tibet, before fleeing into exile in India in 1959, following the Chinese invasion. Although he claims to be nothing more than a 'naughty monk', the Dalai Lama has become Buddhism's first global celebrity, cutting across barriers of race, religion and creed. Remarkably, for someone who has experienced the loss of his entire nation, he is famed for his offbeat sense of humour and his hearty laugh – and for reaching out to ordinary people.

Uncannily, he appears to transcend barriers without the use of language. In 1988, when he visited Mexico, security had to be arranged, but because this was a privately funded visit the budget was low. For security, a bunch of tough Mexican men were assembled – they had not a clue about the Dalai Lama, and the Mexican hosts prayed nothing too terrible would transpire. But by the second day, these tough-as-nails guards were in tears: they were fetching their mothers so the Dalai Lama could bless them, saying he was the sweetest man in the world. The Dalai Lama spoke not a word of Spanish – he communicated by pinching a guard on the cheek and using other wordless gestures. The Dalai Lama somehow radiated his warmth and good karma. His hosts were astonished; the Dalai Lama was just as interested in these guards as in the VIPs he was scheduled to meet.

In a world largely lacking peace and compassion, the Dalai Lama is a beacon in the darkness. His advocacy of a non-violent approach to resolving conflicts earned him the Nobel Peace Prize in 1989. But more than this, the Dalai Lama has become an international icon for peace, an inspiration to millions who believe in nonviolence. He promotes what he calls 'secular ethics': living so that people can achieve a certain degree of happiness and cultivate compassion through 'the warm heart'. These, he maintains, are values that should be promoted irrespective of one's religion. The 'warm heart' is one of the Dalai Lama's core convictions.

THE LOST ART OF READING FACES

Empathy, or guessing what is on another person's mind, is a critical skill for fostering a civil society in which adults are kind to one another, according to the magazine *Psychology Today*. But in truth, most of us perform very poorly at the task of 'mindsight'. Texas-based psychologist William Ickes has conducted research that suggests strangers read each other with an accuracy rate of only 20% – and while married couples may nudge that up to 35%, almost no-one ever scores higher than 60%. Psychiatrist Daniel Siegel worries that mind-reading ability is on the decline in Western culture.

And yet most facial expressions are universally understood. A study by a team of Israeli researchers in 2006 tackled a theory posed by Charles Darwin in 1872 suggesting facial expressions are innate. The Israeli research confirmed that the faces we pull – whether happy, sad, angry or disgusted – are passed from generation to generation. This study analysed the facial expressions of 21 volunteers who had been blind from birth, compared with those of their sighted relatives. Even though the blind volunteers had never seen their relatives' faces, their facial expressions conveyed in emotionally charged situations were nearly identical – a kind of facial 'signature'.

In decades of research, American psychologist Paul Ekman claims he has not found a single emotional expression that isn't universal. He has catalogued over 7,000 facial gestures with different emotional implications; he has studied tribes in New Guinea and compared their facial expressions to those of Americans and found them similar. In the process, Ekman has found ways of becoming a human lie detector by looking for very subtle changes of expression in the subject's face.

When Paul Ekman first met the Dalai Lama in 2000 in India, he marvelled at the Tibetan leader's face. Ekman was attending a conference themed around Destructive Emotions: over the next week he had plenty of opportunity to observe the Dalai Lama in person. In all his years of studying faces, he'd never seen one like the Dalai Lama's – with supple facial muscles that seemed to belong to someone in his twenties. Ekman theorised that this is because the Dalai Lama expressed himself with great precision, using his facial muscles more vigorously than anyone else Ekman had come across.

But the Dalai Lama is not only adept at expressing himself through facial expressions – he is highly skilled at reading them. Compassion is a basic tenet of Tibetan Buddhism and for compassion to happen, empathy is needed – which means in turn the skill of face-reading is vital. It is possible that advanced practitioners like the Dalai Lama can read micro-expressions betraying emotions with great precision, rather like a biometric scanning device.

The Dalai Lama believes in promoting harmony between religions, thus reducing violent conflicts due to religious intolerance. Canadian author Victor Chan draws on 11 September 2001 as an instance of missing heart: 'Basically, the way the Dalai Lama sees it, some highly educated people were able to put together a very complex set of logistics and devise a very complicated plan of a level sufficient to bring down the towers. These are highly intelligent, highly educated people, but because they do not have what he calls a warm heart, they are using this knowledge, this capability, in a very destructive way. That's why it's important to parallel education of the mind with that of the heart. The Dalai Lama thinks that in some ways we would all be better people and the world would be a better place if we have this kind of parallel component in which we can somehow develop a heightened degree of compassion toward our fellow human beings, to instill in people a stronger sense of moral values, and a sense of doing the right thing.'

In his book, *The Universe in a Single Atom* (2005), the Dalai Lama talks about a moral compass. 'Today's challenges are so great – and the dangers of misuse so global, entailing a potential catastrophe for all humankind – that I feel we need a moral compass we can use collectively without getting bogged down in doctrinal differences... How can we find this moral compass? We must begin by putting faith in the basic goodness of human nature, and we need to anchor this faith in some fundamental and universal ethical principles. These include a recognition of the preciousness of life, an understanding of the need for balance in nature and the employment of this need as a gauge for the direction of our thought and action, and – above all – the need to ensure that we hold compassion as the key motivation for all our endeavors...'

In October 2007, when receiving the Congressional Gold Medal, the highest civilian award given by US Congress, the Dalai Lama said: '... my formal education in Buddhist thought exposed me to concepts such as interdependence and the human potential for infinite compassion. It is these that gave me a profound recognition of the importance of universal responsibility, nonviolence, and inter-religious understanding. Today, it is conviction in these values that gives me the powerful motivation to promote basic human values. Even in my own struggle for the rights and greater freedom of the Tibetan people, these values continue to guide my commitment to pursuing the nonviolent path.'

In his book *Re-enchantment: Tibetan Buddhism Comes to the West*, author Tom Paine settles on a startling facet of the faith: 'Tibetan Buddhism won its place late in the modern world by becoming the first religion that apparently can, when necessary, dispense with religion. The distinction between religion and spirituality sounds rather flaky, or New Age, but the Dalai Lama subscribes to it. Religion involves creeds of salvation, and ramifies into dogma and ritual; those, he says, anyone can forgo. Spirituality, or what he calls "qualities of the human spirit" – eg: patience, tolerance, contentment, loving-kindness – are, however, everybody's business, monk and atheist alike.'

Does Tibetan Buddhism hold solutions for bringing about peace and harmony, and fostering compassion? In the 1980s, the Dalai Lama initiated an ongoing dialogue with Western scientists, meeting with them mostly in India every year, and thus catalysing an interest in Buddhist philosophy. He once said that while Western science pursued the physical world (such as in its quest for outer space), Tibetan Buddhism has turned inward, in a quest to understand the workings of the mind (inner space).

Western scientists have long been leery of anything to do with mysticism, but over the past decade some scientists have taken an interest in Tibetan Buddhist practices. Neuroscientists at a handful of US universities have used sophisticated brain-imaging techniques to track activity such as blood flow in the brains of

Tibetan Buddhism is the only form of Buddhism to employ oracles, possibly a throwback to Bon shamanism. In Dharamsala, down the hill from the Dalai Lama's residence, is Nechung, the temple of the state oracle. It was on the cryptic advice of the state oracle that the Dalai Lama left the Potala in 1959 and fled to India. The state oracle wisely fled at the same time, but later died in exile. He was replaced, and about 70 monks study the sacred rituals surrounding the oracle at Nechung.

The Dalai Lama consults three or four oracles, one a woman. Like the ancient Greek oracle at Delphi, these mediums speak in riddles, giving advice and rendering prophecies. While the oracle trance-dances, thrashing his sword above his head, the Dalai Lama and members of his cabinet pose questions. The answers are delivered in high-pitched Tibetan, often in poetic stanzas. The oracle acts as a medium to convey messages to the Dalai Lama from Dorje Drakten, a protector-deity: these messages are used in important decision-making.

Ceremonies where the oracle goes into a trance are secret and few Westerners have ever glimpsed them. The oracle is dressed in a traditional brocade costume and a heavy headdress of precious metals. The ceremonial headdress is thought to weigh 20kg: normally it is too heavy to be worn without support. However, when in a trance, the oracle's strength increases considerably, and attendants quickly strap on the headdress. During the trance, the oracle is said to dance around as if the headdress were made of feathers.

accomplished meditation masters. Research suggests that meditation practices re-orientate the brain from a stress-induced mode to one of acceptance, a shift that increases contentment and calmness. The potential applications for this are wide-ranging: meditation practices have been effectively used by NBA (National Basketball Association) teams to improve concentration and as a stress antidote by those with attention-deficit disorder.

The Dalai Lama is revered by Tibetans as an emanation of Avalokiteshvara, the universal bodhisattva of compassion. To many others, he is a source of great inspiration. He is a superstar without the trappings of stardom: he doesn't care if he stays in a five-star hotel or a tent. He teaches that wealth isn't on the exterior of the self; it is in the interior. He himself may well be the greatest living example of those teachings. And the Dalai Lama's concept of educating the heart may prove to be one of his greatest legacies.

LAHAUL, SPITI AND KINNAUR

The little-visited valleys of Lahaul and Spiti, accessed from Manali, are very Tibetan in character. No special permits are needed to enter Lahaul, but inner line permits are required for parts of Spiti (obtainable in places like Simla). Lahaul is reached over the 3,980m Rohtang Pass, while access to Spiti is via the 4,550m Kunzum La pass. Long ago, both Lahaul and Spiti were ruled by the Kingdom of Guge in far-west Tibet. This is reflected in the now-rare Kashmiri style of artwork found at Tabo Gompa in Spiti, which is similar to that of Tsaparang (Guge kingdom) in west Tibet. Tabo Gompa houses one of the Tibetan world's finest collections of Buddhist art, with seven chapels bearing frescoes and a number of Guge-style *chortens*. May to June is the best time to visit these areas. Getting around is possible by bus, hired taxi or trekking. You might consider a jeep safari – hiring a Landcruiser for the journey, splitting the cost with several others.

For skiers, the major problem with the Himalaya is that there are very few ski-lifts around. Enter a Tibetan called Peter Dorje, who hails from the Indian hill resort of Manali. Pete came up with what is possibly the wackiest extreme sport in the world: yak skiing. I have no idea if the operation is still running, but it has great potential for other parts of the Himalaya, where yaks are generally found in abundance but ski-lifts are rare. Pete takes a small group of skiers – and a herd of yaks – on a hike above Manali, with an overnight camp. The following morning, Pete heads up further on the snowbound slopes with his yaks, trailing a rope behind him. When he reaches the top of a slope, he ties a large pulley to a tree, and threads the rope through it and onto a burly yak. Meanwhile, down at the base of the hill, the skier puts on skis and prepares for the 'lift'. The skier has been given one other essential piece of equipment: a bucket of pony nuts (feed composed of oats and barley). The skier shakes the bucket of nuts and quickly puts it down; the behemoth charges down the mountain in search of the food, pulling the skier up like a rocket. It works like a charm – except if the skier shakes the bucket too soon, or forgets to put it down fast enough.

Southeast of Spiti is the Kinnaur region, where local people wear green felt hats. Like Lahaul and Spiti, Kinnaur was once part of the Guge kingdom. The main focus of pilgrims to Kinnaur is the sacred mountain of Kinnaur Kailash (6,050m), which Hindus set out to circle clockwise. It is thought that Shiva comes from Mount Kailash in west Tibet to winter at Kinnaur Kailash – and to smoke hashish. Kinnaur can be accessed from Simla; there is also a route leading from Kinnaur to Spiti.

LADAKH AND ZANSKAR

The kingdoms of Ladakh and Zanskar (northwest India) originally splintered from west Tibet. Tibetans settled in Ladakh between AD500 and 600. Upon the death of the king of Ngari (western Tibet) around AD930, his kingdom was split between his three sons, one taking Guge and Burang, another Ladakh, and the third Zanskar and Spiti. The kingdoms of Ladakh and Zanskar changed hands numerous times. The most famous king of Ladakh, Senge Namgyal (1616–42), overran the kingdom of Guge in west Tibet, and even threatened central Tibet. By the end of the 17th century, Ladakh's power was in decline, leaving it vulnerable to Muslim incursions.

Due to its strategic location, Leh (the capital of Ladakh) once hosted a busy trading bazaar, attracting caravans from Kashgar, Khotan, Yarkand, Lhasa and Rawalpindi. With India's independence in 1947, Ladakh was absorbed into the Indian state of Jammu and Kashmir. Pakistan contested the borders and seized Baltistan, plus a part of Ladakh and a part of Kashmir. In 1962, the Chinese attacked Ladakh and took over the region east of Nubra, effectively ending any trade. There's now a heavy Indian military presence in Ladakh, to counter potential threats from Pakistan and China.

Dominating Leh is a derelict palace, built in the same monumental fortress style as the Potala. There are many monasteries within easy driving range of Leh; some, such as Hemis Gompa, host traditional festivals and monastic dances. Most imposing of the lamaseries is Tikse Gompa, a fantastic complex that occupies a whole hillside 17km upstream along the Indus River from Leh; the main hall houses a 15m-high seated gold image of Maitreya. Another real high point is

Distinctive Bhutanese architecture

above   Punakha Dzong in central Bhutan has structures dating to the 17th century

below   Ancient wooden covered bridge, Paro

right   Mural of Guru Rinpoche, patron deity of Bhutan

bottom   Parliament buildings in Thimphu, built in the 1960s

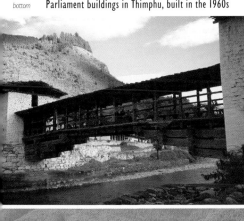

Ancient versus modern

left The kingdom's Thunder Dragon logo appears on Druk Air plane

below left Snow lions painted on taxi, Thimphu

below right Petrol station built in traditional design, Thimphu

bottom Movie theatre with traditional design, Thimphu

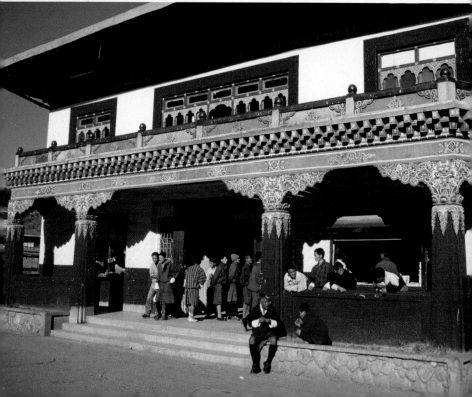

above left Bhutanese monk in burgundy robes

above right Woman in kira and bamboo hat, Trongsa region

below The biggest book in the world, measuring 2m across by 1.5m high, on display in Paro

Festivals in central Bhutan

above   Audience seeks blessing of lama at festival

left   Medieval passion play, pitting good against evil

below   Masked dancers perform outside monastery

opposite page

top   A round of darts at festival venue

middle   Royal marching band, on parade in Thimphu

bottom   Man strumming a *damnyen* (Bhutanese dragon-headed lute) at festival

Scenes from rural Bhutan

above left Family in eastern Bhutan

above School in Laya, with females wearing bamboo hats connected with ancient fertility beliefs

left Bhutanese love spicy food – here, a woman dries out chillies

below Phalluses are painted on farmhouse doors to ensure fertility and to ward off evil spirits

Trekking in Jigme Dorji National Park, NW Bhutan

above   Trek escort of horses and mules

below left   Trek caravan, with lead horse designated by tufts of yak-hair dyed red

below right   The fabled blue poppy puts in an appearance at 4,000m

bottom   Valley with rhododendrons blooming, Laya

above left & right Terrain for trekking in Bhutan runs the gamut from soaring Himalayan peaks to lowland rice terracing

below The classic pyramidal peak of Jichu Drake, 6,989m, NW Bhutan

above The Dalai Lama at an emotional audience for Tibetans, Dharamsala

below Monks attending teachings by HH the Dalai Lama, Dharamsala

above left Tibetan schoolgirls in Darjeeling, a major educational centre

above right St Joseph's School, Darjeeling, where Jesuit fathers educate the sons of wealthy Tibetans and Bhutanese

below Reading room and library with Tibetan books in Dharamsala

above Chortens in upper Sikkim

right Monks at small temple in Gangtok, Sikkim

below Winter festival in Leh, Ladakh, with women weighed down by their finest jewellery

Ladakh region

above Rizong gompa, constructed on a sheer rock face

below right Buddha sculpted in granite at Mulbek

below left Beacon roadsign at hairpin bend

bottom Crossing snowbound Zoji La on foot

top	Sweeping views of Annapurna range, on trail into Mustang
above left	Hand-woven Tibetan saddle rug, with musk-deer saddle-bags
above right	Sherpa crew for trek to Mustang
below	Royal Palace in Lo Monthang

top	Reaching the summit of trekking peak, Langtang, Nepal
above left	Collecting wood for fuel has caused major deforestation in Himalayan Nepal
above right	Cliff riddled with caves, Mustang
below	Village in the Kali Gandaki Gorge, Mustang

Mountainscapes

above left Jeep on the Karakoram Highway, NW Pakistan

above right Yaks cavorting near river in Langtang region, Nepal

right The ethereal peak of Mustagh Ata reflected in lake, Karakoram Highway, far-west China

following page

Granite rock spires loom up in the Karakoram range, Pakistan, dwarfing two trekkers

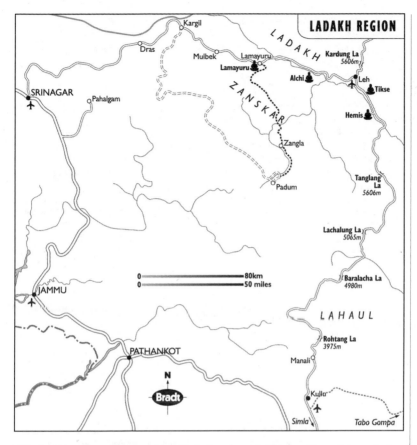

Khardung La, a pass 40km north of Leh that sits at 5,606m and lays claim to being the world's highest drivable roadway. There are excellent trekking and mountaineering opportunities in Ladakh and Zanskar – you can put your own small group together and head out with a guide and donkey to carry gear.

ZANGLA TREK

PADUM TO LAMAYURU

Of the many trekking options for Zanskar and Ladakh, this one stands out because it is challenging yet rewarding – and steeped in history and mythology. You're best off trying to organise supplies and logistics from Leh, as other towns are not well-stocked and offer limited choices. Along the route of the following trek there are lodges and tent-camps, but there's little in the way of food apart from tea-houses. You might consider the assistance of a porter or pack-horse for the journey, arranged in Padum. Getting from Leh to Kargil and Padum (the trailhead) can consume two or three days.

You've got to get your timing right for this one: the season is late June to September. In snow-blocked months, the only way in is to fly to Leh from Delhi, and flights are often overbooked or cancelled, or both. Travellers have also experienced the opposite – they've made it into remote Zanskar but then have been unable to get out due to heavy snowfall. Faced with the prospect of being trapped

In *Lost Horizon*, surveying the views from Shangri-La lamasery, Mallinson notes:

...Fine winter sports centre if it were in the right spot. I wonder if one could get any skiing on some of those slopes up yonder?'...

'I don't suppose anybody here has ever seen a ski-jump.'

'Or even an ice-hockey match,' responded Conway banteringly. 'You might try to raise some teams. What about Gentlemen vs. Lamas?'

'It would certainly teach them the game,' Miss Brinklow put in with sparkling seriousness.

And such things have come to pass, though it took 70 years to get round to the hockey match that Conway bantered about. Not Gentlemen v Lamas, but Sacred Bulls v Ladakhis. And the Ladakhi coach uses a regimen of yoga and meditation to focus his players.

In the Tibetan world, snow and ice have long been considered things to endure. The concept of snow being fun, as in winter sports, is still alien to Tibetan culture. The British Mission in Lhasa brought in some ice-skates, and Heinrich Harrer showed Tibetans how to skate, a sport referred to as 'walking on knives' by Tibetans. Tibetans are not familiar with any snow sports, even snow-shoeing, although there are a handful of ski-resorts in northern India.

In the early 1970s, in an effort to combat their most tenacious enemy – boredom and long winters – the Indian army stationed in the region of eastern Ladakh introduced ice-hockey to the village of Tangtse. The concept of chasing a small, circular object across open ground is not new to the Ladakhis. After all, this is the region where polo comes from. The transition from charging full gallop on horseback to sliding along a skating rink has come easily, especially since the turf surface of the polo grounds is frozen solid and there's precious little else to do during the long winter months. Early efforts used homemade equipment, like black army boots affixed with roughly forged blades. Venues were often frozen lakes, smoothed over with brooms made of bound grass.

Sparking the interest of the Ladakhis is a Canadian team that first came to Ladakh in 2000. The Sacred Bulls is a team made up of ex-pats who work in sweltering New Delhi, where they train at an indoor skating rink on the outskirts of the city. The middle-

in Shangri-La for six months till summer, there are two ways out: radio for an Indian helicopter airlift (expensive), or hike out along the ice on the frozen Zanskar River (slippery, and the ice is becoming unstable due to the effects of climate change).

One of the first Western travellers to penetrate the region of Zanskar was Alexander Csoma de Koros, an eccentric Hungarian scholar who set off from his native Transylvania to solve the mystery of the origins of the Magyar people, thought to be of Mongolian stock. He was constantly thwarted in this endeavour, but found a treasure trove of quite a different sort. Csoma de Koros was a gifted linguist who mastered over a dozen languages. He was arguably the first Western scholar to study and translate sacred Tibetan texts, making them accessible to astounded Europeans, who had overlooked this corner of the world. He spent 1823 to 1824 absorbing Tibetan Buddhist texts at the monastery-fortress of Zangla, subsisting through the freezing winter on little more than *tsampa*. He pored over the two Tibetan canons, the *Kanjur* and the *Tenjur*, and amassed a Tibetan vocabulary of 40,000 words for his dictionary. From here, the emaciated Csoma de Koros staggered back to the refined world of British-run Simla, where he showed up wearing Hungarian national costume – baggy trousers, and a longtailed coat with a waistcoat under it. He needed to attract British patronage to continue his

aged Canadians dazzled the fledgling amateur hockey teams in the Himalayan region of Ladakh with their superior stick handling and strategising skills in a tournament. Chewang Motup Goba, a Ladakhi adventure tour operator (who became the first sponsor to provide equipment for a local team), says: 'This was the first time we had seen how hockey was meant to be played...from stick handling to team strategising, it was a real eye-opener!' The face-off between the Canadian ex-pats and the Ladakhis has become an annual event. The ageing Canadian players have more experience than their Ladakhi counterparts, but the Ladakhis have the altitude edge – they don't huff and puff due to the thin air.

In the winter of 2003, Pat and Baiba Morrow, on location to make a documentary film in Ladakh, mentioned the Ladakhi infatuation with hockey to a friend. The friend suggested they contact the NHL Players' Association Goals and Dreams Program in Toronto, which actively distributes equipment to underprivileged kids both at home and abroad. Within the space of about 10 emails, and one application form later, a shipment of 50 sets of hockey gear was winging its way to New Delhi.

Tashi Rigdzin, president of the 31-member volunteer organisation, the Ladakh Winter Sports Club, was ecstatic. 'The 50 sets sent to us by the NHLPA were placed in a central pool and shared by around 175 kids ranging in age from 6 to 12. He went on,'Our goal is to provide some level of skating equipment and instruction to as many Ladakhi villages as possible. Because the Indian government is understandably largely unaware of the potential of winter ice sports, we Ladakhis need to provide for ourselves in this matter.' That includes Ladakhi women's teams, which compete against each other.

The Canadians call it 'hockey diplomacy': the potential is tremendous for hockey to make important social and cross-cultural inroads into this friendly Tibetan Buddhist enclave. With its many natural ice surfaces – frozen ponds and river ice surfaces – and guaranteed cold weather, Ladakh is ideally suited to adopting Canada's favourite winter pastime. Hockey has reached new heights. At 3,484m, the frozen pond used for all official hockey games at the heart of Leh is the highest altitude in the world where ice hockey is regularly played.

studies. He returned to Zanskar to grapple again with the puzzle of Tibetan Buddhism in the winter of 1825, staying at Phuktal monastery to the east of Padum.

And what on earth has all this got to do with Shangri-La, you might ask? Well, quite a lot, actually. It is highly likely that in Zangla, while poring over the Tibetan canons, Csoma de Koros came across references to the kingdom of Shambhala as part of the Kalachakra teachings. He published his findings about Shambhala in 1833 – the first reference in English to this mythical land. As Shambhala is the probable source of Hilton's Shangri-La, then Zangla would have been the starting point for that mythic shift.

At the time of Csoma de Koros's visit, Ladakh and Zanskar were governed by royal lineages. Although royalty has largely disappeared from Ladakh, the king of Zangla still controls one castle and five villages – which you'll see on the following trek. The trek can be completed in ten days, but you might want to build in a few rest days to stop and soak up the scenery and local ambience. Most of the route is above 4,000m, so you need to acclimatise for a few days in either Leh (3,484m) or Padum (3,650m) before setting out.

A road is being forged toward Zangla from Padum, so you may be able to shorten the first part of this trek. If coming from Kargil, you can go direct by road to Karsha and set out from there. Karsha (3,600m) has a fine monastery dating from the 15th century. This Geluk gompa is arrayed down a rocky mountain slope: it is the largest monastery in Zanskar, with around 200 monks.

Day 1 Karsha to Pishu, 5 hours. There is a gradual ascent to the village of Rinam (3,350m), and then on to Pishu (3,470m). After setting up camp in Pishu, you can cross the hanging bridge of Zangla – the biggest in Zanskar – to visit Zangla gompa, famed for its *tankas* (religious paintings). The ruined fortress of Zangla is where Csoma de Koros spent 16 months decoding Tibetan texts with the abbot, living in a tiny unheated cell. The largest mansion in Zangla belongs to the king, who has a nominal role. The tiny kingdom of Zangla encompasses the villages of Hanumil, Pishu, Pidmu, Chazar and Honia.

Day 2 Pishu to Hanumil, 5 hours. The trail is fairly level and follows the Zanskar River to Hanumil (3,380m).

Day 3 Hanumil to Snertse, 5 hours. A steady uphill to Purfi La (3,850m), and then steep ups and downs for the climb for Snertse (3,850m), which is a shepherd settlement.

Day 4 Snertse to Lingshet, 6 hours. Gradual ascent over Hanuman La (4,650m) and steep descent to Lingshet gompa.

Day 5 Lingshet to Senge-La base, 6 hours. Gradual ascent to Netuke La (4,280m), another climb to Khyupa La (4,300m), and gradual ascent to the base of Senge-La.

Day 6 Senge-La to Photoksar, 6 hours. Over the Senge-La (5,050m), with a gradual descent to Photoksar (4,200m), a splendid village at the base of big mountain walls.

Day 7 Photoksar to Hanupatta, 6 hours. Gradual ascent to Sisir La (4,850m). There are brilliant views of the Zanskar range along this stretch, ending in a gradual descent to Hanupatta.

Day 8 Hanupatta to Wangla, 5 hours. Gradual descent to the small village of Wangla at 3,250m. The village is a quiet oasis with beautiful poplars, walnut and apricot trees.

Day 9 Wangla to Lamayuru, 4 hours. Via Prinkiti La (3,650m), down through lusher growth to Lamayuru (3,430m).

Lamayuru Gompa has a fantastic setting overlooking a deep valley with village and barley fields. Ladakh is called 'Land of the Broken Moon' and in this region you can see exactly why – it resembles a moonscape. Valley of the Blue Moon? Lamayuru Gompa is an impossible structure fused to a rocky outcrop, with dark, brooding hills behind it. It seems to have come off the pages of a book about mythical places; even in its advanced state of decay, it exudes an air of splendour. The monastery, dating from the 10th century, is one of the oldest in Ladakh. It is well worth spending a day or so in this valley, visiting the gompa and walking around. You might be able to stay in the monastery itself in an attached guesthouse. There are several guesthouses in the village below; one of them is called Hotel Shangri-La. Lamayuru is right on the main Srinagar–Leh road: it takes about six hours to reach Leh from Lamayuru. An alternative is to head westward for Srinagar.

SIKKIM

Darjeeling and Kalimpong in northeast India were once controlled by Sikkim, but in the 18th century Kalimpong was lost to the Bhutanese while Darjeeling fell to the Nepalese. Eventually, the lands fell into the hands of the British East India Company, which developed the region as a tea-growing centre. Darjeeling is a former British hill station – a cool place at 2,100m, and the base for trekking in the area. From Darjeeling there are views of Kangchenjunga, at 8,595m the third highest peak in the world. There are several Tibetan monasteries around

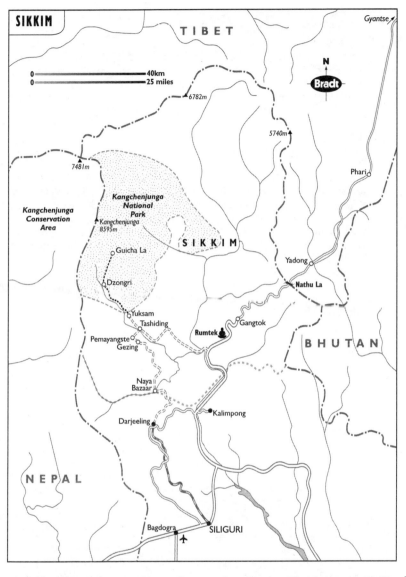

Darjeeling. Great places to visit are the zoo – featuring rare Himalayan animals like the red panda and the snow leopard – and the HMA (Himalayan Mountaineering Institute), which was run by Tenzing Norgay until his death in 1986, and now houses a climbing museum and climbers' training centre. Apart from being a resort, Darjeeling is a major educational centre, attracting the children of wealthy Sikkimese and Bhutanese.

From Darjeeling you can take a bus, jeep or taxi to Kalimpong. Kalimpong is a pleasant trading town – famed for its cheese – with several Tibetan monasteries. The town attracts Indian tourism. In the days of the British Raj, the main wool-trade route to Lhasa was via Kalimpong and Sikkim through Yadong to Gyantse. This route was closed in 1962 as a result of border clashes between China and

WHEN TO GO

The best months to visit northern India are March to end of June (with spring flowers in bloom April–May) and October–November (post-monsoon). Watch out for the monsoon season (July to mid-September). Winters (December through February) are cold in Himalayan India, with occasional snowfalls. However, February is when Losar (Tibetan New Year) is celebrated in Dharamsala.

LOGISTICS

If planning to visit India plus Nepal or Tibet, it would be wise to get a multiple-entry Indian visa, valid for three months or longer. Currency is the Indian rupee (US$1 = 44 rupees).

Agents/guides To arrange treks and onward transport, you can generally find local agencies and guides in key regional towns like Dharamsala, Leh or Gangtok. You can consult a number of travel agent links by going to www.kotan.org/Tibet/ (click on Tibetan Cultural Region Directory, then click on Indian Himalayas). Websites like www.dharamsalanet.com give links to travel agents in the region. A good smaller agent is Himalaya Fun and Tours, based in the Annex Hotel in McLeod Ganj, tel. 221-002, email: info@himalayafundandtours.com; www.himalayafunandtours.com/.

Following up The guidebook *Mapping the Tibetan World* is good for detailed maps. A lot of information on India, including Delhi, Himachal Pradesh, Sikkim and Ladakh is posted at www.roughguides.com/. For more on the Dalai Lama, go to his splendid home page: www.dalailama.com/.

ROUTES

There are regular flights from Delhi to Leh and from Calcutta to Bagdogra (closer to Darjeeling). Otherwise, travel is mostly overland. You can reach Leh by road from Manali. You can take regular buses or hire transport for the run from Delhi to Dharamsala, or from Darjeeling up to Gangtok.

DHARAMSALA

Dharamsala is divided into two very different parts: Kotwali Bazaar and lower Dharamsala, and McLeod Ganj in upper Dharamsala. The centre of activity for the Tibetan exile community is McLeod Ganj, set in forested mountain slopes. You can reach McLeod Ganj by day or overnight bus from Delhi, taking about 12–15 hours for the 495km drive. The closest railway station is Pathankot.

Basics

A slew of mini-guides to Dharamsala appear on www.dharamsalanet.com (click on 'Travel'). McLeod Ganj is a laid-back town of perhaps 7,000, with lots of small restaurants and cafés where travellers hang out. During peak tourist seasons (February and August), the tiny town of McLeod Ganj gets so crowded that it's difficult to find a room in a hotel or guesthouse. People find the place so relaxing they just stay on after the teachings; there's a very real danger of lingering over apple pie or chocolate cake in the cafés of McLeod Ganj and completely losing track of time.

There are some great budget hotels with views over the valleys below. Right where you arrive at the bus stand is the Shangrila Guesthouse and Restaurant – but while the restaurant is good, the guesthouse is noisy. A better choice is to the other side of the square – the Om Guesthouse, which is much quieter. Further along to the east is the Annex Hotel. If you have the funds to splurge, try Chonor House – this hotel has special Tibetan décor in themed rooms like the Wild Animal Suite and the Nomad Suite. It is located near the Dalai Lama's residence.

LADAKH

No special permits are required to visit Ladakh – an Indian visa suffices. However, certain areas may be out of bounds to tourists. There are two roads to Leh: from Srinagar in Kashmir, and from Manali in Kullu. Both routes are dramatic for scenery. A round-trip loop might be to travel by road from Manali to Leh, visit this area, proceed overland to Padum, complete the trek to Lamayuru, and then exit to Srinagar. The 475km Manali–Leh route goes over the 5,330m Tanglang La, one of the highest road crossings in the world. The Manali–Leh and Srinagar–Leh roads are generally open from July to October.

SIKKIM

Getting to Sikkim proceeds in stages: first to Darjeeling, on to Kalimpong and Gangtok, and then into Sikkim proper. Darjeeling is open without permit.

Darjeeling has several 'layers': most travellers ignore the burgeoning industrial town at the lower end and head for the high ground where the resort end of things is located. If you go right to the top here, there are fine guesthouses with direct views of Kangchenjunga. Relics of British days, like Glenary's Bakery and Café, have great views of the peak, too.

You can obtain a two-week permit for Sikkim in either Darjeeling or Siliguri, and an extension of two more weeks should be possible (longer permits for Sikkim may require booking a trek with an agency in advance). Half of the thrill is getting there: the 'toy train' – a narrow-gauge railway completed in 1881 – winds up from Siliguri for the 80km to Darjeeling, passing tea plantations and misty mountains. The closest airport to Darjeeling and Kalimpong is Bagdogra.

Kalimpong can be visited on the way to or from Gangtok. It's a low-key hill station that is much less touristy than Darjeeling and, for that reason, more attractive. The Himalayan Hotel in Darjeeling is the place where Heinrich Harrer started writing his book, *Seven Years in Tibet*, after he departed Tibet in 1950 (see pages 92–3). He might have got the idea for the title from a book on the shelves: *Twenty Years in Tibet*, by David Macdonald, who was the British Trade Agent in Tibet in the early 20th century. The hotel is still run by the Macdonald family; the ambience here is excellent, with a beautiful enclosed garden. On the walls are pictures of those who have passed through over the years, including Alexandra David-Neel.

Gangtok (1,675m), the once-charming capital of Sikkim, has been overrun by commercialism and poor town planning, with trucks and traffic screaming through the lower parts and ugly electrical wiring overhead. To find refuge from this circus, you need to scout out a hotel on higher ground – up toward the former palace.

Longer overland routes to consider: you can travel from Darjeeling via the border town of Kakarbhitta to Kathmandu, Nepal. If the border from Tibet is open to foreigners, you might also be able to cross from Tibet via Nathu La into Gangtok.

India, but was re-opened to cross-border trade in 2006. It has great potential as an overland tour route from Sikkim to Tibet, via Nathu La pass.

Sikkim used to be a Tibetan kingdom – a kind of vassal state. Later, it was run by the rajas of Sikkim. In 1975, it was annexed by India (China also claims the whole of Sikkim). The story of the demise of Sikkim has all the elements of a fairytale – with a bad ending. In Darjeeling in 1959 the crown prince of Sikkim, Palden Thondup Namgyal, met Hope Cooke, an American on a study trip in India. He married her in 1963 at a ceremony at Gangtok Monastery. Two years later he became king and she was given the title of queen. The American press seized on this to romanticise the place as a real-life Shangri-La. But behind the scenes, things were not idyllic at all. The match did not sit well with the people of Sikkim. Hope Cooke remained distant; she never converted to Buddhism and she made frequent trips to Europe and America with the couple's two children.

In 1973 there was a wave of unrest in Sikkim, and Indian troops took advantage of the situation to place the royal family under house arrest. Hope Cooke eventually left the king, returned to New York with her children, and filed for divorce. In 1975, the Sikkim National Congress voted to incorporate Sikkim into India. The monarchy was abolished, and Sikkim was annexed as the 22nd federal state of India. The deposed king died in 1982 in a New York cancer clinic. Hope Cooke later wrote a book about her turbulent time in Sikkim, describing it as a 'coming-of-age' epic. She comes of age, and a 330-year-old kingdom bites the dust.

Gangtok, elevation 1,500m, is the capital of Sikkim. Here you can find the former royal palace and the royal chapel (neither open to the public), and the Institute of Tibetology, with a fine collection of Buddhist literature.

About 25km from Gangtok is Rumtek Monastery, built as a replica of Tsurphu Monastery (near Lhasa) by the 16th Karmapa, the exiled head of the Kagyu sect, who fled Tibet in 1959 and died in 1981. The current incarnate in the lineage is disputed, with two rival Karmapas claiming the seat at Rumtek. One claimant, Ugyen Trinley Dorje, made a dramatic escape from Tibet from Tsurphu Monastery in 2000. He declared that he escaped Tibet to study with his lineage's exiled teachers. He has taken up residence in Dharamsala. There are ongoing battles between rival monk factions at Rumtek over the issue of who is the real Karmapa.

KANGCHENJUNGA TREK

KANGCHENJUNGA NATIONAL PARK

There are excellent treks west of Gangtok, usually arranged in small groups with guide, permits, porters and horses. The prize trek is up toward the base camp of mighty Kangchenjunga (8,595m), the third highest peak in the world, lying on the Sikkim–Nepal border. In Tibetan, Kangchenjunga means 'Five Treasures Snow' – a reference to its five distinct peaks.

The base of Kangchenjunga has been indicated in some texts as one of the *beyuls* of Padmasambhava. Among the earliest Western travellers to this region of Sikkim was Alexandra David-Neel (see page XXX), who in 1915 spent the winter in a cave in the Lhonak Valley, where a learned monk coached her in meditation techniques from his own cave nearby.

The first climbing attempt on Kangchenjunga took place in 1905, with a small Swiss party led by dissolute English mystic, Aleister Crowley. Crowley had a falling-out with the team and retired sullenly to his tent. The team plodded on without him and were hit by an avalanche; only a few survived. Crowley later dallied with a Nepali girl and absconded with the expedition funds. The first ascent of Kangchenjunga was made in 1955 by Joe Brown and George Band in a British team of climbers.

The best times to trek to Kangchenjunga base camp area are April–May and October–November. June–September is the monsoon season. The spring (April–May) is best because of the carpet of rhododendrons. You need about a week for this trek, which uses the village of Yuksam (1,760m) as its start and end point. Yuksam is about a six-hour drive from Gangtok, if the transport is in decent shape.

Day 1 Yuksam to Bakhim, 6 hours. A steady hike, ascending through pine and oak forests to Bakhim (2,750m).

Day 2 Bakhim to Pethang, 5 hours. This day passes through rhododendron forests up to a campsite at Pethang (3,650m).

Day 3 Pethang to Dzongri, 3 hours. A steep ascent with breathtaking mountain views and glimpses of Kangchenjunga. At Dzongri (4,020m) is a grazing ground for yaks. A sidetrip from Dzongri leads to Rathong Valley, with stunning views of glaciers.

Day 4 Dzongri to Samiti Lake, 6 hours. Brisk uphill and down dale leads past Thansing (3,930m) to Samiti Lake (4,200m).

Day 5 Samiti Lake to Guicha La (4,950m), 4 hours. A set of prayer flags at the pass marks the ultimate viewpoint for Kangchenjunga, with sweeping views of the titan, assuming clear weather. This is the furthest point you can reach with present permits. Backtrack to Thansing (another march of 4 hours).

Day 6 Thansing to Tsoska, 7 hours. Heading down will be faster, but can be troublesome for the knees.

Day 7 Tsoska to Yuksam, 6 hours. The end of the trail. You can stay overnight in Yuksam, or carry on the same day by road to Gangtok. An alternative is to start heading south through the old Sikkimese towns of Tashiding, Pemayangste and Gezing to Naya Bazaar, and then onward to Darjeeling.

8

Wild Cards

THE LOST KINGDOMS OF NEPAL AND PAKISTAN – FROM ANNAPURNA TO RAKAPOSHI

The list of lost kingdoms and hidden valleys in High Asia with Shangri-La potential is a long one, but a number are exceedingly difficult to get to – and thus not described here. One instance is Afghanistan: due to war and instability, getting around Afghanistan would be a foolhardy venture, although you can make it close to the Wakhan corridor in the Pamirs (see the end of this chapter).

Way out there in Outer Mongolia is the Altai Shan range, where large snowcaps loom, and where Tibetan Buddhism is the main faith. Mongolia and Tibet have a long association. In the 13th century, at the court of Kublai Khan, a great contest with shamans, sorcerers and priests took place, to see which philosophy had the greatest power – Islam, Nestorian Christianity, Confucianism, Taoism or Tibetan Buddhism. The latter prevailed, and took hold in Mongolia under Altan Khan in the 16th century. Over the centuries, monks and scholars from Tibet and Mongolia engaged in exchange visits. Despite strong Chinese protests, the Dalai Lama has visited Mongolia a number of times since 1990, drawing huge crowds. He has established teachings there through his own monks, reviving Tibetan Buddhism after severe repression under the former Soviet regime.

Mongolia is believed by many Tibetans to be the location of Shambhala – or is that Xanadu? To the north of Mongolia, even more remote and tougher to get to – and even more fascinating – is the tiny republic of Tuva. Tuva's population is around 300,000 – mostly nomadic – scattered over an area of 170,000km², which is a bit larger than England. Kyzyl, the capital, hosts regular competitions of *khoomei* (throat singing). The majority of Tuvans are followers of Tibetan Buddhism mixed in with local shamanist belief.

When he went looking for Shangri-La a second time round, Hugh Conway passed through upper Burma. As it happens, Burma borders Tibet, and there is a tiny pocket on the Burmese side where ethnic Tibetans live. But getting to that part of Burma is completely off-limits, and very dangerous to boot.

Enough conjecture: moving on to some places you can get to (though by no means easily), this chapter presents some wild and wonderful valleys deep in northern Nepal and in northern Pakistan – with other-worldly landscapes and stunning mountain vistas. Among these places is the district of Shangla, which comes close to the sound of Shangri-La. Located in the North West Frontier Province of Pakistan, Shangla is, however, totally Muslim – and likely to be a battleground these days.

Nepal and Pakistan complement each other, weather-wise. Pakistan lies beyond the Himalayan rain shadow: the worst trekking season in Nepal (June–August monsoon) happens to be the best trekking season in northern Pakistan, where it's bright and sunny. Unfortunately, both regions share a reputation for highly volatile politics, which could translate into bombs going off and bullets flying. Travel to these regions could be very risky: read up on the latest news sources to determine how stable the current situation is.

NEPAL

EMERGING FROM THE SHADOWS OF WAR

Nepal experienced a royal meltdown in 2001. On 1 June, crown prince Dipendra went berserk on a shooting rampage in the royal palace in Kathmandu, committing sororicide, fratricide, matricide, patricide, regicide, deicide and, finally, suicide. This was, apparently, triggered by his parents' rejection of his choice of wife, a member of the Rana clan. Following the carnage, the throne was taken over by King Birendra's brother Gyanendra. Conspiracy theories abounded, with many Nepalese of the belief that Gyanendra had engineered the killing of his brother and family. In 2005, Gyanendra abolished parliament and assumed all powers, saying that he needed to do this to take on Maoist rebels.

But in November 2006, a peace accord was signed between the government and the rebels, with a new constitution and a new national anthem. King Gyanendra gave up his absolute rule, and returned the government to an elected parliament, with rebel leaders slated to join, and seats set aside for women. Citizenship rights have been conferred on millions of formerly disenfranchised Nepalese. The Madhesi ethnic group, which by some estimates represents up to a third of Nepal's population of 29 million, has been granted citizenship rights for the first time in the 50-year history of independent Nepal.

A decade of brutal civil war in Nepal resulted in an estimated 13,000 people killed, mostly civilians. Scores of people simply disappeared. Hopefully this has all be relegated to Nepal's dark past. In April 2008, the Maoists emerged as clear victors in elections. Shortly after, Nepal became a republic, ending 240 years of monarchy.

Nepal is a small country sitting on a border shared with an up-and-coming superpower. The Nepalese have no desire to confront the People's Liberation Army, so the Nepalese government has worked closely with the Chinese since their invasion of Tibet, and fully supports the Chinese position in Tibet. About 20,000 Tibetan exiles live in Nepal, but no politicking is allowed – Nepali officials have sworn to cooperate with the Chinese and swear they will not allow any demonstrations by Tibetans in Nepal. In fact, some demonstrations have taken place, but have been blocked by Nepali police in riot gear. The office of the representative of the Dalai Lama in Kathmandu was closed down in 2005, along with a Tibetan refugee organisation. This is directly attributable to pressure from the Chinese. The Nepalese press is blatantly pro-Chinese, muzzling voices that support the Tibetan cause. Oddly, however, Kathmandu is the best place in Asia or the Indian sub-continent to buy materials on Tibet, such as Free Tibet stickers, Free Tibet T-shirts, Tibetan flags, Dalai Lama pictures, books, magazines and tapes. It is this material that roadblock searches in Tibet are directed at if you head toward Lhasa by road from Kathmandu.

Two of Nepal's major foreign exchange earners centre around Tibetans: carpets and tourism. The flourishing Tibetan carpet industry – based in Kathmandu – was initially set up by exiled Tibetans in the early 1960s as part of a Swiss aid project to benefit Tibetan refugees in Nepal. The venture became wildly successful. Tourism in Nepal is largely connected with Tibetans: Kathmandu's most popular temples are Tibetan and the commonest trekking routes are through Sherpa or ethnic Tibetan regions.

Sherpas, a group that migrated from Tibet centuries ago, are directly involved in the tourist, trekking and mountaineering industries. They are often wealthy business people who run lodges, guide groups and so on. Sherpas speak a language similar to Tibetan – they can converse with Tibetans, but have no written language. They are followers of Tibetan Buddhism. Sherpas have been sympathetic to the Tibetan cause, and have formed a kind of 'underground' to help arriving refugees in Nepal. There are probably around 20,000 Sherpas living in Nepal, with the strongest base around the Khumbu area. Sherpas are identified by their last name 'Sherpa', as in Jangbu Sherpa or Tashi Sherpa. Other Tibetan-related groups in Nepal are the Lhobas from Mustang and the Dolpopas from Dolpo.

Nepalese tour operators are keeping their fingers crossed that peace has been restored. While not specifically targeting tourists, the Maoists have certainly scared away the tour companies; the insurgency has sunk the lucrative Nepal tourist trade. If peace ever returns, Nepal would be quickly restored to its former spot as one of the top touring attractions of Asia.

Nepal remains the most 'developed' of any of the trekking destinations in the Himalaya. Tea-house trekking is the easiest way to visit regions with Sherpa or Tibetan-related populations – places like Solo Khumbu, Langtang and Annapurna. This section focuses on the restricted regions – Mustang, Dolpo and Limi regions – which can only be accessed through self-sufficient camping trips by groups, with a liaison officer and special permits. These restricted regions have strong historical and trading links to Tibet; their remoteness and mountain splendour give them a special Shangri-La aura.

MUSTANG TREK

Mustang (pronounced 'moose-tang') is a Nepalese mispronunciation of Lo Monthang, meaning 'abundant fields' in Lhoba dialect. By sheer coincidence, the horse rules here: it is the best way of getting around the kingdom, and wealth is measured by the number of horses owned.

Mustang is a Himalayan kingdom with a real king – King Jigme Parbal Bista – who is the 24th monarch in a line stretching back to the 14th century. His wife, the queen of Mustang, is originally from Shigatse in central Tibet. This is one of the rare Tibetan-style citadels with walls still intact. If the king is around, trekkers can probably drop in for a quick audience over a cup of butter tea. Not having the time or the stamina to trek for a week, Nepalese dignitaries have been known to drop in for tea by helicopter, landing in a wheat field next door to the king's humble palace. The king himself, if he goes out to Jomosom, relies on neither of these transport options. He rides one of his horses out, escorted by a mounted bodyguard. The king breeds the best horses in Mustang; one of his horses can fetch several thousand dollars.

Incredibly, it was not until 1952 that the first Westerner set foot in Lo Monthang – a Swiss geologist and hardy hiker named Toni Hagen. He was followed by a handful of Europeans including Professor Giuseppe Tucci and Peter Aufschnaiter, but it was not until 1964 that French explorer Michel Peissel stayed in the kingdom long enough to study the culture. In his book *Mustang: A Lost Tibetan Kingdom*, Peissel described Lo Monthang as 'the mythical fortress of a lost planet; in a lunar landscape of barren crests with jagged contours'. Getting to Mustang in the early 1960s was not easy. In 1960, Khampa guerrillas, backed by the CIA, chose Mustang as a base to launch punishing raids on Chinese troops in western Tibet. They lived in caves in the high ridges of Mustang. Peissel had trouble finding caravan companions on his trip to Lo Monthang because the Nepalese feared the tall brawny Khampas, who had a reputation for being ruthless brigands. More than once Peissel found himself looking into the muzzle of a sub-machine gun. His knowledge of Tibetan helped smooth things over, and he eventually made friends

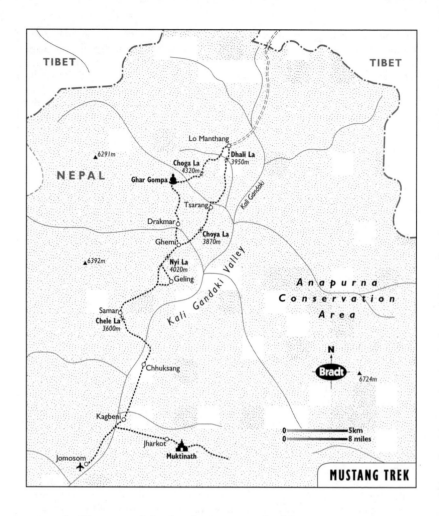

TIBET

TIBET

▲6291m

NEPAL

Lo Manthang

Dhali La
3950m

Choga La
4320m

Ghar Gompa

Tsarang

Drakmar

Choya La
3870m

Ghemi

Kali Gandaki

▲6392m

Nyi La
4020m

Geling

Kali Gandaki Valley

Anapurna
Conservation
Area

Samar

Chele La
3600m

Chhuksang

N

Bradt

▲6724m

Kagbeni

0 ━━━━━ 5km
0 ━━━━━ 8 miles

Jharkot

Muktinath

Jomosom

MUSTANG TREK

among the Khampas and developed great respect for them.

He later published a book that revealed the Tibetan guerrilla campaign, called *Cavaliers of Kham* (1972). Khampa resistance was snuffed out by Nepalese troops in a special operation in 1974. After the Dalai Lama appealed to the Khampas to lay down their arms, the Nepalese Army surrounded the last guerrillas in Mustang and ambushed them. Most were killed; the rest were thrown in jail for lengthy periods.

Because of its connection with guerrilla warfare, Mustang remained closed for tourism until 1992. There are various roads-in-progress snaking into the Mustang region that will dramatically change the traditional way of life. A road from the north, from Tibet, has passed Lo Monthang and is heading for Geling. It is still very rough. Several Chinese truck convoys enter each year, bringing in supplies of rice, kerosene and electrical goods. This is the route that the 17th Karmapa used to escape Tibet – he simply drove across the border in an SUV. The road is planned (eventually) to meet the one coming up from Jomosom. One import from China is home solar units, used by villagers for lighting in Mustang (some villages have their own micro-hydro plant to generate electricity).

Trekking to Lo Monthang

The gateway point to this region is the town of Jomosom, which is reached by air from Pokhara. You can hike into Lo Monthang, and can also arrange to go on horseback. This is usually a 10-day round-trip trek because of permit limitations (time extensions are possible but costly). The restricted zone trek starts from Kagbeni, which is reached by a two-hour march from Jomosom. Groups usually camp overnight here so they can get a good day's march when entering the Mustang region. Kagbeni (2,840m) is a medieval-looking village of adobe housing, set in an oasis of greenery. It lies at the intersection of several trails: the main one goes toward Muktinath on the Annapurna circuit. The other trail heads north for Mustang.

Day 1 Kagbeni to Chele. The trek starts out with sweeping views of the Kali Gandaki Valley – named after the goddess Kali, who can sometimes turn nasty and whip up storms. The wind has, over the millennia, sculpted the canyon walls into surreal shapes – organ-pipe cliffs, fluted pillars, rock spires. Striking bands of colour appear in the hills: blue, grey, rust and green tones. Cliffs are pockmarked with caves that were used as dwellings by early inhabitants, and much later as living quarters for meditating monks. Camp at Chele (3,100m).

Day 2 Chele to Geling. You march up a route hacked out of yellowish rock, poetically known as the Golden Staircase. This is the bizarre portal to the plateau: once you scale this obstacle, you enter the realm of Mustang. The route passes through the village of Samar and carries on to Geling (3,570m), with poplar trees and fields of barley.

Day 3 Geling to Tsarang. Along this stretch are views of ethereal snowcaps in the Annapurna range. There's an arduous crossing of Nyi La (4,020m), followed by a steep descent to the village of Ghemi. The route passes a very long mani stone wall, and traverses Choya La (3,870m) before making a descent to Tsarang (3,560m). Tsarang is the second-largest town in Mustang, with a population of around 500 souls. The town has its own hydro-plant that provides electricity. There's an imposing five-storey Sakya-style temple to the south side of town.

Day 5 Tsarang to Lo Monthang. A hike through a pebble-strewn desert terrain leads steadily up to Dhali La (3,950m). This is the classic Shangri-La entry: the pass is composed of giant boulders, between which flutter strings of prayer flags. From this vantage point, you suddenly glimpse the entire valley where Lo Monthang lies.

Days 6–8: Spend two days exploring Lo Monthang (3,840m). Lo Monthang is enclosed by lofty russet mud-brick walls – the only walled Tibetan town of the Himalaya. You can make an internal circuit of the place in half an hour: it's a maze of 200-odd houses crammed together, supporting a population of perhaps 1,000. There seem to be as many animals as people: rounding a corner, you might encounter a cow, a horse, or a herd of goats. Animals dwell on the ground floor of housing; people occupy the upper floors; the flat roofs are festooned with yak dung or brushwood – the winter fuel source. The town has only one gate, at the north. Close by is the king's palace, a fortress-style white building rising four storeys. It may be possible to arrange to have tea with the king. In its heyday, Lo Monthang was the fulcrum of a lucrative salt-trading route: Tibetans took salt and wool south to exchange for grains from India. In the 15th and 16th centuries, Mustang's prosperity was translated into lavish architecture and artwork. The town has three temples where restoration of fine frescoes has been implemented by foreign experts.

Days 8–10 Head back for Kagbeni (out of permit zone) and Jomosom. Although the return is by the same route, the campsites are different, staying at Ghemi the first night and Samar the second night. A variation is to take another route from Lo Monthang via Chogo La and Drakmar to Ghemi.

DOLPO

The regions of Mustang and Dolpo used to lie on old salt-trading routes from Tibet. Like Mustang, Dolpo has close connections with Tibet. Dolpo's mystique has less to do with James Hilton's *Lost Horizon* and more to do with Peter Matthiessen's book, *The Snow Leopard* (1979), and George Schaller's *Stones of Silence* (1980). Drawing on Schaller's research, in 1985 the Nepalese government created Shey-Phoksundo National Park to protect the habitat of the snow leopard. You might already have glimpsed the magnificent landscape of Dolpo: it is the setting for Eric Valli's film, *Himalaya*.

Dolpo was a Maoist rebel stronghold, so it may be difficult to access. You need to talk with tour agents to find out what the current situation is for trekking in this region. Not all of Dolpo is restricted – treks in south Dolpo just require a $10-a-week permit. To access north Dolpo and Shey Gompa requires the US$700-a-head special fee for 10 days, and US$70 a day after that. There are some long and arduous treks through this region, taking 18 days or longer.

LIMI VALLEY LOOP

Limi Valley, to the extreme northwest of Nepal, can only be reached on foot. It can be a destination in its own right, or can be combined with a foray across the border to Kailash in Tibet.

Some group tours fly into Simikot in far-west Nepal and trek for five days through Humla (via Muchu and Chachena) to reach the Tibetan border at Sher, where they transfer to Landcruisers to reach Darchen and begin the Kailash *kora*. A return by the same route through Humla to Simikot is possible, but an alternate trekking route leads through the Limi Valley to Simikot. However, entering Limi Valley requires the US$700 a head permit fee.

Because of the expense and logistics, not many bother going this way. The region is isolated by snow for much of the year (November–April), so traders are actually closer in touch with Tibetans from Burang. In the remote Limi Valley there are only three villages, each with a monastery founded over a millennium ago. When the Red Guards headed for Tsaparang and Toling in west Tibet in the 1960s Cultural Revolution, the monks loaded up as much of their precious artefacts and texts as they could, and brought them to Limi to safeguard them. Stored at places like Halji Gompa and Jang Gompa are illuminated texts that date from the Guge kingdom.

The people of Limi Valley are Bhotias, an ethnic subgroup with strong links to Tibet. The Bhotias of Limi are astute traders. They sell pashmina wool (high-quality cashmere from goats) to Kashmir, and they are famed for making wooden bowls from pine, birch and maple, which are highly prized in Tibet (where trees are scarce).

The route from Sher (Tibetan border) goes over Lamka Lagna pass (4,300m) to reach Limi Valley at Til. Then it continues to Halji Gompa and Jang Gompa, on to Talung, over the Nyalu Lagna pass (4,990m) and Kuki Lagna (4,900m), and finally toward Simikot (2.960m). Sher to Simikot by this trek route takes about a week.

NORTHERN PAKISTAN

CHILLING OUT IN THE HUNZA VALLEY

Of the world's 14 highest peaks (over 8,000m), five are in Pakistan, including K2 and Nanga Parbat – both mentioned in *Lost Horizon*. That's one link with the novel: the other connection is longevity. Thanks to a diet of nuts, berries and apricots, the inhabitants of the Hunza Valley in northern Pakistan are rumoured to have no cancer or obesity, and to live to well over 100. However, what the

WHEN TO GO

Go in the October–November or March–April trekking seasons. Avoid the mid-June to late September monsoon season – trails are slippery, and roads can be washed out, with frequent landslides and mudslides. Winter can close down approach routes for trekking.

LOGISTICS

One-month visas for Nepal are available on arrival at Kathmandu airport, or when coming in by road from Tibet or India. Visas are easily extended. The currency is the Nepal rupee (US$1 = 70 Nepal rupees). US dollars in cash are handy as back-up.

Agents/guides Mustang, Dolpo and Limi are restricted zones, with a quota system on the number of trekkers allowed to enter each season. You will need to join a pre-arranged group, with a liaison officer and special permit needed for these regions. The cost is US$700 per person for 10 days, and $70 a day per person after that. A reliable agent in Kathmandu is Royal Mountain Travel, tel. 9771-4215364, email: info@royalmt.com.np; www.royalmt.com.np/.

Maoist surcharges The Maoists demand a standard charge of 100 rupees a day per trekker for all trails in Nepal. This is levied as a tariff to support their cause. Checkpoints are set up at strategic junctions to collect the fees. For a group of eight trekkers going around Manaslu for 15 days, the fee levied would be 100 × 15 days × 8 pax = 12,000 rupees (the operator managed to bargain it down to 9,000 rupees, with a receipt issued). Trek leaders report that their bus has been stopped on the road by youths, school groups, women and assorted thugs demanding money – and not related to the Maoists. Payment depended on the diplomatic skills of the driver. There's a definite Wild West mentality in the highlands of Nepal.

Inspiration *The Snow Leopard* (originally published 1978) by Peter Matthiessen is a finely wrought account of a journey to Dolpo. Matthiessen also wrote the text for *East of Lo Monthang* (Shambhala Publications, 1995), a photo book featuring pictures of Mustang by Thomas Laird.

ROUTES

Most trips have a start or end point (or both) in Kathmandu, the capital, which is ideal for buying trekking equipment, as a lot is left behind by expeditions. If passing through Kathmandu, drop into the Shangri-La Hotel and proceed to the Lost Horizon Bar, where you can sip cocktails like The High Lama. The hotel is not part of the Asia-based Shangri-La luxury hotel chain, but a convincing copy, with prices to match.

Air Kathmandu is well-connected to other Asian capitals like Delhi, Bangkok, Lhasa and Thimphu. For domestic flights, why not fly Shangri-La Air? There are flights on twin-otter planes from Kathmandu to trailheads at Jomosom, Dolpa and Simikot. For schedules, consult www.shangrilaair.com.np/. Shangri-La Air also operates mountain flights from Kathmandu to see Everest and the Himalayan range close up.

Overland From the north, there is a fine overland route from Lhasa, crossing the border into Nepal at Zhangmu/Kodari. Another overland route in the far west of Nepal through Limi leads to a border crossing close to Burang (Tibet). Nepal has a number of border crossings with India, one of which leads to Sikkim.

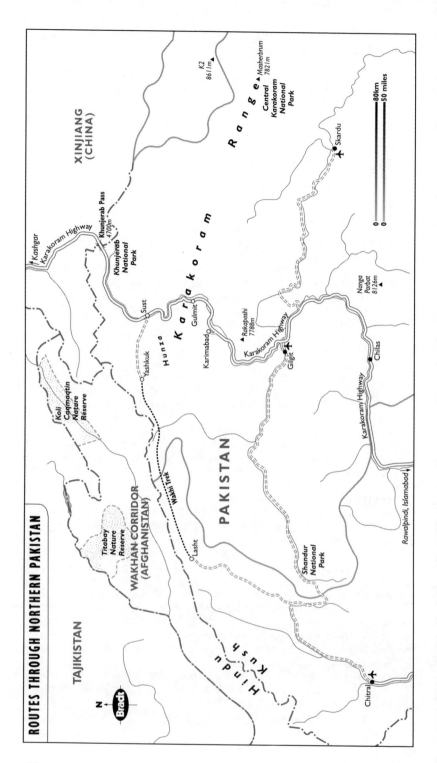

ROUTES THROUGH NORTHERN PAKISTAN

TAJIKISTAN

XINJIANG (CHINA)

Kashgar

Karakoram Highway

Khunjerab Pass 4700m

Khunjerab National Park

Koli Caqmaqtin Nature Reserve

Titabay Nature Reserve

WAKHAN CORRIDOR (AFGHANISTAN)

Wakhi Trek

Sust

Yashkuk

Lasht

Hunza

Gulmit

Karimabad

K a r a k o r a m

R a n g e

K2 8611m

Masherbrum 7821m

Central Karakoram National Park

Skardu

Rakaposhi 7788m

Karakoram Highway

Gilgit

Nanga Parbat 8126m

Chilas

Karakoram Highway

PAKISTAN

Shandur National Park

H i n d u   K u s h

Chitral

Rawalpindi, Islamabad

N

Bradt

80km

50 miles

0

0

brochures from Hunza fail to mention is that the traditional diet has changed in the last few decades. With the introduction of sugar and packaged foods, more disease comes in.

The life-extending properties of a largely vegetarian menu may keep Hunza people active into their 90s, but the brilliant mountain sun and steady glacial winds ensure that, unlike the youthful-looking population of Hilton's fictional land, they look their age. But there are no Buddhists here – they come from different Muslim groups. The people of Hunza are largely Ismailis, one of the 70-odd sects of Muslim. Ismailis are followers of the Aga Khan, an ancient lineage, with the present leader based in Paris. Languages spoken in the region include Burushaski and Wakhi, but Urdu is widely understood.

Tourism in Pakistan has suffered from its proximity to conflicts in Afghanistan. But if you go to Pakistan, you will lose the crowds and experience phenomenal hospitality. In Hunza, there is gentle yet overwhelming hospitality as people greet you, shake your hand, ask where you are from, where you are going, what you are doing, and invite you into their homes for tea. The backdrop here, the mighty Karakoram range, is totally majestic, spectacular, dramatic – choose whichever adjective you like and it will still be pathetically inadequate.

THE KARAKORAM HIGHWAY

The Karakoram Highway is a marvel of engineering that cuts between two colossal ranges – the jagged Karakoram peaks in Pakistan and the more rounded peaks of the Pamir in Xinjiang, far-west China. The road is prone to landslides, so you need to build in time for delays. With stops, you would need about two weeks or longer to cover the route. You could start in Gilgit (Pakistan) and end in Kashgar (Xinjiang, China). Some make a return trip to Kashgar (you would need a multiple-entry Pakistan visa for this). Another option for a starting point is to fly from Rawalpindi to Skardu first and then proceed northward by road via Gilgit to the 4,700m Khunjerab Pass on the Chinese border. Entering China, you pass Karakul Lake, with the snows of Mount Mustagh Ata reflected in its waters. Karakul is very close to the spelling of Karakal, the mountain backing Shangri-La.

SKARDU

Skardu is a small settlement in a rugged valley with excellent hiking: this area is known as Baltistan, or Little Tibet, due to ancient links with kingdoms in Tibet. Although Tibetan influence is long-gone, Shangri-La lingers on. About 20km from Skardu, Shangri-La Resort has set out to recreate the mythical paradise of *Lost Horizon* in detail, with Chinese-looking cottages plonked around a lake. What would Shangri-La be without a crashed plane nearby? A plane that crash-landed on a riverbed in the 1950s was hauled to the site, and turned into the DC-3 Café. You can see all this on the hotel website: www.shangrilaresorts.com.pk/. The same resort group operates another hotel, the Shangri-La Midway, near Chilas.

The road leading down from Skardu to Gilgit cuts through a deep canyon – it is a spectacular ride on winding roads. Gilgit is a busy, noisy market town – the largest in this region.

KARIMABAD

Karimabad is the heart of Hunza – at one time the seat of the Mir who ruled this region. Since 1974, the power of the Mir has been in name only. The fantastic setting of Karimabad gives it the classic outlines of…the Valley of the Blue Moon. There is a deep fertile valley of green terraced fields, with a settlement high up on a ridge, and snowcaps tucked behind. Across the valley looms the dramatic snowcap of Mount Rakaposhi. Strange but true, 15th-century Baltit Fort has strong Tibetan influence in its architecture, as the craftsmen who built it came from Baltistan.

A handful of writers have pinpointed Karimabad's awesome setting and rundown Baltit Fort as the inspiration for Shangri-La. This hobby goes back a long way: in October 1953, *National Geographic* magazine published a story entitled 'At World's End in Hunza'. The subheading for that story ran: 'This Strange Shangri-La Near the Himalayas Has Few Laws or Taxes and No Army; Bridegrooms Take Mother on the Honeymoon.' Sounds like the proverbial good news, bad news. The good news is no taxes; the bad news is the mother-in-law. In a 2001 documentary that aired on the Discovery Channel, David Adams ends up in Hunza Valley and comes to the conclusion that Baltit Fort is the inspiration for *Lost Horizon* (though Adams never actually names the fort). To spin things out, Adams zigzags all over northern Pakistan *en route*, starting out by visiting the Kalash Valley, maintaining that Alexander the Great was on the same quest – a quest for the fountain of youth.

Karimabad offers great rambles in the vicinity, or you can indulge in more ambitious hikes through to Rakaposhi base camp. Further up the line is the small village of Gulmit, which is worth a few days so you can take some hikes to nearby glacial zones.

A WAKHI TREK
Khunjerab National Park

Right up north is a weird strip of land known as the Wakhan Corridor, which is actually part of Afghanistan, and is the only place where Afghanistan borders China. Up around the meeting of Pakistan, Afghanistan and China is a superb high-altitude trek that passes very close to the Wakhan Corridor on the Pakistan side.

To reach this area, you would fly from Rawalpindi to Chitral, and proceed by jeep overland to Lasht, where the trek starts. Negotiating remote glacial valleys requires some river wading – and other times crossing a river by gondola (only one person at a time can go in the gondola). The trail passes through wilderness where the ibex and Marco Polo sheep roam. The wild sheep with the impossibly long curling horns are named after Marco Polo, of course – less well-known is the fact that nobody in Italy at the time believed Polo when he told them the length of the horns; it was thought to be just another of his great fabrications. Unfortunately, those long curling horns are what make this animal attractive to trophy hunters, who continue to come here, paying US$25,000 to shoot a wild sheep. The Marco Polo sheep may soon become a figment of the imagination: numbers have dwindled to 6,000 by rough estimates. The Wildlife Conservation Society, acting through field surveys by biologist George Schaller, is trying to create a peace park of 50,000km^2, encompassing parts of Pakistan, Afghanistan, China and Tajikistan, to protect the last remaining Marco Polo sheep habitat.

The top elevation reached on this Wakhi trek is around 5,100 metres. After a trek of around 14 days, you reach Babajundi (west of Yashkuk). Here, the trail meets a road negotiable by jeep: from this point, it's a bumpy drive into Sust.

THE LOST WHITE TRIBE

The legend of Shangri-La may be the ultimate Lost Race novel. Hero stumbles across lost race of people, hero falls in love with customs of lost race, hero decides to leave anyway, hero desperately tries to find a way back to lost race. The twist in Shangri-La is that it hosts a lost white tribe. Those in command are Europeans.

Improbable though this may sound, there are real-life parallels to this story in northwest Pakistan. Tucked into the high peaks of the Hindu Kush range, bordering Afghanistan's Nuristan province, is the region of Chitral at the northwest tip of Pakistan. Chitral is home to the Kalasha, whose exact ethnic origins are unknown. One legend has it that the Kalasha are descendents of Alexander the Great, who invaded India in the fourth century BC. Some of his soldiers are thought to have stayed behind in this part of Pakistan, which may explain some blue-eyed and blond-haired traits among the Kalasha. The heyday of the Kalasha civilisation was from 900 AD to 1320 AD, when Kalasha kings ruled over much of present-day Chitral.

The Kalasha present startling contrast to Pakistani Muslims: the Kalasha follow pagan beliefs (they are polytheistic), and their men and women mix freely – relaxed and music-loving, fond of wine and dance. In fact, they lead a lifestyle that runs completely counter to the austerities of the Taliban in Afghanistan – who attempted to wipe the Kalasha out. The Kalasha number only about 3,000 today, located in three tiny valleys in southwest Chitral. Their civilisation is on the brink of extinction – their numbers in steady decline due to intermarriage with Muslims, pressure from Islam, and pressure from encroaching roads and modern technology.

WHEN TO GO

The best time to visit Hunza is June–September.

LOGISTICS

Pakistan visas need to be obtained in advance. If heading to Kashgar, you would need a Chinese visa in advance. Currency is the Pakistan rupee (US$1 = 60 Pakistan rupees).

Agents/guides A recommended agent is Concordia Expeditions, with head office in Rawalpindi, tel. 9251-5510308; www.Concordia-expeditions.com.

ROUTES

The main gateway point is Islamabad (Rawalpindi), with many air connections. By road, there are crossings from India and from China.

GILGIT

A quiet end of town to stay is the Serena Hotel, with vistas of snowcapped peaks and tranquil gardens. The hotel restaurant has a panoramic view over the Hunza River, Gilgit River and Danyore Valley.

KARIMABAD

The Hunza Baltit Inn offers 20 rooms (around US$20 each) and commanding views over the Hunza Valley. The Inn is lower in the valley, near the Mir's Palace. Above Karimabad is Eagle's Nest Hotel, which can be reached by the owner's jeep. The hotel charges US$20 for a room with a view – of Rakaposhi by moonlight. And if you want some moonshine to go with that, Hunzakuts have a unique way of getting around Pakistan's prohibition laws: they simply brew their own. The alcoholic 'Hunza water' is fruit-based, and of variable strength. A good restaurant in Karimabad serving Hunza food is The Hidden Paradise.

GULMIT

You can stay at the Marco Polo Inn for US$15 or so for a room. Tea is served in the rose garden. The inn has a Hunza menu with items like apricot soup. Another place to stay is the Silk Road Inn.

9

In Another Dimension

Shangri-La was created out of thin air – and it lives on in fiction, comics, movies, gaming and cyberspace. So finding it in its original milieu – a fictional or virtual realm – could be the way to go. And exploring these realms will fire up dreams for the real road.

Tibetans believe in parallel dimensions and multiple universes. They suggest that the mythical realm of Shambhala can only be found in another dimension – beyond the range of common perception. How is it possible to enter another dimension like this? Tibetan lamas, including the Dalai Lama, claim this can be achieved through the practice of deep meditation. But perhaps there are alternatives. Books are portals to fantastic realms and other planes of reality. And there's the celluloid dimension, with old Tibet captured on film – intangible, yet appearing to be so real.

SHANGRI-LA LIBRARY

The fabled library of Shangri-La contained some 30,000 volumes when Conway saw it in 1931. He was astonished by what was on the shelves there – the finest literature from East and West. He was drawn to a special collection called Tibetana, devoted solely to Tibet. According to Conway, new additions were constantly made to the library, so by now there could equally be a special section devoted to Shangri-La itself at the lamasery. That would be a collection called Shangrilana: there are certainly enough Shangri-La-related books to fill an entire bookcase. Some are listed here, but this is just the tip of the iceberg – there are many more books on Tibet, and travel narrative works with titles like 'In Search of Shangri-La' or 'The Search for Shangri-La' are still going strong. Imagine you are in the great library of Shangri-La and many pleasant hours can be whiled away reading these tomes.

THE POWER OF SHANGRI-LA

In Western minds, the romance of Tibet has been created primarily by novels like *Lost Horizon*. Martin Brauen's *Dreamworld Tibet: Western Illusions* (Orchid Press, 2004) is a marvellous work of myth busting, debunking Western concepts of Tibet, particularly those linked with utopias like Shangri-La – with full-colour illustrations.

Virtual Tibet (Metropolitan Books, 2000), by Orville Schell, is subtitled: 'Searching for Shangri-La from the Himalayas to Hollywood.' The book promises insights into Western fascination with Tibet, but gets sidetracked with its focus on the making of the movie *Seven Years in Tibet*, and an obsession with tracking down Brad Pitt. When finally cornered for an interview, Brad Pitt has absolutely nothing to say about Tibet – a master of emptiness.

Prisoners of Shangri-La, by Donald Lopez (University of Chicago Press, 1998), argues that the 'Shangri-La Syndrome' – Western romanticising of Tibet – is detrimental to the cause of Tibetans in exile and their quest for independence.

The Myth of Shangri-La, by Peter Bishop (University of California Press, 1989), is a scholarly analysis of several centuries of Western travel writing about Tibet, anchored around the concept of a lost, mysterious, forbidden land.

LOST HORIZON LIVES ON

Lost Horizon Companion by John Hammond (McFarland, USA, 2008) is a guide to Hilton's novel, the plot, the characters, film adaptations, and the place of Shangri-La in popular culture. John Hammond is secretary of the James Hilton Society in the UK.

There are several sequels to *Lost Horizon*. *Return to Shangri-La* by Leslie Halliwell, published in 1987, picks up the trail half a century later – with Hugh Conway, Roberta Brinklow and Henry Barnard still at Shangri-La, though 50 years older. Halliwell locates Shangri-La in the south of Tibet, not the north, and at one point a helicopter lands at the monastery, which sounds a bit far-fetched. The three remaining Western characters show up again in *Shangri-La: The Return to the World of Lost Horizon*, published in 1996, by Eleanor Clooney and Daniel Altieri. This sequel is set in the 1960s upheaval of the Cultural Revolution, and pits cryptologist General Zhang, seeking to plunder Tibet's treasures, against Hugh Conway, the guardian of Shangri-La (which is the same as Shambhala, according to the book). Zhang has intercepted a contraband caravan with some odd cargo: phonograph records, modern flush toilets, cameras, aeroplane parts, and other high-tech equipment. He is on the trail of clues that could lead him to Shangri-La; to stop him, Conway must go to Lhasa, but he can only leave the precincts of Shangri-La for ten days at a time – to avoid growing suddenly older.

The characters Conway, Brinklow and Barnard show up in another sequel, also set in the 1960s, entitled *Messenger: A Sequel to Lost Horizon*. This work, self-published by author Frank DeMarco in 1994, follows the escapades of an American pilot in a U-2 spy plane who is forced down by engine failure in remote Tibet: the pilot finds himself the guest – and prisoner – of Shangri-La.

FICTIONAL TIBET

Hilton qualifies as the first Western writer to use Tibet as primary location for a novel. A number of authors have followed in his wake – using similar techniques by warping themes from Himalayan mythology.

Using the setting of Tibet, *The Third Eye* by T. Lobsang Rampa (London: Corgi, 1956, reprinted many times) describes the painful opening of the Third Eye – the wisdom eye, the power to see things profoundly. Lama Rampa claims he was initiated at Lhasa's Chakpori Medical College. In 1958, an English newspaper revealed this bestseller was not written by a Tibetan lama but by Cyril Henry Hoskins, the unemployed son of a plumber from Devon, England. Despite its fanciful gaffes about Tibetan culture, the book remains one of the most widely read tomes about Tibet. *The Rose of Tibet*, by Lionel Davidson (London: Gollancz, 1962), is a page-turner set in 1950 involving the beautiful abbess of Yamdring, in her 18th incarnation, a bumbling British man, sacks of emeralds, and an advancing Chinese army. Davidson made up the location Yamdring by combining Yamdrok Lake and Samding gompa, in central Tibet – which used to have a female incarnate with strange powers. *Stones of the Dalai Lama*, by Ken Mitchell (Vancouver: Douglas & McIntyre, 1993), is a piece of black humour set in the late 1980s about a tourist who pockets some *mani* stones at Lake Namtso as souvenirs. Bad karma: he finds that terrible things befall him back home, so he resolves to put the *mani* stones back where they belong. Tibet, however, is hard to get into – riots have broken out in Lhasa...

Using the setting of Nepal, *Escape from Kathmandu* (first published 1989), by Kim Stanley Robinson, is a hilarious romp through Himalayan mythology and twisted rumours, with marvellous yarns about a yeti encounter, a visit to Shambhala, and an excursion to the Tibetan side of Everest to find Mallory. *Surfing the Himalayas,* first published in 1995, is presented as a first-hand account by Frederick Lenz, who claims to discover mystical insights on his snowboarding style from Master Fwap Sam-dup, a Buddhist monk in Nepal – who looks to be around 70 and whose lineage extends back as far back as Atlantis. The master teaches him 'the metaphysics of snowboarding' – how to become one with the board. *Snowboarding to Nirvana* (1997) is a sequel, continuing on with the snowboarding spiel, but also embracing tantric sex with Nadia. Unfortunately, there was no third book to make that a trilogy because Fred Lenz committed suicide in 1998. Fierce legal battles broke out over his estate, estimated to be worth US$18 million. Apart from his bestselling books, Lenz had a cult following in the USA as a self-styled guru – and had bilked followers of large amounts of cash.

THE YOGA OF SHANGRI-LA

In Shangri-La's version of the Fountain of Youth, the High Lama lives to 250 years of age through a steady regimen of meditation, yogic breathing exercises, and partaking of precious medicinal herbs from the valley. He is somewhat addicted to the *tangatse* berry, and drinks a special scented tea. Plus lots of bracing mountain air, sauna-like temperatures in his personal quarters, and regular doses of Mozart – played by angelic 105-year-old nymphet Lo-Tsen.

But what kind of meditation and yoga can lead to such perennial youthfulness and longevity? Burning questions that we'd all be interested in hearing further about. Offering partial answers, and hinting at secrets of longevity through yoga exercises, has turned into something of a cottage industry: a Shangri-La-style yoga sub-genre. Not long after the release of the movie version of *Lost Horizon* (1937), a slim volume entitled *The Eye of Revelation* appeared. Published in 1939, the book was written by Peter Kelder, an obscure American from the mid-West – obscure because the author claimed to be an intensely private person. *The Eye of Revelation* recounts the discovery of five simple Tibetan yoga exercises taught to Kelder by a man he met in Los Angeles, a retired British army officer named Colonel Bradford (not his real name, according to Kelder, to protect his privacy). Bradford claimed to have stumbled into a Tibetan monastery in the Himalaya in the late 1920s. The location of the monastery is not specified, but is cited as some kind of hidden Shangri-La, a mysterious place without time, where the secret of the fountain of youth had been passed down over a millennium. Bradford, who was 73 when he went to the Tibetan monastery, returned to India looking 30 years younger, or such was the opinion of members of the 'Himalaya Club' in India.

How did he accomplish this amazing feat of rejuvenation? The secret, according to Kelder, is a series of five ancient Tibetan exercises, which anyone can perform in a matter of minutes. And so the legend of the Five Rites was born. But wait – there is a Sixth Rite. The Sixth Rite, according to Kelder, should only be practised by those who are willing to remain celibate for a while. Only this rite guarantees complete restoration of health and youth, he claims. There are some curious lapses in Bradford's story – he mentions his astonishment when he sees his reflection in a full-length mirror at the monastery and looks 15 years younger. But Tibetan monasteries do not have full-length mirrors, and in the 1920s such items very rarely made it over the Himalaya from India, as the only method of transport was on animal-back. Another anomaly is what happened to Bradford? After relating his story to Kelder, Bradford vanished into thin air, never to be heard from again. But no matter: Kelder's book has sold millions of copies, issued under various titles like: *The Five Rites of Rejuvenation*, or *The Five Rites*.

The Five Rites (or is that six?) are still going strong. The book was reissued in 1985 by Doubleday in the USA under the title: *Ancient Secret of the Fountain of Youth*. The tome claimed that Kelder was very much alive and well, but in the same breath declared this edition restored 'the Lost Chapter', recently discovered in the author's personal papers – which would imply that he is no longer with us. Which might also imply that Kelder forgot to follow the rejuvenation practices himself, as otherwise, logically, he would still be around. It is in the interest of publishers of these titles to have Kelder still going strong, so biographical details on the mystery author are non-existent. The same Doubleday book was modernised and expanded into two volumes with copious commentaries by other authors, published in 1998 and 1999. Strangely, there is no commentary from Kelder himself, though his publisher swears black and blue that Kelder is still going strong and still remains an intensely private person.

If Colonel Bradford's incredible story is true, then spiritual copyright has been broken – the exercises would legally belong to the monastery in Tibet that guarded its fountain of youth secrets for a millennium. However, it seems that while there is a form of Tibetan yoga (using simple stretch and warm-up exercises in monasteries, and specific breathing exercises to focus meditation), none of the movements match those in Kelder's book. And no lineage holder from Tibet supports anything to do with The Five Rites. The First Rite involves a clockwise whirling routine that is completely alien to Tibetan practices; it appears to derive from the Sufi tradition of Whirling Dervish dances.

Kelder's book is just a series of yoga poses that any Hatha yoga class could teach you, like downward dog, camel or cobra poses. Essentially, what is being marketed here is ordinary Hatha yoga re-packaged in extraordinary Shangri-La spiritual wrapping. Hatha yoga is of Indian origin, not Tibetan. In 1990, an American yoga instructor, Christopher Kilham, revamped Kelder's tome and reissued it as a very slim book under the title *The Five Tibetans* – which went on to become a bestseller too. Another yoga guru, Carolinda Witt, revamped the concept as *T5T: The Five Tibetan Exercises Rites*, published in 2005 by Penguin Australia. This has done so well that a new version is out in 2007 entitled *The 10-minute Rejuvenation Plan* (subtitled 'T5T: the Revolutionary Exercise Program that Restores your Body and Mind'). One book on sale through Amazon is entitled: *The Secret Art of Seamm-Jasani: 58 movements for Eternal Youth from Ancient Tibet*. And so the rites go on.

All of these books carry glowing testimonials vouching for how well they work and how easy it all is, and how it can be done in 20 minutes a day or less. There are testimonials that claim supercharged energy levels, better memory, improved potency, improved eyesight, hair growth, restoring full colour to grey hair. If you go to Amazon.co.uk or Amazon.com and search these titles, you will find lots of positive recommendations. But you will also find some entries from puzzled acolytes who are not so sure, like these two comments:

> I wonder where those positive reviews come from… I've practised the 5 rites for 2 years now…hardly ever skipping a day, but have not noticed any change… I don't look any younger than other people my age… How come they seem to work miracles for others but don't produce any results for me?

> To all those people who claim to look younger because of the rites, I have one thing to say: show me. Show me a before and after picture. Doesn't it explain a lot that so far all

these miracles were only described on paper? Why are there no pictures of Colonel Bradford?

The Ancient Fountain of Youth Video has yet to appear on the market. Along with the Fountain of Youth Cookbook. There is, however, *The Shangri-La Diet*, a 2006 cult book about effortless weight loss – without feeling hungry or exercising.

COMIC BOOKS

Tintin in Tibet (1958) has done wonders for yeti lore, extending the mythical beast's reputation worldwide, in many languages. This Belgian story is the only Tintin comic ever to appear in the Tibetan language. Belgian cartoonist Hergé has a lot of fun with levitating monks and bizarre customs of the Land of Snows.

Tomb Raider: Chasing Shangri-La (2002) visualises a very Chinese version of Shangri-La, with pagodas and Chinese rooftops straight out of the 15th century. Lara Croft must evade the claws of huge lion-like watchdogs to make her escape.

Bulletproof Monk (2002) embodies every single cliché about Tibet you can imagine – monks with supernatural powers, a monk over 90 who looks to be 30, Nazi treasure-seekers... In 2003, it was made into a B-grade movie of the same name, starring Yun-Fat Chow and Seann William Scott. Yun-Fat Chow plays the nameless monk who protects a sacred Tibetan scroll possessing mystical powers so great that anyone who reads the scroll would be endowed with the ability to turn the world into a paradise or a living hell. The monk is apparently not so much bulletproof as uncanny in his ability to dodge bullets. He's also trained in the ancient art of how to bring down an attacking helicopter with little more than his bare hands.

THE CELLULOID UNIVERSE

Find Shangri-La where it was originally created – in the intangible celluloid dimension, with larger-than-life celluloid deities. Advanced computer graphics make the return to hidden Shangri-La much easier for today's directors. The 2004 movie *Sky Captain and the World of Tomorrow* takes a side-trip to Shangri-La (alias Shambhala) in northern Tibet. And you can indulge in Time Travel to Old Tibet through a number of films. You might already have come across the Buddhist code of ethics in other movies. The Jedi code in *Star Wars* is based on Buddhist principles, particularly the wisdom of Yoda. In fact, on census forms in places like Australia, Star Wars fans have entered 'Jedi' as their religion.

SHANGRI-LA REDUX

After *Lost Horizon* was released in 1937, there was a 60-year gap before Hollywood tackled Tibet again as a setting for a full-length movie. The same studio that produced *Lost Horizon*, Columbia TriStar, was at the forefront again, with a 1997 movie bearing a very Shangri-La-type theme: *Seven Years in Tibet*. Two Austrian climbers, Heinrich Harrer and Peter Aufschnaiter, escape a British POW camp in India during World War II, and find sanctuary in a world ruled by Tibetan reincarnate lamas. One of the escapees, Heinrich Harrer, befriends the young Dalai Lama.

This time, the director worked with Bolivian extras, but also flew in real Tibetans – refugees from a land obliterated by the Chinese. French director Jean-Jacques Annaud said that Tibetan monks make splendid actors because they know how to live in the moment. Directing unknown Tibetan actors, he found they performed with remarkable grace and dignity. They didn't even need stuntmen. The question is: are the Tibetans really acting? Most of the time, they seem to be playing themselves. *Seven Years in Tibet*, based on a true story, employed real

9

Tibetan-exile monks – enthralled to be a part of translating their culture to the silver screen. The role of the young 14th Dalai Lama is played by Jamyang Wangchuk, son of a Bhutanese diplomat, who is used to being in the public gaze. The movie produced the first Tibetan movie star to hit the big screen – the alluring Lakpa Tsamchoe, from Sikkim, who plays opposite David Thewlis and Brad Pitt. She later starred in the movie *Himalaya*.

For the making of *Seven Years in Tibet*, director Jean-Jacques Annaud was rebuffed from filming in the Indian Himalaya (due to pressure from China), so he set about recreating Lhasa in the mountains of Argentina. The climbing scenes were shot in British Columbia, Canada. During filming, some scandalous information came to light. The German magazine *Der Stern* revealed Harrer had voluntarily become a Nazi storm trooper in 1933 and a sergeant in the SS five years later – he had his picture taken shaking hands with Hitler. He had neglected to come clean about this in his 1955 bestselling book. In 1997, when confronted with it, Harrer said he needed Nazi sponsorship to climb in the Himalaya. There were a few other things missing from his book: he left a pregnant wife behind when he set off for India. What a tale of redemption Harrer missed out on in his own book! Controversial snippets found their way back into the movie version. Harrer passed away in 2006; Aufschnaiter died much earlier, in 1973.

DOCUDRAMAS ON TIBET

In 1931, there were no DVDs to speak of, but would the lamas of Shangri-La be spending time watching movies? If so, there would be a number of Tibetan stories to watch, including films made by Tibetans themselves – even films made by Tibetan high lamas. The majesty of Tibet – and the ugliness of Chinese occupation – are shown in these films. Recent films made about Tibet are often based on real events that have been dramatised and re-enacted – a blend that directors call 'docudrama'. Here are some of them.

Kundun, though filmed in Morocco, brings pre-1950 Tibet back into sharp focus in a superb biopic about the early years of the Dalai Lama. This 1997 film, directed by Martin Scorsese, used unknown Tibetan actors.

Windhorse, directed by Paul Wagner (released 1998), is partly based on the true story about a singer who must flee Tibet. At great risk, the director took video of actors on location in Lhasa. The docudrama was filmed in Tibetan and Chinese languages and stars Dadon, a famous Tibetan singer who escaped into exile in 1992 and now lives in the USA.

Himalaya, directed by Eric Valli (released 1999), is a stunning French-Nepalese co-production with an all-Tibetan cast speaking in Tibetan. It was filmed on location in Dolpo, Nepal, under very taxing conditions. The movie offers great insight into the nomadic way of life.

Kekixili: Mountain Patrol starts out with the cold-blooded murder of a volunteer on an anti-poaching patrol. This 2005 docudrama is based on real patrols in northern Tibet to stop the killing of the Tibetan antelope for its prized underwool. The movie is a rare thing – a Chinese-made docudrama about conservation and saving the Tibetan antelope.

10 Questions for the Dalai Lama is an electrifying documentary on one of the greatest spiritual figures of all time. Filmed by Rick Ray, this 2006 documentary includes rare historical footage; it is part biography, part philosophy, part adventure and part politics.

TIBETAN MOVIE MAKERS

'I am a little bit out of line,' says Khyentse Rinpoche, joking. What he refers to here is his lineage: he is a reincarnate Tibetan lama. Who has made a movie. About soccer. He is actually way out of line – doing things his predecessors would not have even dreamed of doing.

It seems like some sort of contradiction to have a high Tibetan lama indulge in movie-making. But Khyentse Rinpoche doesn't see it that way. He says film is a potent force – and it is better to 'understand the power of this influence, than be its victim... Making a good film, I suppose, is a bit like doing good Buddhist practice. It all begins with an awareness of how we're conditioned.' By writing and directing a movie like this, he can reach far more people than by building temples. 'Films tell us a lot about who we are,' he says. Khyentse Rinpoche says movies can indeed be used for spiritual practice and 'visualisation' just as religious scroll art (*tankas*) are used for spiritual training.

And who exactly is he? Well, in his past life, he was a Tibetan saint: at the age of seven, he was recognised as a reincarnate lama in a non-sectarian lineage dating to the 19th century. Khyentse Rinpoche is throne-holder to a monastic seat in eastern Tibet. Although he has travelled to that part of Tibet, he remarks that it is difficult for a religious teacher to function under a watchful Chinese Communist regime. Born in Bhutan, Khyentse Rinpoche was educated in Sikkim and Bhutan, receiving rigorous philosophical training in the Tibetan Buddhist tradition. He travels on a Bhutanese passport, embossed with a double-thunderbolt design on the cover. Though he has no formal film training, Khyentse Rinpoche learned the ropes when hired as a special consultant on the set of Bertolucci's *Little Buddha*, mainly filmed in Bhutan. The rest he gleaned from simply watching countless videos.

The Cup, shot on a shoestring budget of US$670,000, is based on a true story about soccer-crazed monks at Chokling Monastery in Bir, Himachal Pradesh, northwest India. They fall over themselves trying to rent a TV set and satellite dish to watch the 1998 World Cup final between Brazil and France. This sets up tension between austere monastic rules and the exhilarating thrills that go with football viewing. Academic pursuits are imperilled; in its own irreverent fashion, the movie raises the absurd question: which force is more powerful – religion or soccer?

That's the thorny question that came up in 1943, in Lhasa, when the incoming conservative Regent banned soccer games and motorcycles, among other newfangled foreign ideas. Football was introduced to Tibet by the British: there were over a dozen teams in Lhasa in the 1940s – the game was all the rage. Monastic opposition to soccer – and the passions it generated – was behind the soccer ban (as it was behind most opposition to modernisation). Monastic officials saw it as a threat to social and cultural stability; movie-making and viewing were also regarded with deep suspicion.

Questioned about this, Khyentse Rinpoche says officials were mistaken to reject European ideas and sporting values. 'That's why I want to tell my fellow-Tibetans that modern things – Western things – are not necessarily a threat to our spiritual part, or the traditional life. In fact, they can be an aid.' It's a subject that he handles deftly in *The Cup*: the clash of modern technology and traditional cultural values – a problem not just for Tibetans or Bhutanese, but for cultures everywhere. 'Movies are our modern-day *tankas*,' says Khyentse Norbu, speaking about painted Tibetan religious scrolls that are used for meditation and teaching. 'Rather than fear modernisation, we should see it as a tool that can help us express our culture more powerfully.'

Khyentse Rinpoche took *The Cup* to the Cannes Film Festival in 1999, making him the first Tibet/Bhutan director ever to appear there – and a Rinpoche at that. He didn't receive any awards, but 'just getting there was an award in itself'. *The Cup* was well-received by audiences and critics at Cannes, perhaps because it handles a subject that is embedded in the French psyche – as triumphant winners of the 1998 football World Cup. But who wins is not the point of *The Cup*: Khyentse Rinpoche throws us for a loop by not revealing the actual winners of the big match.

The movie focuses instead on monastic life, using real monks as actors, and a real abbot. In fact, just about everyone in the movie plays a real-life part. Kunzang Nyima, the Tibetan refugee shown, arrived two weeks before shooting for the movie began; he lost his brother and sister when they fell into an ice crevasse attempting to escape from Tibet over the Himalaya. Khyentse Rinpoche gets across the message that monks have their ups and downs, their passions and aggressions, just like anybody else. And they happen to love watching football – and playing it.

The camera takes us into a very different world – as seen through a very different eye, offering novel perspectives. *The Cup* is filmed in Tibetan and Hindi, with English subtitles. In a dialogue with Geko (the head monk), the abbot is puzzled about why two great nations would fight over a ball. When he finds out that the reward for all this is a cup, he is even more incredulous. He ponders, deep in thought: 'A cup....hmmm,' as he sips butter tea – with a trace of a smile on his face.

For a movie with a first-time director and unknown actors, *The Cup* made quite an impression. The movie garnered several awards, and was accepted as the Bhutanese entry in the Academy Awards (Best Foreign Film category). Tongue-in-cheek, *Esquire* magazine called it the best sports movie ever directed by a lama. Meanwhile, back in Bhutan, the film premiered in the country's grand total of three movie-theatres (ticket price: 12 cents).

If you think that's a poor showing, consider that there is only one large movie theatre in the centre of Lhasa, and foreign content is pretty well non-existent under the watchful Chinese masters of Tibet. Officials only allow about 20 carefully vetted Hollywood movies into China each year – even knocking productions with famous stars like Jet Li. To bridge the gap, pirated movies are in huge demand. Tibetans within Tibet are not free to watch movies made in Hollywood about Tibet, nor movies made by their Tibetan compatriots in exile. And watching DVDs or videos featuring the Dalai Lama can lead to a jail sentence.

Khyentse Norbu's success with his first movie inspired thoughts of a second. He followed up with *Travellers and Magicians* (2004), which was shot in Bhutan and tells the story of a Bhutanese official, Dhondup, who sees America as his Shangri-La. Movie fever has caught on in Bhutan, with the tiny nation releasing 24 new films in 2006.

An assistant to the director in *Travellers and Magicians* (and a stunt-rider too) was Neten Chokling Rinpoche, whose monastery was the setting for *The Cup*. Using an Australian crew, Neten Chokling embarked on his own ambitious two-movie project to tell the life of the great Tibetan sage, Milarepa. One of the monks appearing in *The Cup* plays the young Milarepa, in a story focusing on revenge and compassion. The movie *Milarepa* was shot on location in the Spiti Valley, and was released in 2006. The Dalai Lama, addressing the crowd attending the premiere screening of *Milarepa*, in California in September 2006, said: 'Our intention is not the propagation of Buddhism, but helping the world. Hollywood has the power to affect the world through cinema and spread compassion.' Having failed to get the nations of the world to recognise his government-in-exile, the Dalai Lama has resorted to going a different route via Hollywood.

While Hollywood may spread the word, some Tibetans see that as harmful because it perpetuates the image of Tibet as Shangri-La, where everyone is happy. Blasting this image is *We're no Monks* (2004), a film by Pema Dhondup, exploring the discontent of four young Tibetan exiles in Dharamsala, and their dreams about emigrating to America. One of them becomes a human bomb killing a visiting

Chinese diplomat. The film was mostly shot around Dharamsala by Dhondup, a graduate from film school in California. *Karma* (released in 2006) is a movie about the life-altering journey of a young exiled Tibetan nun, mostly filmed in the remote region of Mustang, Nepal. The director is Tsering Rithar, a Tibetan based in Kathmandu. Another film about disaffected Tibetan exiles is *Poison Charm* (2007), the creation of Indian-Tibetan filmmaking couple Ritu Sarin and Tenzing Sonam.

SACRED VIBES

Getting to Shangri-La in another dimension could simply be a matter of finding the right doorway. Here's a clue: 'Shang' is the Tibetan for a flat bell used in Bon rituals. Here's another clue from the New Age-type album, *The Singing Bowls of Shangri-La*: 'The listener automatically resonates with the higher vibrations of the subtle realms, wherein the body heals itself. These sacred bowls open a vibrational doorway to another reality…a dimension depicted in the legend of Shangri-La.' In other words, good vibrations could get you there. Shangri-La is good New Age material, and has appeared in the titles of a number of albums by Western singers and musicians.

Music is very important to the lamas of Shangri-La, but singing bowls have nothing to do with Tibet. The singing bowl meditation fad was started by some savvy Westerners in Nepal. In Tibet, brass bowls are only ever used for offerings in temples. If anything, the concept of musical brass bowls comes from Central Asia, not Tibet. If you want to be transported to another dimension through Tibetan music, then sacred temple chanting of the Gyuto monks might do the trick. They're based in Dharamsala, and are featured on a number of albums as well as soundtracks for movies about Tibet, including *Kundun*. These dirges are not for everyone. The exiled monks have mastered the Tibetan meditation technique of chanting with a deep three-note chord, which places such strain on the vocal chords that the singer is in danger of becoming mute if he overdoes it. The same throat-singing technique is practised in Mongolia and Tuva, and, strangely enough, in the high Arctic in Canada, among the Inuit people.

Among the Tibetan nomads, there is a rich tradition of folk songs, with the high-pitched yodelling from Amdo being an acquired taste. In the West, exiled Tibetan musicians like Yungchen Lhamo and Nawang Kechog have produced albums.

IN CYBERIA

Armchair travellers, rejoice! Finding Shangri-La need not cost you an arm and a leg – you don't need to shell out for elaborate expeditions. It may well be that all you need is a fully loaded computer and a high-speed internet connection. *Journeyman Project 3: Legacy of Time* (Red Orb Entertainment, 1998) is a videogame that will take you through virtual environments of Atlantis, El Dorado and Shangri-La. *Beyond Atlantis* (Dreamcatcher videogame, 2000) will launch you into virtual Tibet and China, and on to virtual Shambhala.

VIRTUAL TOURING

On the web, the Tibetosphere is just a few keystrokes away.

Put together your own Shangri-La circuit. Get on board at www.shangrilaair.com.np, pick out a tour at www.shangrilatours.com, and stop for the night at Shangri-La Resort (www.shangrilaresorts.com.pk). To assist with further journeys, here are a few ideas. Be careful if trying to access these sites from within China or Tibet; some show material that is highly sensitive to view, and could be blocked or banned – or cause a lot of trouble. Under normal viewing conditions – in the free world – you can find an archive of many websites about Tibet at www.tibetsites.com/.

earth.google.com. Fantastic free web access that allows you to zoom over the Himalaya and fly low over Lhasa, Kathmandu, Gangtok, Thimphu and other parts, though it's sometimes sketchy on these regions. These 'moving maps' offer a quasi 3-D simulated view, similar to virtual maps that pilots use in the cockpits of modern planes. Start by flying in low over Lhasa, and take your virtual journey from there. You can visit both north and south approaches to Mount Everest with considerable detail on the mega-peaks of the area. A virtual approach to the summit of Everest will, of course, be a lot safer than a real one. And a hell of a lot cheaper. You can drop in on Yunnan and see the peaks in Shangri-La County.

www.wnnasia.com. Worldnews Network has thousands of themed virtual newspapers, with stories cobbled together from CNN, BBC, Reuters and other sources. Apart from country-based themes, there are themes like sports, politics and human rights. You can check out newspapers that only exist in cyberspace, like the *Himalaya Post* (www.himalayapost.com), *Tibet Daily* (www.tibetpost.com), *World News India* (www.worldnewsindia.com), *Nepal Post* (www.nepalpost.com) and *Bhutan Post* (www.bhutanpost.com).

www.tibetgame.com. Virtual Lhasa is portrayed in this cool interactive travellers' game with sweeping panoramas that can be moved around. You have limited money and three Dalai Lama pictures: the object is to give possessions away, thereby building your karma to attain nirvana. As you do good things, your karma will build. This site, created by Sydney-based photographer Peter Danford, gives you the feeling of being on the ground, exploring Lhasa via 24 linked panoramas with some audio. You need some plug-ins to run this game.

www.damanhur.org. Although the Shangri-La community has no website, there are other utopian groups that do. The most prominent is Damanhur, located in Italy, where a massive underground temple has been constructed (you can see the results on their website gallery). The eco-society of Damanhur has gained recognition from the UN as a model of a sustainable society. It has no particular religious slant, except following meditation practices.

www.zaadz.com. Utopian online community aiming to change the world through social networking. It is based in...cyberspace.

Part Three

BEING THERE

10

Being There

The trouble with practical advice for paradise is that you don't *find* Shangri-La, you stumble into it. That's how the High Lama found it – he was totally lost. Conway got there by crash-landing. Those are hard acts to follow.

Whatever you stumble into will likely be in remote areas at high altitude. The following section provides a brief sketch of some of the peculiar problems posed by travel to remote parts of the Tibetan plateau and by ascending to altitude. That's not just concerning health: high altitude is a potential hazard for computer hard drives and a big problem for helicopters. And altitude makes it doubly difficult for you to run around or to carry luggage. The good news is that mosquitoes do not like cold and altitude – over 3,000 metres is too high for them.

EMBARKING ON YOUR QUEST

As a huge swathe of the Himalaya is covered in this book, with half a dozen countries, there are inevitable gaps in material. High detail would need to come from other guidebooks. A good web listing for details is: www.kotan.org/Tibet/. This resource has been set up by the authors of *Mapping the Tibetan World*. On the site you will find a complete listing of Chinese, Indian, Nepalese and Bhutanese embassies and consulates abroad. If you click on 'Tibet Cultural Region Directory' on this site, it leads to listings of agents and other contacts.

Due to restrictions in remote border areas, a number of routes described in this guidebook can only be accessed in small group tours, organised by an agent. Embarking on your quest depends on juggling the money and time available. Use agents to save time and aggravation when getting permits. Some reliable agents are listed with the regional chapters in this book.

Small group touring is one of the best options for getting around these regions. If you have a group of, say, four people, this will reduce costs for hired transport like a jeep or Landcruiser. You could, for instance, arrange a month of touring in northwest India, through Ladakh, Lahaul and Spiti for around US$100 a day for jeep and driver. In Tibet, a Landcruiser rate (with driver and guide) would run to about US$150 a day. Touring in Bhutan costs around US$200 a day (per person) no matter what transport you use.

In large gateway cities like Bangkok, Hong Kong, Kathmandu or Chengdu, there's easy access to ATM machines, but elsewhere you can't count on finding any. Credit cards are fairly useless in the Himalayan region. The main forms of money to carry are travellers' cheques and US cash. You need to load up on local cash like Chinese yuan in a bank or ATM in Lhasa before heading off to the remote Kailash region, where there are no banks in sight. If all else fails, US cash should work: carry larger bills (US$50 bills are good) to reduce bulk, and smaller bills for tips. All prices in this book are quoted in US dollars to save on conversion confusion.

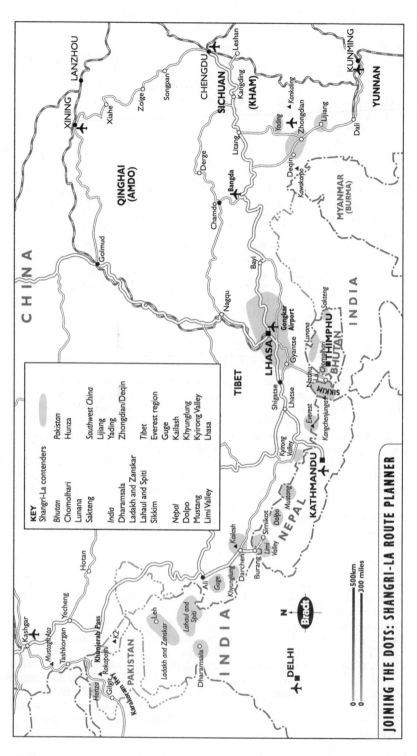

JOINING THE DOTS: SHANGRI-LA ROUTE PLANNER

KEY

Shangri-La contenders

Pakistan
Hunza

Bhutan
Chomolhari
Lunana
Sakteng

Southwest China
Lijiang
Yading
Zhongdian/Deqin

India
Dharamsala
Ladakh and Zanskar
Lahaul and Spiti
Sikkim

Tibet
Everest region
Guge
Kailash
Khyunglung
Kyirong Valley
Lhasa

Nepal
Dolpo
Mustang
Limi Valley

JOINING THE DOTS

When planning a trip to these regions, start with identifying the high-interest destinations and looking at the best weather choices for those. Choose the best season and the second-best season to go, and work around those options. That's because the icy doors of high passes can swing shut for the winter, leaving you no way in (or out). Some regions can only be accessed for a few months a year.

What's your grail? Poring over maps is the most important part of trip planning. Pick the destinations of high interest, mark the dots on the map and then start joining the dots. Think about combination touring. Combining southwest China with Tibet would be on the same visa. Hunza combined with the Karakoram Highway into China and back to Hunza would require a multi-entry Pakistan visa. Not all embassies and consulates are created equal. The Chinese embassy in Nepal may grant you just two weeks to tour Tibet, while the visa-issuing office in Hong Kong can set you up with a three-month visa for China (covering Tibet). You might want to consider touring with an agent, and then staying longer in a region to explore on your own.

OFF-KILTER TOURING

For unusual encounters, try going off-season: go to Tibet in winter – Losar (Tibetan New Year celebrations) in January or February would be an ideal target. Monsoon in Bhutan is wet, yes, but it brings out the very best of Bhutan's spectacular flora. For any kind of specialist touring, you're best off assembling a small group, say four people, to guarantee the trip will get off the ground. Agents can arrange special tours for flora lovers, bird watchers, and so on. How you travel can reveal a totally different side of these regions – consider the slower pace of trekking, mountain biking or horseback riding tours. To find out how powerful Tibet's rivers are, trying whitewater rafting – a company in Lhasa runs rafting and kayaking tours, with multi-day trips possible if you assemble your own small group. Whitewater rafting sorties are much more common in Nepal.

Yak safari There are parts of the Himalaya where trekking with yaks as pack animals is possible, which allows you to get to know these remarkable beasts better. Yaks may be used as pack animals on treks like Samye to Ganden, the Kailash *kora* (Tibet), and also in northern Bhutan (the Snowman Trek), where they are sure-footed over snowbound passes that mules and horses cannot handle.

Deluxe trekking Treks in Bhutan stipulate that all camping supplies are self-sufficient, and packed in and out by horses and mules, including tents, food, and so on. Restricted regions of Nepal (like Mustang) use the same system. The style is a vestige of the British colonial presence: your day starts with 'bed tea', which means a cup of hot tea is delivered to your tent as a wake-up call. This might be called 'Shangri-La-style trekking'. On these deluxe treks, the cook is second only to the guide in importance. Mules and horses carry all the gear, and assistants set up camp well before you arrive, with folding chairs and folding dinner table in the mess tent. Hard trekking and tasty carbohydrate-rich food: these two are a great match.

Homestays Staying with Tibetan families is not possible within Tibet (in the Tibet Autonomous Region) because authorities want to keep track of foreigners through hotel registration, but rules are laxer in Kham and Amdo, outside the TAR. Agencies like those in Zhongdian can suggest Tibetan B&Bs, and can arrange longer stays with rural or nomad families in the vicinity.

Voluntourism: For volunteering ideas, see 'Giving Something Back', below.

GEAR

Carrying luggage at altitude is much harder work than at sea level: the emphasis in your gear should be on strong, lightweight stuff that performs multiple functions.

1 *Why Shangri-La?*
Because in a screwed-up war-mongering world, Shangri-La embodies the ultimate in peace and harmony – a shot at saving civilisation from total annihilation. There's a lot to learn from this reclusive Himalayan utopia.

2 *How much will all this cost?*
Change must come from within. You cannot put a price on paradise.

3 *How long will this quest take?*
Could take a lifetime. Or several lifetimes. You might have to put the quest on ice and leave it till the next lifetime.

4 *Will it hurt?*
Shock-absorbers in the knees will certainly take a pounding. Jangled kidneys a distinct possibility, plus lungfuls of dust.

5 *What about the altitude?*
High altitude can knock the wind right out of you, lower your sails, and send your normal functions into a tailspin. It is also a very humbling experience. As you engage in a monumental struggle to trek over a high pass – certain that you are about to die in the attempt – you may see, out the corner of your eye, a 75-year-old Sherpa cruising past you with a fridge on his back.

6 *Where can I pray for divine intervention on road trips?*
There are convenient shrines around Lhasa and Kathmandu to appease the gods. Take a good supply of prayer flags for the journey to tie on at high passes along the way to ensure safe passage.

7 *What kind of personal talismans should I take?*
Recommended are the following: a large chunk of turquoise, a three-eyed *dzi* stone, two sacred mantras, and a well-travelled teddy bear.

8 *What else do I need to take?*
An open mind, a strong heart, lots of cash, some crampons, and a set of plumbing tools. Or, at the very least, a Swiss Army knife.

9 *How will I know if I have reached Shangri-La?*
The aura of spirituality will be strong; signs will manifest themselves, like the appearance of yaks. Keep an eye out for folks with Nordic features who look well over a hundred, and for the shell of an old aeroplane.

10 *How long should I plan on staying there?*
Conway spent about four months in Shangri-La after crash-landing in the region. But he escaped. Shangri-La is zealous in guarding its secrets. No dilettante jet-setters are admitted to this secret community – and leaving is *verboten*. In your mind, you can never leave the Himalaya behind – the mountains stay with you. As the Eagles croon: 'You can check out any time you want, but you can never leave.'

Before you go travelling, assemble all your gear in bags, and then carry it a few blocks – or perhaps up the stairwell of a ten-storey building. After this exercise, you may well want to reduce your load. You have to figure out where the weight lies, and how to reduce it without compromising on essentials like medical supplies.

In Lhasa you can buy or rent camping gear, made in China. There is lots of cheap outdoor clothing for sale in Lhasa, including silk items, fleece sweaters and knock-off North Face jackets. On sale in Kathmandu is an array of left-over expedition equipment of good quality.

A top priority for gear is a good pair of hiking shoes with ankle support – lightweight, strong and well broken-in. You rely on your feet a lot in these regions. Next on the list would be a hat of some kind and a set of high-quality sunglasses or glacier glasses that block UV rays (ideal are dark polarising lenses). And you definitely need a strong torch with a long battery life. Due to erratic or non-existent electrical supply, you constantly need a torch – for finding the lock to your room, for illuminating dark frescoes in monasteries, and so on. In the gadget line, an altimeter may be helpful – make sure it goes to 6,000m. Some wristwatches have in-built altimeters, so the question is not what time, but how high. It's advisable to pack a well-stocked medical kit as you may have trouble finding items like plasters.

Clothing for dealing with extremes of heat, cold and wind is essential. Rain and dampness are less of a problem unless you visit in the monsoon season. Pure cotton clothing is of dubious value in the mountains because it takes too long to dry – if you sweat, the sweat stays, and you can freeze as a result. Quick-dry synthetics are preferable, such as nylon/polyester mixes with the feel of cotton, or else cotton/polyester mixes. Silk items favoured by skiers are ideal for insulating because they're lightweight and durable. A thick pile sweater and a windproof (Gore-Tex) jacket should provide protection against biting wind and cold.

Even if you are not going off the track, it's a good idea to pack a sleeping bag rated to sub-zero temperatures. A down-filled sleeping bag would be preferable. Guesthouses are often not heated, and the bedding supplied may not be adequate. And finally, consider loading all this into a duffle bag with lockable zips for easy transport. Duffle bags are easy to load on horses when trekking, with 50kg to 60kg being an average load per horse (equivalent to two 30kg duffle bags – one on each side of the pack-animal).

This may all sound like a lot to pack, but things have lightened up considerably since Hilton's heyday in the 1930s, when porters would tote around tents weighing 30kg apiece, and climbers attempted Everest in tweed jackets and hobnailed boots. Here are some tips on winter clothing by British Trade Agent David Macdonald, appearing in his booklet, *Touring in Sikkim and Tibet* (1930):

For the heights, in winter, and for travelling in Tibet, where the wind is trying, the following additions should be made:

1 Warm Greatcoat.

1 Extra Set Very Warm Underclothing.

1 Warm Tweed Suit.

A leather coat is very useful on the Tibetan Plateau as a protection from the wind, and a hot water bottle of rubber variety should be included for those who suffer from cold feet at night.

DIGITAL SHERPA

Manufacturers are reluctant to tell you this, but hard-drives are not guaranteed to function at over 3,000 metres. Hard-drives are hollow seal units, so the pressure differential as you go up to altitude affects them. The cushion of air that the disk spins on is not the same at 3,000 metres as it is at sea level. That means an iPod may crash; it means a computer may crash. No way of telling. Some computers work fine at Everest base camp; others do crash. Take lots of back-ups, whatever you decide to do. And stick to solid state media if you can: there are computers with solid state hard-drives.

Electrical supply in the regions described is erratic, intermittent or unreliable, and prone to blackouts. It's best to bring good battery back-up for any electronic devices, and use the power supply to recharge those batteries. A surge protector is a good idea. Some multi-plug units have a surge protector built in.

Digital cameras are mostly solid state; the biggest problem with them is power supply. Digital cameras are notorious battery hogs: there are not a lot of opportunities to recharge in remote areas, so you are best off carrying extra batteries. Another problem is cold temperatures, which can rapidly sap battery strength. Digital cameras have the advantage of being able to show people in remote areas their own image, which will certainly break the ice and arouse excitement. In some places you can arrange for digital pictures to be printed out; these would make excellent gifts.

ON THE ROAD

UNPLUGGED

Entering remote areas, things are not going to function well, if at all. Forget about phones or email working, or finding ATM machines. These things may exist, but don't count on them. Lower expectations, step back in time – and enjoy that feeling of being unplugged. You may have little choice in the matter anyway: there is a blackout on foreign news coverage in Tibet, due to heavy censorship. Cybercafés in places like Lhasa or Chengdu provide some access to news through websites, but sensitive ones like the BBC may be blocked.

Shopping in Shangri-La? Well, there are lots of yak-tail whisks on sale around Shangri-La Town (Zhongdian) and lots of caterpillar fungus, but those wouldn't be high on my list. The Shangri-La ethos is non-materialism. The greatest gift you can buy in Shangri-La is Time.

LODGING

The deluxe Shangri-La Hotel group has not reached any Shangri-La regions yet, but probably will at some point. Accommodation in the Himalayan zone runs the gamut from a tent to a palace, and everything in between. You might find yourself shivering in a Spartan room in a monastery guesthouse at Rongbuk; out of the door is a view of the highest peak on earth. If you can find them, cosy family-run guesthouses are the best places to stay. These can be located in places like Darjeeling (superb views of Mt Kangchenjunga) or Karimabad (views of Mt Rakaposhi) – and at very reasonable rates. There are even some Tibetan B&Bs around Zhongdian, in castle-like converted farmhouses. Family-run guesthouses give you a chance to get closer to the culture. For this reason, when in Tibet try to stay in Tibetan-managed hotels rather than Chinese ones.

FOOD

The characters kidnapped to Shangri-La dined quite well on Chinese food. But the Tibetan world is not known for its cuisine: do not expect gourmet dining experiences. In the interests of maintaining your sanity, it is advisable to drop all food and drink expectations to the lowest possible threshold. This will save you and your stomach considerable angst. The staple diet in Tibet is *tsampa* (barley flour), with yak-meat and rancid yak-cheese providing protein, and the whole lot washed down with yak-butter tea. Or the whole lot barfed up with yak-butter tea – depends how you react. And here's something to think about: food may taste different at altitude. Exposure to mildly hypoxic conditions (meaning a reduced supply of oxygen) throws your taste buds off – it results in a significant increase in sensitivity to sweet tastes, a mild increase in salt sensitivity, and a decrease in sensitivity to sour and bitter tastes. Scrambling your sensitivity levels to different tastes upsets the balance of flavour in your food. This will explain why food tastes worse when you are airborne.

On the ground in Tibet, faced with the bleak Tibetan diet, you could well start to drool when thinking of even the most humdrum food back home. Back in the 1930s, at the time when Hilton's novel was written, explorers solved the Tibetan food problem by packing their own home-cooking. Giuseppe Tucci could not stomach *tsampa* or yak-butter tea, so he got the sponsorship of various Italian companies and loaded up with olive oil and Italian canned meat, ravioli, lasagna and so on.

Austrian-American explorer Joseph Rock went a few steps further and trained Naxi assistants to serve four-course Austrian menus. He carried a folding table and chairs, eating in style with European dishware and cutlery. To ease the digestion, he had a portable phonograph that played Italian opera at his campsite. The Naxi cooks were instrumental to the success of Rock's exploration. That point is illustrated by what happened when he returned to camp one day and discovered the head cook smoking opium. Rock hated the use of this drug. Flying into a rage, he fired the man on the spot. But a few days later he was forced to eat his words: no-one else had mastered the art of cooking Austrian food to the same degree. The head cook was re-instated, but given that opium is highly addictive, it's not clear if he carried on smoking. Rock may well have chosen to overlook the cook's opium habit in the interests of getting his own daily fix of Austrian food.

A similar approach to food is today followed by many trekking companies: they pack everything along. This has to do with a policy of not taking any food from slim local sources. Treks in Nepal and Bhutan include a cook and assistant, with Western-style supplies.

In larger centres on the Tibetan plateau like Lhasa or Leh, you can be pleasantly surprised by tasty local dishes. A memorable dish of golden mushrooms (*sersha*) in central Tibet. Or exquisite yak cheese – made using Swiss or Norwegian cheese-making technology. This highly palatable yak-cheese has a distinct nutty flavour. Similar high-tech yak cheese is made in Nepal, in northwest India (Manali) and in Bhutan. Yak cheese is much richer and more nutritious than cow cheese. It is apparently possible to make yak ice cream, and in the meatier line are attempts at yak meat pie, yakburgers, yak pizza and yak chow mein.

There are other cuisines available in the Tibetan world. In Lhasa, the best restaurants are Nepalese-run, offering Nepali, Indian, Tibetan and Chinese dishes. Call that Nepalese Fusion. And here's something that won't appear on the menu in Tibet: the Rangzen Platter (Free Tibet Platter). Served up in Everest Restaurant, Toronto, it is described as 'an appetizing dish of our popular Tibetan *momos* completely surrounded by Chinese chow mein.'

LEAVING A SMALL FOOTPRINT

The following guidelines are adapted from the Himalayan Tourist Code, developed by the Annapurna Conservation Area Project. The guidelines are for trekkers in Nepal, but equally applicable to other regions of the Himalaya. For minimal impact, take nothing away: leave only footprints.

PROTECTING THE ENVIRONMENT

Plants should be left to flourish in their natural environment – taking cuttings, seeds and roots is illegal in most parts of the Himalaya. Ensure that your guides are following conservation measures. Remove litter. Burn or bury paper, and carry out all non-degradable litter. Keep local water clean and avoid using pollutants such as detergents in streams or springs. If no toilet facilities are available, make sure you are at least 30m away from water sources, and bury or cover waste. Limit deforestation by not making open fires. Where possible, choose accommodation that uses kerosene or fuel-efficient wood stoves. Solar panels are often used to heat water. Where water is heated by scarce firewood, use as little as possible.

CULTURAL INTERACTION

As a guest, respect local traditions, protect local culture and maintain local pride. Be patient, friendly and sensitive. Respect sacred places – never touch or remove religious objects. Shoes should be removed when visiting temples, though this is not always the case (check with the monks first). Follow local customs – use only your right hand for eating and greeting. Do not share cutlery or cups. Avoid revealing clothing. Hand-holding and kissing in public are disliked by local people. Giving money or gifts to children encourages begging – and makes children think that foreigners are like ATM machines, readily dispensing gifts and sweets and pens. Donating to a project, health centre or school is a more constructive way to help. Photography can be intrusive. Respect privacy – ask permission before taking pictures, and use restraint. Ego-tourism (*carry my bags, speak my language, pose for my camera*) is not going to endear you to the locals. You are the guest here.

WHEN VISITING TIBET

Because of the dire human rights situation in Tibet, as a visitor you need to be sensitive about what you talk about. Do not endanger Tibetans by asking them their opinions about risky matters. You may take your freedom for granted, but Tibetans have none.

Do what you can to support Tibetan culture when visiting Tibet. Avoid patronising Chinese-run shops, restaurants and hotels. Avoid using Chinese guides and tour operators – they invariably speak no Tibetan. Donations in religious institutions tend to go to the Chinese authorities, not the monks.

GIVING SOMETHING BACK

For many living in the Himalaya, life is far from paradise. For starters, there are Tibetan refugees in India in need of your compassionate help. How is your karma meter? Gold, silver or bronze? Giving doesn't have to mean money. Voluntourism means giving your expertise in education, medical care, or assistance with computer operations. If you go to these websites, you can glean some ideas:

www.volunteertibet.org Has current postings for volunteer opportunities in Dharamsala and elsewhere in India. Gives ideas on who is needed – teachers, computer experts, other expertise. These volunteer positions range from a few months up to a year, with accommodation often provided.

www.guchusum.org Gu Chu Sum, an organisation in Dharamsala for former political prisoners, needs assistance with teachers of English and computer skills, as well as medical assistance. On their website, click on 'Your Help' to get volunteer information.

www.tibetanliberation.org/volunteer.html The San Diego Friends of Tibet website gives good ideas on volunteering opportunities that include teaching English to new arrivals from Tibet to requests for physiotherapists, doctors and nurses.

www.rokpauk.org A British-based worldwide charity founded in 1980, with projects in Tibet and Nepal from eye care to education.

www.tras.ca The Trans Himalayan Aid Society has projects in Tibet, Nepal and northern India to assist in building schools and medical centres. This non-profit organisation relies on volunteers. It was established in 1962 by the late George Woodcock after meeting the Dalai Lama in India.

www.seva.org Tibetans suffer from a very high rate of blindness from cataracts due to exposure to intense UV radiation at altitude. The Seva Foundation in the USA and its sister organisation Seva Canada (www.seva.ca) are among the few NGOs working in the Himalayan region to address the problem of reversible blindness. Volunteer medical and administrative staff are needed.

Here's what ophthalmic surgeon Dr Pratt-Johnson says of his volunteer work in Nepal, India and Bangladesh: 'You return with an afterglow that warms your heart and soul. This psychologically resets the equilibrium of one's life, fulfillment and joy. We ophthalmic surgeons need to be conscious of having skills that place us in a privileged position, coming close to performing miracles – restoring sight to the blind. Share it with as many as you can. Giving through volunteering is such an adventure and a lot of fun.'

YOUR WELL-BEING

If you make it to the Valley of the Blue Moon, you're fine. There's no sickness or disease in this valley. Otherwise, your greatest problems are likely to be speedy drivers and high altitude – both of which can be life-threatening. Since medical facilities in remote areas vary from very limited to completely non-existent, it's wise to travel with a friend and watch out for each other. Before setting off, you should purchase good evacuation insurance like that offered by Singapore-based International SOS (www.internationalsos.com).

The most common problems encountered on the Tibetan plateau result from exposure to the harsh elements – sunburn, windburn, cracked lips, chapped hands. This is largely because of intense UV rays at altitude. Arm yourself with the right clothing (a good hat and sunglasses) to ward off the sun at altitude, and bring sunblock cream and moisturisers. The air is extremely dry at altitude: coughs, colds and sore throats can turn quite nasty because of the dryness. Protective clothing, cough and cold medicines, and proper fluid intake are necessary to combat dryness. You need to drink about four litres of water a day to stay hydrated. If you have a case of diarrhoea, you will lose a lot of body fluids: you need to keep drinking (filtered) water and to increase your intake of sodium and potassium.

On the road, the biggest potential threat for travellers is possible injury caused by vehicle collisions or road accidents. There are no safety devices along precipitous mountain roads and few warning signs. Your fate rests with your driver's road skills. Drivers range from excellent to downright dangerous. Make sure yours is in the former class. If he is going too fast or taking unnecessary risks, tell him. Explain that there is no rush to reach the destination. Get the driver used to the idea of going slower so you can take in the scenery and make photo stops. Avoid travel at night – visibility is much reduced, and drivers may choose not to turn on their headlights, preferring to navigate in total darkness.

ACUTE EXPOSURE

It can get *very* cold overnight on the Tibetan plateau. Silk articles, favoured by Western skiers, are especially useful for countering the cold – they're light and pack easily (balaclavas, long-johns, T shirts, scarves, gloves). Wool and polypropylene clothing also insulates well. A woollen tuke or similar headgear will go a long way toward countering the cold. A dangerous condition, caused by rapid heat loss, is hypothermia: this is brought about by physical exhaustion when cold and wet. Symptoms include uncontrolled shivering. Shelter is the most important thing here: strip off wet clothing and replace with dry. In severe cases, the person should be stripped and placed in a sleeping bag with another person to share body heat. Do not rub affected limbs.

Frostbite is the most extreme result of rapid body-heat loss. It affects the tips of the extremities first – toes, fingers and nose. In these areas the blood freezes, preventing circulation as ice crystals expand in the cells. Again it is essential to find shelter, and immerse the affected part in lukewarm water if available. Surface frostbite can be thawed with another person's body heat – do not rub the affected part. Snow blindness results when bright sun reflected off snow (or ice or water surfaces) burns the cornea of the eye. The eyes feel like there is grit in them, appear bloodshot, and eyelids may puff up and swell shut. The condition is alarming but temporary – rest and soothe the eyes with cold compresses or eyedrops, and the condition should clear up in a few days. Wearing glacier glasses with total UV block is the way to prevent this condition.

ALTITUDE SICKNESS

The first Westerners known to enter Tibet complained of debilitating 'poisonous vapours' in the mountains. A lot more is known about 'mountain sickness' today, but mysteries remain. When Sherpas say climbing is in their blood, they may mean it literally. Sherpas have a physiology adapted to the high-altitude environment – their blood has a higher red-cell count, and their lung capacity is larger. Ability to adapt to altitude is thought to be in your genes. That may mean you either have the high-altitude genes or you don't. If you do, you can adapt quickly; if you don't, it will take longer – or so the theory goes. At higher altitudes, air pressure is lower, and the air is thinner. Although it contains the same percentage of oxygen as it does at sea level, there's less oxygen delivered in each lungful of air. So you have to breathe harder, and your body has to convert to more red blood cells to carry the oxygen through the system.

Altitude sickness does not appear to depend on being in shape: athletes have come down with it, and it may occur in subjects who have not experienced it before. Altitude sickness can occur at elevations above 2,000m, and about 50% of people will experience some symptoms at 3,500m. The higher you go the more pronounced the symptoms could become. So adjustment is required at each 400m of elevation gain after that. Terrain above 5,000m is a harsh, alien environment; above 6,000m is a zone where humans were never meant to go. Like diving at depth, going to high altitudes requires special adjustments. To adapt, you have to be in tune with your body. You need to travel with someone who can monitor your condition – and back you up (get you out) if something should go wrong. The study of altitude sickness is still evolving. Recent studies suggest that altitude sickness may be due to leaky membranes – which are more permeable as you go up in elevation.

It was unknown if a person could survive above 7,500m without oxygen until 1978, when Messner and Habeler reached the summit of Everest. Messner was told he would come back from Everest a raving madman or, at the very least, a brain-damaged automaton if he attempted the peak without oxygen. Messner got his timing right, got to the top, and went on to bag all the 8,000m peaks without oxygen. Climbers like Messner, however, will admit to impaired functions at higher elevations – and to strange encounters. Messner recalls talking to his ice axe, talking to his feet, talking to an imaginary companion and having hallucinations.

Altitude strategy

It is essential to take it easy for the first three or four days after arriving at altitude; most acclimatisation takes place within the first ten days (it can take two or three months to fully acclimatise). When reaching altitude, most travellers experience discomfort – headaches, fatigue, nausea, vomiting, lack of appetite, swelling of the hands or feet, difficulty sleeping. This condition is usually mild and short-lived. Headaches can be treated with aspirin: if a headache persists, or intensifies – or if the person wakes up with a headache – this is a sign of real altitude sickness. The critical question is how to distinguish between mild altitude sickness and more serious cases – read on. You don't acclimatise by sitting around doing nothing – get some simple exercise like walking, and drink lots of water. Do not drink alcohol, as it contributes to dehydration. Smoking, of course, will be a major problem at altitude.

Never underestimate altitude – it can be a killer. Go slow, be careful, and experiment before you go higher. The climber's maxim is 'walk high, sleep low' – climbers may trek higher during the day, but retire to lower levels to sleep. The maximum rate of ascent when trekking should be about 400m a day. If you're acclimatised to Lhasa (3,650m) you really need to undergo a second acclimatisation phase to handle a visit to Mount Everest base camp (5,150m). On a brighter note, once you've acclimatised to a particular altitude, the altered blood-chemistry should stay with you for about ten days. So if you acclimatise to the 5,000m level and then go down to 3,500m, you should be able to go back up to 5,000m again without ill effects, provided you do so within ten days.

The drug Diamox (acetazolamide) can help alleviate the symptoms of altitude sickness. It does not prevent you getting altitude sickness, nor does it solve the problem, but may ease your passage when, say, arriving in Lhasa by air from Chengdu, or when going up and over and down a pass within the same day. Since it's a diuretic, it leads to increased urination and dehydration, so you need to keep drinking more if you use it. The normal dosage is 250mg every 12 hours, but you could take half the recommended dosage (cut the tablets in half). If a person comes down with acute mountain sickness, the dosage can be increased slightly to 250mg every six hours. The use of Diamox is controversial, and it's a sulphur drug, which some have allergies to.

Acute mountain sickness

Acute mountain sickness (AMS) is a general term for a whole raft of altitude-related maladies. Symptoms of AMS include gastro-intestinal turmoil (loss of appetite, nausea, vomiting), extreme fatigue or weakness, dizziness or light-headedness, and difficulty breathing or sleeping.

A case of severe AMS may result in high-altitude pulmonary edema (HAPE), when a small amount of fluid that appears in the lungs at altitude is not absorbed normally. Instead, it accumulates, obstructing the flow of oxygen and drowning the victim in his or her own fluids. Symptoms include rapid respiratory rate and rapid pulse, cough, crackles or wheezing in one or both lungs, frothy or bloodstained sputum, and severe shortness of breath. Another serious complication is high-altitude cerebral edema (HACE), where the fluid problem is in the brain. A person with HACE is disorientated, has an unsteady gait and trouble using the hands, is irritable, suffers from drowsiness and nightmares, and may suffer hallucinations. Memory, judgement and perception are impaired.

To counter HAPE and HACE, mountaineering expeditions sometimes tote a Gamow bag, which weighs about 8kg. It is a body-enclosing bag that can be hand-pumped to replicate atmospheric pressure at much lower levels. Recent studies suggest that a one-hour treatment corresponds to a descent of 1,500m; this leads to short-term improvements, but nothing lasting. Some group tour operators carry a tank of oxygen to deal with cases – but that tank may only hold 30 minutes of oxygen (Landcruiser drivers sometimes carry oxygen). Drugs like Diamox are also used to counter the effects of altitude. The best solution, however, in all cases, is simply to transport the patient to a lower elevation – as fast as possible (if this means moving in the middle of the night, do so). Unfortunately, on the Tibetan plateau, quick descent to lower elevation is not always feasible.

Risky situations and evacuation

The best advice that can be offered in risky medical situations in Tibet is this: when in doubt, evacuate. Get on a regular scheduled flight to a lower elevation like Kathmandu or Chengdu. When sufficiently pressured, airline authorities will bump passengers off a regular flight to create space for an emergency case. Although helicopter evacuation is employed for injured trekkers in Nepal, it is simply not an option in Tibet. Although the Chinese military have Sikorsky and Boeing CH-47 high-altitude choppers, these are strictly for military applications and under no circumstances will be diverted for civilian use. The elevation limit for conventional helicopters is around 6,000m. This is because the air is so thin that helicopter rotors have nothing to cut into.

If the condition of the patient is not so critical, and there is leeway of a few days to transport, then another option is use of a Landcruiser or jeep as an ambulance – getting the patient off the Tibetan plateau as fast as possible. In the meantime, it may be possible to get oxygen supplies in some places. This evacuation advice is suggested because medical facilities on the Tibetan plateau range from primitive to appalling. You would do a lot better taking a good hotel room rather than going to a clinic. There's a shortage of sterile equipment and supplies; the most basic facilities for diagnosis and treatment are generally absent; doctors and nurses are poorly trained. Major cities in Asia, especially ones with lots of foreign embassies, have clinics and hospitals with Western standards, often staffed by Western doctors. The best are found in Singapore and Bangkok.

HEALING WATERS

Arriving in Shangri-La, Conway is astonished to find central heating and some very high-end plumbing within the monastery, combining Western and Eastern features:

> The bath, for instance, in which he had recently luxuriated, had been of a delicate
> green porcelain, a product, according to the inscription, of Akron, Ohio. Yet the
> native attendant had valeted him in Chinese fashion, cleansing his ears and nostrils,
> and passing a thin, silk swab under his lower eyelids.

This mystified Conway and his fellow travellers – where did these elaborate bathing rituals come from, and how had the porcelain tubs reached Shangri-La from America? Similar questions could well be asked about the origins of the rising Tibetan spa fad on the Tibetan plateau. Where does all this come from? There is no tradition of luxurious bathing in Tibet. If anything, Tibetans are the Great Unwashed. River water is icy-cold, and dirt provides a layer of protection from the sun. The only time you see Tibetans bathing is at bubbling natural sulphur hotsprings. Otherwise, women smear their faces in yoghurt or smelly yak butter, as a combination of moisturiser and sunblock. And Tibetan monasteries reek of the same yak butter, used as offerings to deities within.

Maybe Hilton took the bathing side from Chinese rituals. Latecomers to the Tibetan plateau, mountain spas are now starting to show up in luxury hotels, hinting at longevity and rejuvenation. The Bhutanese have a traditional method of soaking – a sunken wood bath where hot stones are added. This is offered at Uma Paro luxury hotel, along with a range of spa treatments (see page 111). The Banyan Tree Ringha in Zhongdian has a wooden hot tub in each lodge, as well as a dedicated spa facility on-site (see page 68). And at the House of Shambhala in Lhasa is Tibetan Secret Spa, which claims to use products made from healing herbs gathered in the mountains (see page 91).

10

On arrival at Shangri-La, Conway suspects that his food has been doctored with some sort of herb or drug from the valley to relieve respiration problems, caused by altitude. And the Valley of the Blue Moon seems to host a variety of wondrous herbs to take care of ailments, ranging from the mildly narcotic *tangatse* berry to locally brewed fragrant teas.

One thing that will definitely make you woozy in the Himalaya is altitude sickness. Is there any truth to rumours of herbal antidotes to the effects of altitude? It's possible that herbal medicines can reduce symptoms of altitude sickness such as migraines, high blood pressure and so on – but that might also mask symptoms. Cashing in on vague belief is a thriving trade in herbal remedies targeting Chinese tourists to Tibet – but what is in these remedies is often not exactly specified.

The fruits of the Chinese wolfberry are thought to be efficacious for altitude problems. This is the same Goji berry that Hollywood celebrities are fond of, touted as having miraculous properties. In a slick campaign in North America, bottles of Goji juice and other dubious concoctions appeared on health-food shelves, marketed as being an amazing Tibetan cure-all. That is unlikely, since the Goji berry does not actually grow in Tibet – it comes from arid regions like Ningxia, and is only briefly described in Tibetan medicinal cures.

The plant that shows up most frequently in altitude-countering herbal remedies is the Tibetan *Radix rhodiolae* plant, which grows on the plateau at elevations of 3,500 to 5,000m. Also known as 'plateau ginseng', this plant, according to Chinese sources, is efficacious for relieving high blood pressure, high blood fat, diabetes, senility, and 'internet addiction'. In any case, it appears to improve blood flow, which is good at altitude. Rhodiola concoctions are sold in Lhasa in capsules, as a liquid in glass vials, and in various teas. Cans of rhodiola drink (on sale in Lhasa) list rhodiola, honey, water and citric acid as ingredients.

With a surprisingly similar composition, but using ordinary ginseng, is a carbonated herbal drink called Tibetan Tea, manufactured in Hong Kong. The blurb on the can goes on about caravanners in Tibet lacing their black tea with ginseng, ginger, honey and exotic herbs to endure the harsh climate. But the blurb stops short here, because this product is sold in the USA, under the watchful eye of the Food and Drug Administration. The small print on the Tibetan Tea can carries this disclaimer: 'Not intended to diagnose, treat, cure, or prevent any disease'.

Available in Lhasa is a kind of high-altitude tea that claims to relieve headaches, insomnia, nausea and dizziness brought about by altitude. Similar in concept to *maté de coca* (the Andean remedy, from coca leaves), this 'altitude-relax tea' is called Gaoyuanan, and is made in Tibet. You can buy a box of sachets in Lhasa at several of the hotels. Just sprinkle in a cup and add hot water. What's in it? Who knows.

Showing some promise in countering altitude sickness is the herb Gingko biloba. Dr Stephen Bezruchka, in his book *Altitude Illness: Prevention and Treatment*, says 'Ginkgo biloba, 80mg to 120mg twice a day, beginning five days before ascent and continued a day at altitude, appears to prevent AMS. It interferes with platelet activity in the blood, so its safety for those taking other drugs that have such effects is unknown. It also improves blood circulation to the hands in the cold. Its role at altitude remains to be clarified, but it has few side effects and should be considered.'

Doyen of Tibetan-style spas is the signature Chi Spa of the Shangri-La Hotel group. Chi Spa is slated to be set up at all the Shangri-La Hotels worldwide, along with customised local spa treatments. The stronghold of the group is China itself, with more than 30 luxury hotels scattered from Beijing to Chengdu. Flavour of the month at Chi Spa is not Thai-style massage, nor Swedish, but a mix of Tibetan and Chinese. For female spa-goers, Chi Spa offers an exotic alternative to the routine spa offerings that proliferate. But the market for the new Shangri-La spa is as much male as female, targeting executives staying in the high-end Shangri-La Hotel. Executives are at ease with the monkish décor, making this the perfect spa for the jet-lagged road warrior.

Like myself. Just back from Tibet, passing through Bangkok, I set out to investigate. The first thing that strikes me is the décor – which attempts to replicate the atmosphere of a Tibetan monastery, complete with dark lofty halls, lit by candles. For mood music, there's a Tibetan monkish dirge of chanting in the background. The creators claim that the spa is derived from ancient Tibetan and Chinese healing methods, but the finger points in a quite different direction – at the Shangri-La logo, based on a work of fiction. Hotel brochures and the blurb on the hotel website (www.shangri-la/spa) smooth-talk about finding your inner Shangri-La: 'Find serenity in our spacious suites. Find vitality in our healing therapies. Find harmony in our ancient rituals. Find beauty within yourself. Find the new paradise within Shangri-La.'

I am ushered into a large, private treatment room. The spa starts with the eerie sound of Tibetan singing bowls, and proceeds with a Tsampa Rub. The last time I saw a *tsampa* bowl was in Tibet. *Tsampa* is barley-flour, the Tibetan staple food. At Chi Spa the *tsampa* is mixed with herbs and used as a kind of sandpaper for exfoliating. The *tsampa* is real – imported from Nepal, like all the other artefacts and ritual objects at Chi Spa.

This is followed by a hot stone treatment with Tibetan lucky symbols and sacred mantras inscribed on stones, which are heated in oil. The masseuse has a deft touch. She massages the length of the body with the heated stones, wielding a stone in either hand – a strange but quite agreeable sensation. Sometimes she applies deep pressure; other times she leaves them on parts of the body because heated rock supposedly improves the flow of energy. There are even tiny hot stones left between the toes. But when hot stones are paired up with New Age music, a spa-goer can only be left suspicious as to the origins. The cost of all this could burn a hole in your pocket: a Mountain Tsampa Rub runs to US$60 and the Himalayan Healing Stone Massage goes for a cool US$130.

Provided with a luxurious cashmere gown, I feel like some sort of shaggy goat. And so, after three hours of being thoroughly massaged, pummelled, scrubbed, rubbed with *tsampa*, healed with hot stones, detoxified and exfoliated, I emerge glowing from the spa, batteries fully charged. My head still ringing from New Age music and singing bowls, I sip some herbal tea from a jade teacup – a very Shangri-La moment. Is it a gimmick? Yes, but a curious one: the spa mystique repackaged in Himalayan myth and New Age hokum. Give me four or five more sessions like this and I might even become a convert.

Being There **YOUR WELL-BEING**

10

Appendix I

FAUNA EXTRAORDINARY

Adapting to the harsh high-altitude conditions of the Tibetan plateau is some remarkable wildlife. Some animals, like the wild yak, are so well-adapted to the altitude that they cannot live at lower elevations.

This is a brief introduction to some of the unusual mammals and birds of Tibet, and their links to mythology. Sadly, rather than a listing of fauna you might be able to spot, it is more a listing of endangered species – these species may soon end up being mythical. In the 1940s, American adventurer Leonard Clark reported about Tibet: 'Every few minutes we would spot a bear, a hunting wolf, herds of musk deer, kiang, gazelles, big horned sheep, or foxes. This must be one of the last unspoiled big game paradises.' Tibetans only took what wildlife they needed, so impact was minimal. The coming of the Chinese in the 1950s changed all that: Chinese soldiers machine-gunned wildlife not only for food but for export to China – and for sport. Tibet's once-plentiful wildlife now faces extinction: in the last 50 years, large mammals have gone the way of the bison in North America.

Due to poaching for its valuable undercoat, the Tibetan antelope's days are numbered. The fleet-footed Tibetan antelope can easily outrun any predator, but it cannot evade poachers equipped with 4x4 vehicles and high-powered guns. The Tibetan antelope's undercoat is the finest wool in the world, gossamer in weight and texture, soft, yet incredibly warm. Poachers feed an underground network that supplies shawls to wealthy Indians and Westerners. The snow leopard is hunted for its pelt and for parts used in Chinese traditional medicine. Unfortunately, Tibetans themselves have been involved in the smuggling of skins, supplying otter and tiger-skins from India to Tibetans in Amdo and Kham for use as trim on their coats. This market crashed in January 2006, when the Dalai Lama addressed a huge gathering of Tibetans in India, telling them never to use, sell or buy wild animals, their products or derivatives. His talk resulted in Tibetans in Amdo cheerfully burning skins of endangered species worth millions of yuan.

If you want to view Himalayan wildlife and birds, the best bet is Bhutan, which has a network of national parks and strong conservation policies in place. American biologist George Schaller has worked for the last two decades to get reserves established in parts of Tibet and Pakistan; he has been instrumental in the creation of a huge Changtang reserve in northern Tibet.

The species at the start of the list are 'flagship species' and are given longer text. The names in parentheses are Latin, followed by the Tibetan name(s).

MAMMALS

Tibetan antelope
(*Pantholops hodgsoni*) *chiru, tso*
The Tibetan antelope inhabits high desert plateau. The females are hornless, but the males sport a pair of long slender upright horns, which could make the antelope the source of unicorn myths in Tibet that date back several centuries (viewed in profile, the *chiru* would

appear to have one long horn). The *chiru*'s fine wool is a special adaptation that traps layers of warm air close to its body so it can survive snow blizzards where the thermometer plummets to –40°C. The *chiru*'s underwool, known as *shahtoosh*, is the finest animal fibre in the world. The *chiru* has never been tamed or reared in captivity: the only way to get *shahtoosh* is through killing the animals and skinning them. Although the trade in *shahtoosh* is illegal, it has pushed the *chiru* to the brink of extinction, with fewer than 100,000 remaining. Their last hope is the creation of a Changtang nature reserve.

Snow leopard

(*Panthera uncia*) *ganzig, saa*

Unique in its camouflage – a greyish spotted coat, blending in with its terrain – the snow leopard is a nocturnal hunter, mostly active at dusk and dawn, and particularly fond of stalking blue sheep. By day it sleeps in caves or on rocky ledges. It inhabits remote high-altitude terrain from 3,000 to 5,500m, with the largest numbers left in Ladakh, Spiti and Lahaul. The snow leopard is about the size of a large dog. It has adapted ingeniously to life in extreme snowy terrain: its large paws act like snowshoes, and its enormous tail is used to stabilise acrobatic leaps – and at night it is wrapped around body and face like a scarf to withstand freezing temperatures. Because of its throat-bone structure, the snow leopard is a non-roaring cat, but is known to make strange howling cries during the January–March mating season. So elusive and stealthy is the snow leopard that the first movie film to capture it in action was not taken until the dawn of the 21st century. The snow leopard is highly endangered, with numbers remaining estimated at under 7,000 – it may soon become as mythical as the snow lion. Seeing one: captive animals are held at the Darjeeling snow leopard breeding programme.

Takin

(Budorcas taxicolor) bamen, dong gyemtsey

The takin is a hairy hoofed herbivore with a bulbous nose and backward facing horns. It is a strange mix of moose, musk-ox and wildebeest, and can weigh up to 400kg, with a body 2m long. The takin favours the forested slopes of the Tibetan plateau, particularly in southeastern Tibet and Bhutan, where it inhabits dense forest. There are four subspecies – the Bhutan takin, Mishmi takin (Tibet), Shensi takin and Sichuan takin (China). There are probably fewer than 5,000 remaining. Seeing one: the takin is the national animal of Bhutan – a handful of captive takins are kept at a reserve overlooking Thimphu.

Wild yak

(Bos grunniens) drong

An enormous creature: an adult male can weigh up to 1,000kg (equivalent to double the weight of a domestic yak), and can stand almost 2m high at the shoulder. Wild yaks graze on grass, herbs, moss and lichen. They are sure-footed over rough terrain: herds travel on snow in single file, carefully stepping on footprints left by the lead yak. The wild yak's long shaggy coat enables it to withstand violent winds and snowstorms.

Tibetan wild ass

(Equus kiang) kyang

The largest of the Asiatic asses, this animal actually shares a lot in common with the zebra, minus the stripes. It is now mostly found in the Changtang in Tibet. The British army attempted to domesticate them in 1904 for use as pack animals, but failed. Huge herds of kyang used to graze the highlands of Tibet, but today sightings are rare – they are only spotted in groups of five to ten.

Alpine musk deer

(Moschus sifanicus) lawa, larna

The musk deer does not have antlers. Instead, both males and females have two large fang-like extruding upper canines for defence purposes. The musk deer has been hunted for centuries for the male's musk pod, located in front of the genitals. The musk obtained fetches a high price, used for its medicinal qualities and in the preparation of perfume. For these reasons, hunting has severely depleted numbers of the musk deer.

Blue sheep
(Pseudois nayaur) naya

Blue sheep combine features of both goat and sheep. They have a slate-gray coat that appears more bluish in winter but turns brownish in summer – to blend in with their surroundings. Adult rams have large horns that curve up, outward, and downward. The females have smaller horns. Blue sheep can congregate in herds of up to 200 during mating season.

Marco Polo sheep
(Ovis ammon hodgsoni)

Huge males have massive curling horns, and are thus prized in hunting as trophy animals. The sheep is found in the Pamir region, at the intersection of China, Afghanistan and Pakistan. It is named after Marco Polo: in his day, nobody in Italy believed his story about the preposterous horns of this wild sheep. An estimated 6,000 remain. There is a close Tibetan cousin, the Tibetan argali sheep.

Himalayan brown bear
(Ursus arctos pruinosus) dremo
A Himalayan brown bear can stand up to 1.8m – as tall as a man, which is probably why the species (and its footprint) is likely to be mistaken for a yeti. The highly endangered Himalayan brown bear ranges into higher altitude zones. Lower down in forests is the Himalayan black bear (*Ursus Thibetanus laniger*).

Appendix I FAUNA EXTRAORDINARY

Red panda
(Ailurus fulgens) og dong kar

This mammal has long been thought to be a distant relative of the giant panda, because it shares the peculiar habit of feeding largely on bamboo. But the red panda is actually more closely related to raccoons: this chestnut-coloured 'cat-bear' is small, with a ringed bushy tail half its length. It is a tree-dweller, inhabiting dense bamboo forests to the eastern side of the Tibetan plateau, including parts of China, Nepal, India, Bhutan and Burma. The red panda is hunted for its pelt, used to make traditional hats in Yunnan. Seeing a live one: Darjeeling Zoo holds several.

Tibetan sand fox
(Vulpes ferrilata) wa, wamo
This species is endemic to the Tibetan plateau, and inhabits open steppe like the vast desert of the Changtang. Its sandy colouring allows it to blend in easily with the desert. The Tibetan sand fox has a peculiar chunky head and is bigger than the common fox, which is also present in Tibet (mostly found in forested zones). The Tibetan sand fox keeps the rodent population in check, especially *pikas* (mouse-hares). The sand fox is hunted for its pelt, which is made into hats.

Himalayan marmot
(Marmota himalayana) kunpo, sho, jibi
Also known as the 'Tibetan snow pig', this species is commonly seen throughout the plateau on the plains and in grassy mountain valleys. It is a large rodent related to the North American marmot. Himalayan marmots live in large colonies in networks consisting of deep burrows. Their shrill whistling call alerts all animals in the vicinity to danger from predators. The marmot is hunted for its thick golden-brown fur.

HIGH-FLIERS
There are over 500 species of birds recorded in Tibet, 660 recorded in Pakistan, and 800 in Nepal. Bhutan is the best place for bird-watching in the Himalaya, with over 700 species, including magnificent pheasants like the satyr tragopan. For many years it was believed that no birds flew over the high peaks of the Himalaya. However, Himalayan griffon vultures have been sighted flying at 9,000m, over the summit of Everest, and yellow-billed choughs have been sighted at 7,000m by climbers attempting Everest. Snow pigeons and bar-headed geese have been sighted flying over peaks at 8,300m.

Lammergeier

(Gypaetus barbatus) gobo

Also known as the bearded vulture, this bird soars across the length of the Himalaya, and may be sighted riding thermals high overhead. It has a wingspan up to 2.8m, making it Eurasia's largest raptor. An unusual feeding routine: this vulture drops bones from its talons from a great height and then swoops down to feed on the exposed bone marrow.

Bar-headed goose

(Anser indicus) kalaha, gangpa

The name comes from several black bars visible at the back of its head. This bird can fly long distances in a single day when migrating. The honking of the bar-headed goose in the mountains is a sure sign you are in Tibet. Seeing one: some have been sighted in parks in Lhasa, mixed in with other geese.

Black-necked crane

(Grus nigricollis) trung trung

This is the tallest of the birds in Tibet, up to 1.5m high: much of its height is in the neck, which is black with a red cap. There are estimated to be fewer than 6,000 black-necked cranes remaining in the wild. In mating rituals, pairs of cranes leap into the air and utter loud bugling sounds. The birds migrate every year from Tibet to Bhutan. Gangtey Gompa (central Bhutan) hosts an annual festival to welcome the flocks of cranes, arriving in late October, and departing again for Tibet in mid-February.

APPENDIX 2

TIBETAN LANGUAGE   *Tibetan script by Chung Tsering*

Although there is a Babel of languages spoken in the regions covered in this book – Chinese, Hindi, Urdu, Nepali – the main ethnic group under focus speaks Tibetan. The existence of many dialects makes it difficult for Tibetans to communicate with each other. Even within Tibet, a person from Amdo may have trouble understanding a person with a Lhasa dialect. However, Tibetan script is fairly uniform throughout the Tibetan world: this elegant script consists of 30 consonants plus four vowels. Although different writing styles are employed, they more easily understood from one end of the Himalaya to the other than the spoken word.

There's one catch here: the very high illiteracy rate. In Tibet itself, learning how to write in Tibetan language has a low profile due to Chinese domination of the educational system, which insists that children learn Chinese characters instead. In Bhutan, by contrast, the literacy rate is quite high: the official language, Dzongkha, is a unique variety of Tibetan.

Tibetan is the Latin of High Asia: it is hardly geared to the modern world. The ancient language lacks the vocabulary range for innovations like 'barcode' or 'mobile phone'. Tibetan is flexible enough that English or foreign words can be imported phonetically, or Tibetans can try to make up new compound words. The Tibetan word for movie, for instance, is *log-nyen*, meaning 'electric picture', and the word for aeroplane is *namdru* ('ship of the sky'). But new vocabulary requires consensus among widely scattered groups of Tibetans to gain wide acceptance and thus to be widely understood. There could be one term used within Tibet (taken from Chinese) and a completely different one used in India (deriving from English or Hindi).

Any attempt you make to speak Tibetan, no matter how bad your pronunciation or your enunciation is, will be warmly received in these lands. A few useful phrases for pidgin Tibetan speakers: *tashi delek!* is an all-purpose opener, meaning: greetings! how are you? congratulations! best wishes! *Yapodu* or *yagodu* means 'good' (thumb up) while *yapo mindu!* means 'bad' (little finger down). Vital to your survival is the phrase *kale kale*, which means 'slow down', when spoken to a maniacal driver. Etiquette when you reach the prayer flags on top of passes in Tibet requires you to shout, at the top of your lungs, *Sso-so-so-so-so! Lha Gyalo!*, which means 'Victory to the gods!' You can derive a lot of dialogue from learning numbers in Tibetan, and not just for shopping. Numbers can be used in other creative ways: how many children do you have? How many yaks?

Bon	pre-Buddhist religion of Tibet, strong on shamanism and sorcery
beyul	sacred hidden valley of the Himalaya, one of a number consecrated by 8th-century sage Padmasambhava
chan	fermented barley-beer, a potent milky liquid
chorten	inverted bell-shaped shrine containing relics, or the ashes or embalmed body of a high lama (*stupa* in Sanskrit)
dharma	the word of the Buddha and his teachings
dorje	'thunderbolt.' A sceptre-like ritual object, made of brass and used against the powers of darkness
dzong	castle or fort, usually grafted onto a high ridge
Gelukpa	Yellow Hat school – the most politically influential of the four main schools of Tibetan Buddhism. The leader of this school is the Dalai Lama
gompa	active monastery

gonkhang	protector chapel at a monastery
Kalachakra	the 'Wheel of Time', a complex supreme *tantra* associated with the mystical land of Shambhala
kata	white greeting scarf, made of cotton or silk, presented on ceremonial occasions or offered at monasteries
Khampa	ethnic group of the Kham area in eastern Tibet, famed for their toughness and warrior-like demeanour
kora	clockwise circuit of a sacred temple, lake or mountain
la	Tibetan for 'high mountain pass', as found in the name Shangri-La
lakhang	chapel or inner sanctuary
lama	master spiritual teacher or guru
Losar	Tibetan New Year, usually celebrated around February
mandala	mystical circle (often enclosing a square) representing the Buddhist cosmos and used as a meditational aid (*chilkor* in Tibetan)
mani stone	stone tablet inscribed with a mantra, often included as part of a *mani*-wall, composed of many such stones
mantra	sacred syllables repeated many times as part of spiritual practice, such as *om mani padme hum* ('hail to the jewel in the lotus heart,' a phrase addressed to the Buddha)
momo	Tibetan steamed or fried dumpling, filled will meat, cheese or vegetables
Monlam	the Great Prayer Festival, around the time of Losar
nirvana	release from the cycle of mortal existence and rebirths
Padmasambhava	a great sage from the 8th century, instrumental in founding Tantric Buddhism in Tibet. He is the patron saint of Bhutan, where he is known as Guru Rinpoche
potrang	palace
prayer flag	small flag printed with sacred prayers, activated by the power of the wind
prayer wheel	large fixed wheel or small hand-held wheel containing mantras and activated by the spinning of the wheel
prostrator	pilgrim who measures the distance to a sacred destination with the length of his or her body, flung prone along the ground
rinpoche	'precious one'. A reincarnate lama, also known when young as a *tulku*
Saka Dawa	day of Buddha's enlightenment, celebrated around June
shaman	oracle or medium attuned to linking with supernatural powers to give advice and direction in ritual ceremonies (*ngakpa* in Tibetan)
Shambhala	Buddhist 'Pure Land', a Tibetan utopia where disease and ageing are unknown, said to be located deep in the mountains to the north of the Himalaya
Sutra	sacred text, the written or spoken teachings of the Buddha
tanka	painted portable scroll, usually depicting a deity, on fine cotton or silk; can be used as a teaching aid
tantra	the 'web of life', or *vajrayana*, is the form of Buddhism most often associated with Tibet. It employs radical steps to seek enlightenment within a single lifetime
terma	transliterates to 'treasure', and is closely associated with sacred texts and artefacts hidden by Padmasambhava and followers in the 8th and 9th centuries. *Terma* were widely scattered around the Tibetan plateau to await revelation in more propitious times
terton	'treasure revealer': a great sage who discovers *terma*, or treasure texts and other sacred items
tsampa	ground barley-flour, a Tibetan staple food
tulku	reincarnate lama
yak	hairy high-altitude cattle, or 'cow with a skirt'

Appendix 3

GLOSSARY

OPENERS

greetings (good fortune)	*tashi delek*	བཀྲ་ཤིས་བདེ་ལེགས།
goodbye (spoken to the person staying)	*kaleshu*	ག་ལེར་བཞུགས།
goodbye (spoken to the personleaving)	*kalepay*	ག་ལེར་ཕེབས།
pleased to meet you	*kerang tukpa gapo chung*	ཁྱེད་རང་ཐུག་པར་དགའ་པོ་བྱུང་།
how are you?	*kerang debo yinbe?*	ཁྱེད་རང་བདེ་པོ་ཡིན་པས།
I'm fine	*nga debo yoe*	ང་བདེ་པོ་ཡིན།
where are you going?	*kerang kawa droga?*	ཁྱེད་རང་ག་པར་འགྲོ་ག
what's your name?	*kerangi mingla karey re?*	ཁྱེད་རང་གི་མིང་ལ་ག་རེ་རེད།
my name is . . .	*nge mingla . . . yin*	ངའི་མིང་ . . . ཡིན།
I only speak a little Tibetan	*nga perkay teets teets shingi yur*	ངས་བོད་སྐད་ཏོག་ཙམ་ཏོག་ཙམ་ཤེས་ཀྱི་ཡོད།
I don't understand	*ngay hako masong*	ངས་ཧ་གོ་མ་སོང་།
Do you understand?	*kerang hakosong ngay?*	ཁྱེད་རང་གིས་ཧ་གོ་སོང་ངམ།

GETTING PERSONAL

where are you from?	*kerang lungpa kane yin?*	ཁྱེད་རང་ལུང་པ་ག་ནས་ཡིན།
I am from X	*nga X ne yin*	ང་ X ནས་ཡིན།
UK / Canada / Australia	*injilungpa /kanada / ostrelia*	ཨིན་ཇིའི་ལུང་པ་ / ཀེ་ན་ཌ་ / ཨོ་སེ་ཊི་ལི་ཡ།
America / France	*ahri / farenci*	ཨ་རི་ / ཧྥ་རན་སི།
Tibetan / Chinese / Nepalese	*perpa / gyami / pelpo*	བོད་པ་ / རྒྱ་མི་ / བལ་པོ་
How old are you?	*kerang lo katsay yin?*	ཁྱེད་རང་ལོ་ག་ཚོད་ཡིན།
nomad / farmer	*drokpa / shingpa*	འབྲོག་པ་ / ཞིང་པ།
monk / pilgrim	*trapa / nekorpa*	གྲྭ་པ་ / གནས་སྐོར་བ།
married / single	*changsa / migyang*	ཆང་ས་ / མི་རྐྱང་། (མི་རྙེང་)
husband / wife	*kyoka / gyemen*	ཁྱོ་ག་ / སྐྱེ་དམན།
mother / father	*ama / apa*	ཨ་མ་ / ཨ་པ།
children / son / daughter	*puku / pu / pumo*	ཕུ་གུ་ (ཕྲུ་གུ) / བུ་ / བུ་མོ།

younger brother	*chungpo*	གཅུང་པོ་
younger sister	*chungmo*	གཅུང་མོ།
older brother	*jojo*	ཇོ་ཇོ་ (ཅོ་ཅོག)
older sister	*aja*	ཨ་ཅེ།

FLATTERY

good / very good	*yapo du / yapo shedra re*	ཡག་པོ་འདུག / ཡག་པོ་ཞེ་དྲགས་འདུག
The food is great!	*kala shimpo du!*	ཁ་ལག་ཞིམ་པོ་འདུག
I love this place!	*nga sacha dila gapo yur!*	ང་ས་ཆ་འདི་ལ་དགའ་པོ་ཡོད།
beautiful	*nying jepo du*	སྙིང་རྗེ་པོ་འདུག
very interesting	*nangwa dropo shedra re*	སྣང་བ་འགྲོ་པོ་ཞེ་དྲགས་རེད།
I feel happy	*gyipo du*	སྐྱིད་པོ་འདུག
we had a good time!	*ngantso gyipo chung!*	ང་ཚོ་སྐྱིད་པོ་བྱུང་།
good luck	*lamdro yongbar shok*	ལམ་འགྲོ་ཡོང་བར་ཤོག

NEGATIVES, QUESTIONS, REQUESTS

yes, that's it	*re, de rang re*	རེད། དེ་རང་རེད།
yes, okay	*digi re*	འགྲིག་གི་རེད།
no problem	*kay chegi mare*	གང་ཡང་(ག)བྱེད་ཀྱི་མ་རེད།
no	*mare (mindu)*	མ་རེད་ (མིན་འདུག)
not okay, no good	*yapo mindu*	ཡག་པོ་མི་འདུག
thank you	*tujeche*	ཐུགས་རྗེ་ཆེ།
that's enough	*dik song*	འགྲིག་སོང་།
need	*gerh*	དགོས།
don't want (don't like)	*mo gerh*	མི་དགོས།
I don't know	*nga shingi meh*	ངས་ཤེས་ཀྱི་མེད།
sorry, excuse me	*gohnda*	དགོངས་དག
can I take a photo?	*nga par gyapna digi rebay?*	ངས་པར་བརྒྱབ་ན་འགྲིག་གི་རེད་པས།
what's this called in Tibetan?	*perke nangla di kandres lab gire?*	བོད་སྐད་ནང་ལ་འདི་ག་འདྲས་ལ་བགྱི་རེད།
what does this mean?	*di thondak karey re?*	འདིའི་དོན་དག་ག་རེ་རེད།
where / where is?	*kapa / kaba du?*	ག་པར / ག་པར་འདུག
what?	*karey?*	ག་རེ།
when?	*kadu?*	ག་དུས།
who? / why? / how?	*su? / karey jeni? / kandres?*	སུ་ / ག་རེ་བྱས་ནས་ / གང་འདྲ་སེ།
how much (how many)?	*katsey?*	ག་ཚོད།
how far?	*ta ringpo rebay?*	ཐག་རིང་པོ་རེད་པས།

RED TAPE

passport	*chikyur lakteb*	ཕྱི་སྐྱོད་ལག་དེབ།
permit	*chokchen*	ཆོག་མཆན།
PSB office	*gonganju (Chinese word)*	གུང་ཨན་ཇུད། (རྒྱ་སྐད།)
	sangwe nyen tokbe lekung! (Tibetan)	གསང་བའི་ཉེན་རྟོགས་ལས་ཁུངས། (བོད་སྐད།)
tourist	*takorwa*	ལྟ་སྐོར་བ། (ཡུལ་སྐོར་བ།)
I need a translator	*nga la gegyur cheken chik gerh*	ང་ལ་སྐད་སྒྱུར་བྱེད་མཁན་གཅིག་དགོས།
what's the problem?	*gang ngel karey tresong?*	དཀའ་ལས་ག་རེ་འཕྲད་སོང་།

MEDICAL

sick / very sick	*nagi du / shedra nagi du*	ན་གི་འདུག / ཞེ་དྲགས་ན་གི་འདུག
altitude sickness	*zatuki natsa*	ཟ་དུག་གི་ན་ཚ། (ལ་དུག)
headache / fever	*gonagi du / tsawa pargi du*	མགོ་ན་གི་འདུག/ ཚ་བ་འཕར་གྱི་འདུག
diarrhea / stomach ache	*troko shegi du / troko nagi du*	གྲོད་ཁོག་བཤལ་གྱི་འདུག/ གྲོད་ཁོག་ན་གི་འདུག
cold / cough	*champa nagi du / lo gyabgi du*	ཆམ་པ་ན་གི་འདུག / གློ་བརྒྱབ་གྱི་འདུག
feel dizzy	*goyu korgi du*	མགོ་ཡོམ་འཁོར་གྱི་འདུག
I was bitten by a dog	*khi chik gi sogyab song*	ཁྱི་གཅིག་གིས་སོ་བརྒྱབ་སོང་།
I need a doctor right away	*nga la gyokpo amchi laten gerh*	ང་ལ་མགྱོགས་པོ་ཨེམ་མཆི་ (སྨན་པ་) དགོས།
oxygen	*sog lung*	སྲོག་རླུང་། (འཚོ་རླུང་།)
emergency	*zatrak*	ཟ་དྲག
hospital	*menkhang*	སྨན་ཁང་།
pharmacy	*men tsongkhang*	སྨན་ཚོང་ཁང་།
medicine	*men*	སྨན།

TRANSPORT

ticket	*pasey (Indian-Tibetan word)*	པ་སེ། (དབྱིན་སྐད།)
	zinyik (Tibetan)	འཛིན་ཡིག (བོད་སྐད།)
plane	*namdru*	གནམ་གྲུ།
motor vehicle	*mota (Indian-Tibetan)*	མོ་ཊ།
	noomkor (Tibetan)	སྣུམ་འཁོར། (བོད་སྐད།)
bicycle	*gangkor*	རྐང་འཁོར།
horse	*ta*	རྟ།
I'd like to hire a jeep	*nga jip chik lander yur*	ང་འཇི་བ་ཅིག་གླ་འདོད་ཡོད།

English	Romanization	Tibetan
I'd like to hire a Landcruiser	*nga landkrusa chik lander yur*	ང་ལནྡི་ཀུ་རུ་ས་ (སྐྲ་འཁོར་ཏེ་ཡོ་ཏ་) གཅིག་བླ་འདོད་ཡོད།
Do you rent bicycles?	*gangkor laya yurbe?*	ཀང་འཁོར་གླ་ཡལཡ་ལ་ (རྒྱ་) ཡོད་པས།
how much for an hour?	*chutsu chik la katsey re?*	ཆུ་ཚོད་གཅིག་ལ་ག་ཚད་རེད།
how much for a day?	*nyima chik la katsey re?*	ཉི་མ་གཅིག་ལ་ག་ཚད་རེད།
what time is the bus?	*jijger lun korte chutsu katserla drogi re?*	སྤྱི་སྤྱོད་རླངས་འཁོར་དེ་ཆུ་ཚོད་ག་ཚད་ལ་འགྲོ་གི་རེད།
guide	*lamtriken*	ལམ་འཁྲིད་མཁན།
driver	*siji (Chinese word)*	སི་ཧི། (རྒྱ་སྐད།)
	kalowa (Tibetan)	ཁ་ལོ་བ། (བོད་སྐད།)
go slowly please	*kale kale drorok nang*	ག་ལེ་ག་ལེར་འགྲོ་རོགས་གནང་།
please stop here	*dila kag rok nang*	འདི་ལ་བཀག་རོགས་གནང་།

TREKKING

tent	*kur*	གུར།
sleeping bag	*nyeche*	ཉལ་ཆས།
stove	*tapga*	ཐབ། (བབ་ཀ)
I want to hire a yak	*nga yak chik ladoe yur*	ང་གཡག་ཅིག་གླ་འདོད་ཡོད།
porter	*jalak kyerken*	ཅ་ལག་འཁྱེར་མཁན།
is this the trail to X?	*di X la dro sai lamka rebay?*	འདི་ X ལ་འགྲོ་སའི་ལམ་ཁ་རེད་པས།
how many hours will it take to reach X?	*X pardu chutsu katsey gorgi re?*	X བར་དུ་ཆུ་ཚོད་ག་ཚད་འགོར་གྱི་རེད།

PLACES

I want to go to X	*X la drondoe yur*	X ལ་འགྲོ་འདོད་ཡོད།
airport	*namtang*	གནམ་ཐང་།
post office	*drakhang*	སྦྲག་ཁང་། (ཡིག་ཟམ)
bank	*ngukhang*	དངུལ་ཁང་།
PSB office	*gonganju*	ཀུང་ཨན་ཅུ།
temple	*lakhang*	ལྷ་ཁང་།
market	*trom*	ཁྲོམ།
photo shop	*barkhang*	པར་ཁང་།
bookshop	*teb tsongkhang*	དེབ་ཚོང་ཁང་།
museum	*dem tonkhang*	འགྲེམས་སྟོན་ཁང་།

LODGING

English	Romanization	Tibetan
hotel	*drukhang*	འགྲུལ་ཁང་།
guesthouse	*dronkhang*	མགྲོན་ཁང་།

room	khangpa	ཁང་པ། (ཁང་མིག)
bed	nyetri	ཉལ་ཁྲི།
can I see the room?	khangpa la migtana digi rebay?	ཁང་པ་ལ་མིག་བལྟས་ན་འགྲིག་གི་རེད་པས།
do you have a room with private toilet?	khang panang lola sangcher yur rebay?	ཁང་པའི་ནང་ལོགས་ལ་གསང་སྤྱོད་ཡོད་རེད་པས།
where can I leave luggage?	nge jalak dintso kawar shakka?	ངའི་ཅ་ལག་འདི་ཚོ་ག་པར་བཞག་ག (འཇོག་གས)
telephone	kapa	ཁ་པར།
key	deymi	ལྡེ་མིག
blanket	nyejay	ཉལ་ཆས། (གམ་པ་ལི)
candle	yangla	ཡང་ལ།
toilet / paper	sangcher / sangcher shuku	གསང་སྤྱོད། / གསང་སྤྱོད་ཤོག་གུ
shower / hot shower	trukhang / chu Tsapoe tru	ཁྲུས་ཁང་། / ཆུ་ཚ་པོའི་ཁྲུས།
towel	ajo	ཨ་ཙོར།
thermos of hot water	chu tsapo chadam gan	ཆུ་ཚ་པོ་ང་དེམ་གང་།

FOOD

hungry	trokok toki du	གྲོད་ཁོག་ཏྩོ་གས་ཀྱི་འདུག
thirsty	kha komgi du	ཁ་སྐོམ་གྱི་འདུག
restaurant	sakhang	ཟ་ཁང་།
tearoom	jakhang	ཇ་ཁང་།
can you bring me . . . ?	. . .chig kyer yongrok nang?	· · · ཅིག་འཁྱེར་ཡོང་རོགས་གནང་།
bowl of noodles	tuk pa porpa chig	ཐུག་པ་ཕོར་པ་གཅིག
meat dumplings	sha momo	ཤ་མོག་མོག
stir-fried vegetables	tsoma ngowa	ཚོད་མ་རྔོས་པ།
meat	sha	ཤ
yoghurt	sho	ཞོ།
water	chu	ཆུ།
boiled water	chu kolma	ཆུ་འཁོལ་མ།
sweet Indian tea	cha ngarmo	ཇ་མངར་མོ།
yak butter tea	cha suma	ཇ་སྲུབ་མ། (བོད་ཇ)
homebrewed beer	chang	ཆང་།
salt	tsa	ཚ།
sugar	che makara	ཕྱེ་མ་ཀ་ར། (ཅི་ནི)

BARGAINING

| how much is this? | gong katsey re? | གོང་ག་ཚོད་རེ་ད། |
| do you have any. . . ? | kerang-la . . . yurbe? | ཁྱེད་རང་ལ་ · · · ཡོད་པས། |

big / small	chenpo / chung chung	ཆེན་པོ་ / ཆུང་ཆུང་།
old / new	nyingpa / saba	རྙིང་པ་ / གསར་པ།
too expensive	di gong chenpo shedra du	།འདི་གོང་ཆེན་པོ་ཞེ་དྲགས་འདུག
can you give me a better price?	gong jak tupki rebe?	གོང་གཅག་ཐུབ་ཀྱི་རེད་པས།
discount	gong jakya yurbe	གོང་གཅག་ཡས་ཡོད་པས།

TIME

today	tering	དེ་རིང་།
now	tanda	ད་ལྟ།
tonight	togong	དོ་དགོང་།
yesterday / tomorrow	kesa / sangyin	ཁ་ས་ / སང་ཉིན།
morning / afternoon / evening	shoke / chitro / gongtak	ཞོགས་ཀ། / ཕྱི་དྲོ། / དགོང་དག (དགོང་དྲོ།)
year / month / week / day / hour	lo / dawa / zankor / nyima / chutsu	ལོ་ / ཟླ་བ་ / གཟའ་འཁོར། / ཉི་མ། / ཆུ་ཚོད།
Monday	sa dawa	གཟའ་ཟླ་བ།
Tuesday	sa migma	གཟའ་མིག་དམར།
Wednesday	sa lhakba	གཟའ་ལྷག་པ།
Thursday	sa pubu	གཟའ་ཕུར་བུ།
Friday	sa pasang	གཟའ་པ་སངས།
Saturday	sa pemba	གཟའ་སྤེན་པ།
Sunday	sa nyima	གཟའ་ཉི་མ།

NUMBERS

zero	lekor	ཀླད་སྐོར།	one	chik	གཅིག
two	nyi	གཉིས།	three	sum	གསུམ།
four	shi	བཞི།	five	nga	ལྔ།
six	druk	དྲུག	seven	dun	བདུན།
eight	gye	བརྒྱད།	nine	gu	དགུ།
ten	ju	བཅུ།	eleven	ju chik	བཅུ་གཅིག
twelve	ju nyi	བཅུ་གཉིས།	thirteen	jok sum	བཅུ་གསུམ།
fourteen	jub shi	བཅུ་བཞི།	fifteen	jo nga	བཅོ་ལྔ།
twenty	nyi shu	ཉི་ཤུ།	thirty	sum ju	སུམ་ཅུ།
forty	shib ju	བཞི་བཅུ།	fifty	ngab ju	ལྔ་བཅུ།
sixty	druk chu	དྲུག་ཅུ།	seventy	dun ju	བདུན་ཅུ།
eighty	gyeb ju	བརྒྱད་ཅུ།	ninety	gub ju	དགུ་བཅུ།
one hundred	gya tamba	བརྒྱ་ཐམ་པ།	five hundred	nyab gya	ལྔ་བརྒྱ།
one thousand	chik tong	གཅིག་སྟོང་།	two thousand	tong-trak nyi	སྟོང་ཕྲག་གཉིས། (ཉིས་སྟོང་།)
one million	sayachik (or: bumju)	ས་ཡ་གཅིག (ཡང་ན་ འབུམ་བཅུ།)			

GEOGRAPHICAL TERMS, MAP FEATURES

river	*gyuk chu (also: tsangpo)*	རྒྱུག་ཆུ། (དེ་བཞིན་ གཙང་པོ)
spring	*chumi*	ཆུ་མིག
hotspring	*chutsen*	ཆུ་ཚན།
village	*trongsep*	གྲོང་གསེབ།
town	*trongte*	གྲོང་སྡེ།
fort	*dzong*	རྫོང་།
monastery	*gompa*	དགོན་པ།
ice / snow	*kyakpa / kang*	འཁྱགས་པ་ / གངས།
rain	*charpa*	ཆར་པ།
pass	*la*	ལ།
hill, mountain	*ri*	རི།
plain, plateau	*tang*	ཐང་།
lake	*tso (also: yumco, caka, nor)*	མཚོ།
map	*sabtra*	ས་ཁྲ།
compass points:	*chang (N), lho (S), shar (E), nub (W)*	བྱང་། ལྷོ། ཤར། ནུབ།

Index